GYNAECOLOGY

Cavendish
Publishing
Limited

London • Sydney

TITLES IN THE SERIES

ACCIDENT AND EMERGENCY

CARDIOLOGY

CLINICAL CARE

DENTISTRY

EAR, NOSE AND THROAT

GENERAL PRACTICE

GENITO-URINARY

GYNAECOLOGY

MEDIATION AND ARBITRATION

NEPHROLOGY

NEUROLOGY

ONCOLOGY

OPHTHALMOLOGY

PSYCHIATRY

RESPIRATORY DISORDERS

UROLOGY

VASCULAR SURGERY

GYNAECOLOGY

Trevor P Dutt, RD, FRCOG
Consultant Gynaecologist
with
Margaret P Matthews, BSc, MRCOG

SERIES EDITOR
Dr Walter Scott, LLB (Hons),
MBBS, MRCGP, DObstRCOG

Cavendish
Publishing
Limited

London • Sydney

First published in Great Britain 1999 by Cavendish Publishing Limited, The Glass House, Wharton Street, London WC1X 9PX, United Kingdom.

Telephone: +44 (0) 171 278 8000   Facsimile: +44 (0) 171 278 8080

e-mail: info@cavendishpublishing.com

Visit our Home Page on http://www.cavendishpublishing.com

Dutt, Trevor

Gynaecology for lawyers – (Medico-legal practitioner series)

1. Gynaecology – Law and legislation – England

I. Title II. Scott, W

344.2'04412

Every effort has been made to trace all the copyright holders but, if any have been overlooked, the publishers will be pleased to make the necessary arrangement at the first opportunity.

ISBN 1 85941 215 7

Printed and bound in Great Britain by
Biddles Ltd, Guildford and King's Lynn

FOREWORD

When I first conceived the idea of the *Medico-Legal Practitioner Series*, in the Summer of 1994, I had been preparing reports for lawyers on cases of alleged medical negligence for about five years. I had also been looking at other doctors' reports for the same length of time and it was becoming increasingly apparent to me that one of the lawyers' most difficult tasks was to understand the medical principles clearly. To be fair to the lawyers, there were some doctors who did not always make matters very clear. This, coupled with the difficulty which many doctors have in understanding the legal concept of negligence and related topics, merely served to compound the problem.

A little more than two years have now passed since I wrote the foreword for the initial launch of the series and, already, the number of titles available in the series has reached double figures, with many more imminent. Therefore, this seems to be an appropriate moment to take stock of our efforts so far and to assess the way in which matters are likely to unfold in the future.

Since the publication of the first book in the series, there have been some exciting developments in the medico-legal scene and there can be no doubt that this is becoming an increasingly specialised field. That trend is likely to continue, with the establishment of legal aid franchise firms of lawyers. Such firms will find it more and more necessary to identify strong cases and eliminate weak ones in an economical fashion, and with as little risk as possible.

An interesting development in some of the newer titles is the coverage of areas that do not relate to clinical negligence. With the series becoming more comprehensive, we have felt able to expand into other medico-legal areas. Examples include *Respiratory Disorders*, which deals with industrial lung disease and *Psychiatry*, which covers testamentary capacity and the defence of insanity to criminal charges.

So much, then, for the latest developments in the *Medico-Legal Practitioner Series*. Our aim remains as it was at the outset, with regard to uniformity of approach and clarity of presentation. In this way, I hope that our readers, mostly the practitioners who are engaged in unravelling the complexities of the medical evidence that is the subject of so much litigation, will continue to rely on us as an invaluable source of reference.

Walter Scott
Series Editor
Slough

ACKNOWLEDGMENTS

The authors wish to express their thanks to Walter Scott, who first suggested the idea of writing this book and who maintained the impetus with his constant enthusiasm and support. We are also very grateful for the sympathetic and helpful guidance given by Jo Reddy and Tristan Rogers of Cavendish Publishing.

TPD
MM

CONTENTS

Foreword   *v*
Acknowledgments   *vii*

1 INTRODUCTION   **1**

    CHAPERONES AND OTHER MATTERS   4

2 ESSENTIAL ANATOMY AND PHYSIOLOGY   **7**

    ANATOMY   7
    Terminology   7
      The anatomical position   7
    An overview of pelvic anatomy   10
      The bones   10
      The pelvic blood supply   12
      The pelvic nerve supply   12
      The pelvic organs   13
      The gynaecological organs or reproductive tract   13
        The ovaries   13
        The fallopian tubes 13
        The uterus   15
        The vagina   17
      The external female genitalia   17
      The urinary tract   18
        The ureters   18
        The (urinary) bladder 18
        The urethra   18
      The gastro-intestinal tract   19

    PHYSIOLOGY   19
    Basic genetics   19
      Chromosones, genes and DNA   19
      Sexual differentiation   20
    The sexual physiology of the unborn   20
    Childhood   21
    Puberty   21
    The menstrual cycle   22
      Follicular phase   22
      Ovulatory phase   24
      Luteal phase   25
    Pregnancy   25
    Lactation   26
    The menopause   26
      Effects of the menopause/climacteric   26
      Hormone replacement therapy (HRT) 27
        Contra-indications and side effects   28
        Progestrogen HRT   29

3 COMMON OPERATIVE PROCEDURES IN GYNAECOLOGY   **31**

THE D & C   31
Indications   32
   Diagnostic   32
   Therapeutic   33
The procedure   33
Hazards of the procedure   37
The operation notes   38

HYSTEROSCOPY   39
Indications   40
   Diagnostic   40
   Therapeutic   40
The procedure   40
   Operative hysteroscopy   41
Hazards of the procedure   42
The operation notes   42

LAPAROSCOPY   42
Indications   43
   Diagnostic   43
   Therapeutic   43
The procedure   43
Hazards of the procedure   46

HYSTERECTOMY   48
Types of hysterectomy   48
   Sub-total abdominal hysterectomy   49
   Total abdominal hysterectomy (TAH)   49
   Hysterectomy with right/left/bilateral salpingectomy   49
   Hysterectomy with right/left/bilateral salpingo-oophorectomy   50
   Extended hysterectomy   50
The vaginal operation   50
   Schauta's operation   51
The abdominal operation   51
The operation notes   53

4 DEVELOPMENTAL ANOMALIES   **55**

OVARIAN ABNORMALITIES   55

TUBAL ABNORMALITIES   55

UTERINE ABNORMALITIES   56
Failure of development   56
Failure of fusion   56

VAGINAL ABNORMALITIES   58
Failure of development   58
Failure of fusion   58

WOLFFIAN DUCT REMNANTS   58

URINARY TRACT ANOMALIES   59

5   **MENSTRUAL DISORDERS**   **61**

CYCLICAL PROBLEMS   61
Menorrhagia   61
Examination   62
Investigation   62
Treatment   63
Medical treatment   63
   Non-steroidal anti-inflamatory drugs   63
   Progestogens   63
   Tranexamic acid   64
   Ethamsylate   64
   LHRH analogues   64
   Danazol   64
   Progesterone releasing intrauterine contraceptive devices   64
Surgical treatment   64
   Hysterectomy and the alternatives   64
   Myomectomy   65
   Pre-operative assessment   65
Dysmenorrhoea   65
Polymenorrhoea   66
The normal range   67
The altered cycle   67
'Twice in a month'   67
Stress   67
Miscalculation of a normal cycle   67
Prolongation of bleeding   67
Intermenstrual bleeding   68
Oligomenorrhoea   68

ACYCLICAL PROBLEMS   68
Amenorrhoea   68
Primary amenorrhoea   68
   Cryptomenorrhoea   68
   True primary amenorrhoea   69

Secondary amenorrhoea 69
Amenorrhoea of pregnancy 70
Mechanical obstruction 70
Hyperprolactinaemia 71
Disturbance of the pituitary-ovarian axis 71
Anorexia nervosa 71
Thyroid dysfunction 72
Inter-menstrual bleeding (IMB) 72
Break-through bleeding (BTB) 72
Post-coital bleeding (PCB) 72
The torn hymen 72
Local lesions of the vagina or cervix 73
Lacerations 73
Cervical 'erosion'/ectropion and polyp 73
Cervical carcinome 73
Post-menopausal bleeding (PMB) 73
Vaginal lesions 73
Atrophic vaginitis 73
Carcinoma of the vagina 74
Other vaginal and cervical lesions 74
Foreign bodies 74
Carcinoma of the body of the uterus 74

PRE-MENSTRUAL SYNDROME 75
Management 76
Differential diagnosis 76
Treatment 76
'Over the counter' remedies 77
Hormonal regimes 77
Symptomatic treatments 77
Second line treatments 78
Conclusion 78

6 INFECTIONS 79

INTRODUCTION 79

PHYSIOLOGICAL VAGINAL DISCHARGE 79
Ectropion 80

PATHOLOGICAL VAGINAL DISCHARGE 81
Non-infectious 81
Infections (not necessarily sexually transmitted) 81
Candida, also known as 'thrush' or 'monilia' 81
Bacterial vaginosis, anaerobic infections, gardnerella vaginalis 82

Contents

Sexually transmitted infections 82
Herpes simplex, cold sores, genital herpes 82
Trichomonas vaginalis 82
Gonorrhoea 83
Chlamydia 83
Management of vaginal discharges 83
Effects and sequelae of sexually transmitted infections 84
Pelvic inflammatory disease 84
Recurrent pelvic infection (chronic PID) 85
Pelvic adhesions 86
Psycho-sexual problems 86

7 ENDOMETRIOSIS 87

DIAGNOSIS 88
Symptoms 88
Delay in diagnosis 89
Signs 89

MANAGEMENT 90

TREATMENT 90
Medical treatment 90
Analgesics 90
Hormones 90
Progestogens 91
Danazol 91
Gestrione and dimetriose 91
Surgical treatment 91
Laparoscopy 92
Laparotomy 92

LONG TERM OUTLOOK 92

8 CONDITIONS OF SPECIFIC ORGANS 95

THE VULVA 95
Pruritis vulvae 95
General conditions 95
Allergic reactions 96
Infections 96
Viral infections 96
Genital herpes 96
Condylomata acuminata (genital warts) 97
Bacterial infections 97
Folliculitis 97
Syphilis 97

Fungal infections 98
  Monilial vulvitis 98
  Tinea cruris ('Dhobic itch') 98
Parasitic infestations 98
  Scabies 98
  Pediculosis pubis 98
  Strongyloides stercoralis 99
Vulval dystrophies 99
  Lichen sclerosus 99
  Vulval intra-epithelial neoplasia 99
Vulval carcinoma 100
Miscellaneous vulval swellings 100
  Trauma 100
  Abnormalities of the Bartholin's gland 100

THE VAGINA 101
Normal vaginal discharge 101
Pathological vaginal discharge 102
  Monilial vaginitis (thrush) 102
  Bacterial vaginosis 102
  Trichomonas vaginalis 102
  Chlamydia 102
  Other organisms 103
Congenital defects 103
Utero-vaginal prolapse 103
  Causes 103
  Symptoms 104
  Examination 104
  Treatment 105
Vaginal adenosis and clear cell carcinoma 106
Vaginal carcinoma 107

THE UTERINE CERVIX 107
Erosion/ectropion 107
  Treatment 108
  Nabothian follicles 108
Cervical polyps 109
Cervical fibroids 109
Exfoliative cervical cytology 109
Malignant disease of the cervix 111
  Squamous cell carcinoma 111
    Cervical intra-epithelial neoplasia (CIN) 113
    Microinvasive carcinoma (FIGO Stage Ia) 114
    Invasive cervical carcinoma 116

Contents

Cervical adenocarcinoma 116
Sarcoma botryoides 116

THE UTERINE CORPUS 117
Infections 117
Tuberculosis 117
Endometrial hyperplasia 118
Endometrial polyps 118
Fibro-leiomyomata 119
Adenomyosis 120
Malignant disease of the body of the uterus 120
FIGO staging 121
Treatment 121
Other malignancies of the uterine corpus 122

THE FALLOPIAN TUBES 122
Infection 122
Fimbrial cysts 123
Malignant disease of the tubes 123

THE OVARIES 123
Infection 123
Polycystic ovarian disease 124
Ovarian tumours 124
Complications which may affect any ovarian tumour 124
Torsion 125
Haemorrhage 125
Rupture 125
Incarceration 125
Infection 126
'Physiological' cysts 126
Benign ovarian tumours 127
Endometrioma 127
Dermoid cysts 127
Fibroma 128
Serous cystadenoma 128
Mucinous cystadenoma 128
Uncommon ovarian tumours 128
Malignant ovarian tumours 129
Endometrioid carcinoma 129
Malignant carcinoma 129
Serous and mucinous cystadenocarcinoma 129
Other ovarian malignant disease 129
Metastatic tumours 129

General considerations 129
Management of suspected ovarian malignancy 130
Special investigations 130
   Imaging 130
   Needle biopsy 130
   Paracentesis abdominis 130
   Tumour markers 131
   Laparoscopy 131
Surgical treatment 131
Radiotherapy 132
Chemotherapy 132
'Second look' operations 132
'Well woman' screening 132
Medico-legal significance 133

THE PITUITARY GLAND 133
Sheehan's syndrome 133
Pituitary adenoma 134

9 SEXUAL DYSFUNCTION 135

VAGINISMUS 135

DYSPAREUNIA 136
Superficial dyspareunia 136
Deep dyspareunia 137

PSYCHOSEXUAL PROBLEMS 137

TREATMENT OF SEXUAL DYSFUNCTION 138

10 CONTRACEPTION 139

COUNSELLING AND CONSENT 140

'NATURAL' BIRTH CONTROL 140
Coitus interruptus 140
The 'rhythm' method 140
The 'Persona' 141

THE MALE CONDOM ('SHEATH') 141

VASECTOMY (MALE STERILISATION) 142

FEMALE BARRIER METHODS 143

INTRAUTERINE CONTRACEPTIVE DEVICES (IUCDS) 144
Types of IUCD 144

Side effects and complications   145
   Insertion   145
   Perforation   146
   Expulsion   146
   Missing threads   146
   Pelvic infection   147
   Menstrual problems   148
   Pregnancy   149
   Ectopic pregnancy   149
Contraindications   149

HORMONAL METHODS OF CONTRACEPTION   150
Oral combined contraceptive pills (OCCPs or COCPs)   150
Non-contraceptive uses   151
Unwanted side effects   151
Assessment   152
Progestogen only contraceptives   152

POST-COITAL CONTRACEPTION   153

11 ELECTIVE STERILISATION   155

METHODS   157
Historical methods   157
   Ovarian irradiation   157
   Burying of the ovaries   157
Current procedures   157
   Laparoscopic sterilisation   158
      Electrocautery to the tubes 158
      Thermocoagulation and unipolar diathermy 159
      Fallope rings   159
      Hulka and Filshie clips   159
      Steptoe rods   160
   Open operation methods   160
      Madlener's operation   160
      Pomeroy's operation   161
      The Oxford technique   161
      Cornuectomy   161
      Bilateral salpingectomy   161
   Hysteroscopic sterilisations   161

OPERATIONS FOR OTHER INDICATIONS   162

STERILISATION FAILURES   162

12 INFERTILITY — **165**

DEFINITION — 165

ASSESSMENT — 166
Clinical history — 166
Examination — 166
Special investigations — 167
    Ovulation — 167
    Semen — 167
    Tubes — 168
    Sperm-mucus interaction — 169

TREATMENT — 170
Medical treatment — 170
    Bromocriptine — 170
    Anti-oestrogens — 170
    Exogenous FSH and LH — 171
Mechanical treatment — 171
Surgical treatment — 171
Advanced treatment — 172

13 ABORTION — **173**

DEFINITION — 173

SPONTANEOUS ABORTION — 173
Septic abortion — 174
Non-septic abortion — 175
Threatened abortion — 175
Inevitable abortion — 175
Incomplete abortion — 175
Complete abortion — 175
Missed abortion — 176
Recurrent spontaneous abortion — 176
Anembryonic pregnancy — 177
    Management — 177

INDUCED ABORTION — 178
Legal termination — 178
    Mifepristone (RU486) — 179
    Surgical termination (vaginal) — 180
    Hysterotomy — 181
    Prostaglandin termination — 181
Criminal termination — 182

Contents

14 ECTOPIC PREGNANCY   **185**

DEFINITION   185

MEDICO-LEGAL SIGNIFICANCE   185

MECHANISM   185

PRESENTATION   186

DIAGNOSIS AND INVESTIGATION   187

MANAGEMENT   188

THE 'MISSED ECTOPIC' AND CLAIMS FOR NEGLIGENCE   189

15 TROPHOBLASTIC DISEASE   **191**

INCIDENCE   191

TYPES OF TUMOUR   191

CLINICAL FEATURES   192

MANAGEMENT   193
The importance of follow-up   193

Appendix – Glossary of terms   195
Abbreviations   195
Surgical sutures   197
Glossary   197

Index   235

CHAPTER 1

INTRODUCTION

One of the most frequent cocktail party questions put to those doctors who specialise in 'women's health' is 'What is the difference between a gynaecologist and an obstetrician?'; perhaps, therefore, this would be a good place from which to start.

The short answer to the question is that a *gynaecologist* deals with problems of the reproductive system of women who are not pregnant whereas an *obstetrician* is concerned with pregnancy and its complications. Unfortunately, like most short answers in medicine, this one tells only part of the story since a pregnancy in the process of miscarrying is considered to be gynaecological while obstetricians may continue to care for their patients for several weeks after they have been delivered of the baby.

The vast majority of gynaecologists in the United Kingdom are also practising obstetricians and the converse is also true so that the current trend to substitute the appellation 'specialist in women's health' is to be applauded. Nevertheless, it is likely to be a long time before the Royal College of Obstetricians and Gynaecologists in Regent's Park, London, changes its name to the Royal College of Women's Health!

Historically, gynaecologists owe their origins to the surgeons and, until very recently, most were Fellows of the Royal College of Surgeons (FRCS) as well as of their own College which was only founded in 1929. This was initially called the British College of Obstetricians and Gynaecologists but became the Royal College in 1938, and its members and fellows use the letters MRCOG and FRCOG respectively. The Royal College of Surgeons of England (originally of London) is much older, having been in existence since 1800. In contrast with gynaecologists, obstetricians have more in common with the 'man-midwives' of the 18th and 19th centuries.

Although a pregnant woman may be booked for her obstetric care from very soon after the conception has been confirmed, any complications of the pregnancy needing admission to hospital before about the 16th week are likely to result in her being placed on the gynaecological ward while, after 16 weeks, she is more likely to go to an obstetric ward. This artificial separation can result in problems of management.

The gynaecological medical staff in any Hospital will include up to four grades. Having passed the qualifying examination, a new doctor must complete 12 months as a pre-registration house surgeon (HS) or house physician (HP) before receiving full registration with the General Medical Council. He or she will then become a senior house officer (SHO) which is now the most junior grade employed in gynaecology. Gynaecological SHOs may intend to pursue a career in the speciality or may be gaining experience before moving into general medical practice or other specialist branches.

After two or three years as an SHO, career gynaecologists will become registrars. In addition, the registrar grade includes a number of overseas graduates, termed 'visiting registrars', who have come to the United Kingdom for higher training before returning to their own countries to take up consultant posts. The grade also contains some doctors who are primarily engaged in academic research but who may also do some clinical work. Those who hold university, as opposed to National Health Service (NHS), appointments may be designated 'lecturer' rather than 'registrar', and the titles 'Research Registrar' and 'Research Fellow' may also be encountered, sometimes at SHO level.

Until recently, after about three years at the registrar grade, those doctors wishing to continue their career in this country would have aspired to a post as a senior registrar which they would normally have held for a further four years or so before being appointed to a consultant post. All appointments up to and including the third year as a senior registrar were regarded as training posts but, from the final year in the grade, specialist training was considered to be completed.

This system changed in 1996 with the introduction of 'structured training', whereby trainees now remain registrars ('specialist registrars' or 'SpRs') for a period of five years. In the final year, they can qualify for a certificate of 'Completion of Specialist Training' (CST) which enables them to apply for consultant posts. The senior registrar grade has been abolished.

Under the old system, the equivalent grades in NHS and university appointments were:

NHS	University
house surgeon	no equivalent
senior house officer	no equivalent
registrar	lecturer
senior registrar	lecturer
consultant	senior lecturer
no equivalent	reader
no equivalent	professor

Clearly, the specialist knowledge possessed by a newly appointed SHO will be little more than that of a medical student but, in a reasonably busy unit, he or she will soon be instructed in the performance of the simpler procedures and, before becoming a registrar, would normally be competent to perform a dilatation and curettage, the evacuation of retained products of conception and perhaps uncomplicated laparoscopies and hysteroscopies. The specialist training at the registrar grade is more intensive and the aspiring senior registrar (now 'specialist registrar year 4') should certainly be competent to carry out all the standard gynaecological operations of a moderately difficult nature.

In the past, a consultant was expected to be fully conversant with all gynaecological techniques but, with the advent of sub-specialisation, some procedures may be outside his or her field of expertise. For example, not all consultant gynaecologists will be trained in colposcopy nor will all have had sufficient experience of endoscopic surgery to perform such procedures safely. Such limitations need cause no problems provided they are recognised by the consultant who then acts responsibly and does not undertake operations for which adequate training has not been received.

A woman's first encounter with a gynaecologist will usually be following referral by her general practitioner (GP) and may take place in a hospital out-patient clinic or, in the case of a private referral, in the gynaecologist's own consulting rooms. At this first consultation, the specialist will first take a clinical history and it is no accident that a considerable part of a medical student's time is occupied in learning how to take a complete but concise history. Not only must details of the presenting complaint be obtained but it may also be essential to enquire about other, apparently unrelated, conditions. For example, a woman referred for investigation of post-menopausal bleeding may also suffer from osteoarthritis of the hip and the potential significance of this is emphasised in chapter 3, when discussing dilatation and curettage.

After taking the history, a clinical examination is performed. Sadly, this is frequently limited to the region of immediate concern and the author has, himself, recently found a very obvious cancer of the breast in a woman with a pelvic complaint who had previously been examined by three other doctors. When surgical treatment is envisaged, it is particularly important that consideration is given to the patient's fitness for anaesthesia. The nature of gynaecological complaints means that, in the vast majority of cases, a pelvic (vaginal) examination will be required and, in some cases, a rectal examination is also advisable.

Before the consultation is concluded, the gynaecologist should explain the probable diagnosis and the intended plan of management to the patient *in language which she can understand*. Sometimes, of course, further investigations such as blood tests or X-rays may be required and these, too, should be properly explained. The medico-legal situation in the US has resulted in the details of such explanations being fully documented in the doctor's records but this is not yet routine procedure in this country where the extent of the explanation, particularly with regard to possible risks, is largely left to the discretion of the doctor.

Every woman is different, and gynaecological complaints are so protean that it would be impossible to give a precise account which would cover every case but it is hoped that this brief summary of gynaecologists and the gynaecological consultation will provide some insight into the background of a client's experiences.

CHAPERONES AND OTHER MATTERS

It has long been an accepted recommendation that every male gynaecologist should be accompanied by a female chaperone during the examination of any woman and preferably during the preceding interview as well. If this should be impossible for any reason then, at the very least, a chaperone should be present for any examination of the genital organs. It has been suggested that the presence of a chaperone is reassuring to the patient and also offers protection for the gynaecologist in the event of a later claim by the patient that he acted improperly.

More recently, this advice has been extended to include female gynaecologists who, though less often than their male colleagues, may occasionally be accused of improper behaviour.

A Working Party of the Royal College of Obstetricians and Gynaecologists considered this question in some detail and its report was published recently: 'Intimate Examinations', 1997, London: RCOG Press. After considering published literature on patient preferences (all the available studies were of US origin), the Working Party recommended that 'a chaperone should be offered to all patients undergoing intimate examinations in gynaecology and obstetrics irrespective of the gender of the gynaecologist' but that, if the patient preferred to be examined without a chaperone, 'this request should be honoured and recorded in the notes'. Furthermore, where a chaperone cannot be offered, the Working Party felt that the patient should be offered the option of proceeding without a third party, or of deferring the examination to some other occasion.

The senior author is aware of many gynaecologists who would never consider examining a patient without a chaperone but this is not, and has never been, his practice. However, exceptions apply to children (when the child's mother will often be the best chaperone) or when, for whatever reason, he feels that the presence of another person would be beneficial (for example, very nervous patients). It need hardly be added that the request for a chaperone would never be refused! The reason for the author's practice is that he believes that the presence of another individual may, in a significant proportion of cases, detract from the very personal relationship that exists between the patient and her gynaecologist, thereby causing the patient to feel inhibited and discouraged from revealing potentially relevant information. He accepts that it might be difficult to justify his actions to the medical defence societies and hopes that it is not tempting fate to observe that, in over 30 years

4

of gynaecological and obstetric practice, he has never been accused of impropriety nor has he ever had occasion to regret the absence of a chaperone.

Going beyond the question of chaperones, it may also be worth mentioning the place of the general medical examination in gynaecological practice. Breast examination is considered to be a gynaecological responsibility in the US but is not universally performed by British gynaecologists.

It is the senior author's practice to perform a (brief) general examination on all new patients and this, of course, includes examination of the breasts. By applying this routine, he has found several abnormalities of significance including, as already mentioned, a cancer of the breast which had been missed by three other doctors. In this context, the RCOG Working Party observes that clinical examination does not give better results than mammography but it does not go on to point out that not all patients will have, nor want, mammography to be performed.

To conclude this section, mention may also be made of the place of medical students. The letter to the patient communicating the date and time of the clinic appointment will usually also contain an indication of whether or not medical students are likely to be present but it is surely only simple courtesy to obtain the patient's agreement before suggesting that a medical student should perform any examination. The majority of patients are very willing to co-operate and it is sad that the greatest number of refusals come from those patients who are themselves doctors or nurses!

CHAPTER 2

ESSENTIAL ANATOMY AND PHYSIOLOGY

ANATOMY

The anatomical descriptions given here are only intended to provide the basic minimum information. If a detailed account is required, reference should be made to an appropriate textbook. The most famous is probably *Gray's Anatomy* which was first published in 1858 and which, at the time of writing, has reached its 38th edition.

Terminology

Anatomy is the detailed study of the structure and form of living, or recently dead, animals. In common with most other specialist areas of interest, anatomy has developed its own terminology, some of which must be learned if anatomical descriptions are to be intelligible.

The following list is very abbreviated but should make the succeeding text more understandable.

The anatomical position

Irrespective of the actual position adopted, the anatomist always describes the relationships between the various parts as if the body were in the 'anatomical position'. In the case of the human body, this is defined as standing erect with the arms by the sides and the palms of both hands facing forward.

It is important to grasp the implications of this convention, especially as most gynaecological procedures take place with the woman lying on her back with her knees drawn up. In this position, her hips are actually below her knees but, because of the use of the standard position, in any anatomical description the hips will remain anatomically above ('superior') to the knee joints.

The body is divided by a number of *planes* or imaginary 'slices'.

The *median plane* is a vertical slice through the middle of the trunk which divides the body into symmetrical right and left halves. It passes through the sagittal suture of the skull and any slice parallel to it is described as a *sagittal plane*.

Vertical slices at right angles to the median plane will pass through or parallel to the coronal suture of the skull and are termed *coronal planes*.

Horizontal planes are, of course, at right angles to the other two.

Anterior refers to a position nearer the front when in the anatomical position or a surface directed forwards. Thus, the face is on the *anterior* surface of the head and the breasts are *anterior* to the underlying rib cage. The term *ventral* is sometimes substituted.

Posterior, similarly, describes a position nearer the back of the body or a backward facing surface and may be replaced by *dorsal*.

Superior, meaning 'above', and *inferior, meaning* 'below', are also always used with reference to the anatomical position. Thus, the head is always *superior* to the thorax (chest), irrespective of the actual position of the body. In some descriptions, the terms *cranial* (nearer the head) and its opposite, *caudal*, may be preferred.

Medial means nearer to the midline whereas *lateral* is further away. For reference points other than the midline, the terms *proximal* and *distal* are used. The reference point may be implied rather than explicitly stated, especially in the case of the limbs, when 'proximal' will mean 'nearer to the torso' (that is, the shoulder is *proximal* to the elbow and the wrist is more *distal*).

Superficial and *deep* are used to describe distances from a surface, often, but not always, the skin. *Internal* and *external* are used for the surfaces of hollow structures such as the thoracic (chest) cavity.

Figure 2.1   **Anatomical planes and relationships**

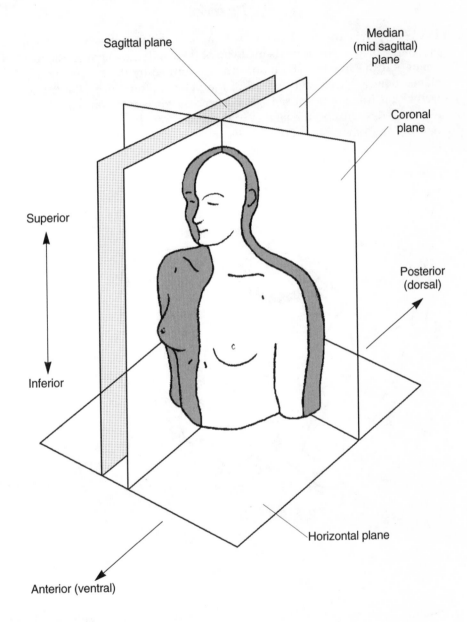

An overview of pelvic anatomy

The bones

The bony pelvis (the word 'pelvis' is from the Latin for 'a basin') has the form of a ring which, in the adult, is made up of three individual bones, the two hip bones and the sacrum. These, in turn, are formed by the fusion (joining) of eleven bones. The posterior wall of the pelvis is formed by the triangular *sacrum* consisting of five fused spinal vertebrae whereas the *innominate bone* on each side develops by the joining of the ilium, ischium and pubis. The pubic parts of the innominate bones meet in the midline anteriorly at the *pubic symphysis*, thereby completing the circle.

Figure 2.2   The pelvic bones

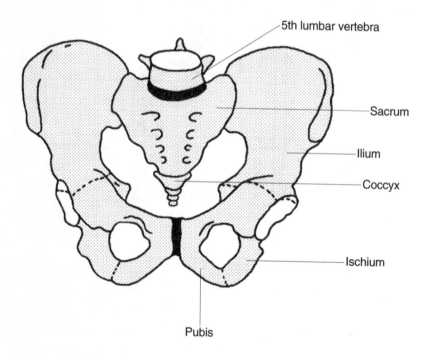

Outside the bony pelvis lie muscles, fat and skin, together with associated blood and lymphatic vessels and nerves. Many of the muscles find attachment to the strong pelvic bones and either support the spine or act upon the *femur* (thigh bone) in the upper part of the lower limb.

The bones of the pelvis are also lined by muscle groups within which are situated the organs of three functional systems, the *reproductive tract* (the ovaries, fallopian tubes, uterus and upper vagina), the lower part of the *urinary tract* (part of the ureters, the bladder and the urethra) and the *digestive tract* (the rectum and anal canal).

The bladder is placed anteriorly in the midline behind the pubic symphysis and in front of the uterus which has a tube and ovary on each side. Behind the uterus, but separated by a space (the *pouch of Douglas*) usually occupied by loops of small bowel, lies the rectum.

The pelvic organs are partly covered by a thin, smooth, surface layer called the *peritoneum*, which is continuous with the similar surface lining the abdominal cavity itself. This normally separates the organs and allows them to slide freely against one another. Inflammation can cause adjacent peritoneal surfaces to adhere to one another.

The lower pelvis is filled by a muscular sheet (the *pelvic floor* or *pelvic diaphragm*) perforated by openings for the urethra, vagina and anal canal. The pelvic floor supports the structures above it and it is primarily a stretching and weakening of this muscular sheet which results in vaginal prolapse (described in Chapter 8).

Figure 2.3   Muscles of the pelvic floor (viewed from above)

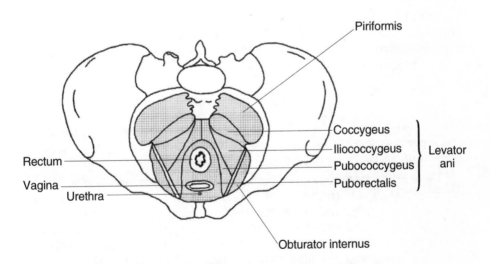

The constituent parts of the levator ani, together with the adjacent muscles of the pelvic side wall, fill in the pelvic opening, except where apertures are left for the rectum, vagina and urethra.

The pelvic blood supply

Oxygenated blood leaves the left ventricle of the heart via the *aorta* which, after giving off branches to supply the head and neck, curves over to pass down on the posterior wall of the thorax and abdomen. Shortly before entering the pelvis, the aorta divides into the two *common iliac arteries* which, in turn, separate into the *external* and *internal iliac* vessels. The former mainly supplies the lower limb whereas the blood in the latter is largely directed to the pelvic organs.

As elsewhere in the body, the arteries divide into arterioles and eventually into the smallest vessels (capillaries) where oxygen and other nutrients are able to diffuse out of the blood and into the surrounding tissues whilst the waste products of metabolism, including carbon dioxide, diffuse into the blood to be carried back via venules and veins to the heart for onward circulation to the lungs (where the carbon dioxide is extracted and oxygen added) and to other organs for disposal.

Some fluid also leaves the capillaries and is eventually returned to the blood circulation via a separate group of tubules called the *lymphatic system*. These tubules never reach the size of the major blood vessels and are interrupted at intervals by the interposition of the *lymph nodes* which act as filters. The final pathway by which much of the contained fluid (lymph) reaches the blood is the *thoracic duct* which drains into the left subclavian vein in the root of the neck though lymph also returns to the blood stream at the lymph nodes.

The clinical importance of the lymphatic system is that it provides a potential route for the spread of cells from malignant tumours and the earliest distant deposits (metastases) from a cancer are often found in the neighbouring lymph nodes.

The pelvic nerve supply

The nervous system is divided into a central part, the brain and spinal cord, and a peripheral part (the nerves themselves) but division can also be made into *somatic* and *autonomic* systems.

The somatic system includes both sensory and motor nerves. The former carry neural signals from the peripheral sensors to the central structures allowing the appreciation of both internal events such as muscle position (proprioception) and external stimuli (touch, temperature, smell, etc) whilst the motor nerves are concerned with the central control of distant structures (mainly the muscles). In contrast, the autonomic system carries signals which rarely reach consciousness and are concerned with the unconscious and automatic control of body functions (for example, control of the muscular walls of arterioles to regulate blood flow).

The nerves arising from the spinal cord (carrying both somatic and autonomic fibres) emerge from the spine by passing out through small spaces between the vertebrae, the *intervertebral foramina*. The nerves then divide into *dorsal* and *ventral rami*.

The largest and most important neural structure within the pelvis is formed by the intermingling of nerve fibres from the ventral rami of the fourth lumbar to the fourth sacral nerves and is called the *sacral plexus*. This lies on the posterior wall of the pelvis on the deep surface of the piriformis muscle and behind the internal iliac blood vessels and the ureter.

The pelvic organs

The gynaecological organs or reproductive tract

As mentioned above, the pelvic reproductive organs consist of the two ovaries, the fallopian tubes, the uterus and the vagina (see Figure 2.4, overleaf).

The ovaries

Normal ovaries are greyish white, almond shaped structures about 30 mm long, 15 mm wide and about 10 mm thick. They are situated laterally on either side of the uterus lying close to the pelvic side-wall in the ovarian fossa where they are not far distant from the ureter. They are attached to the posterior aspect of a fold of peritoneum called the *broad ligament* by an additional fold, the *mesovarium*, in which run the blood vessels supplying the ovary. Unlike the remaining pelvic organs which mostly obtain their blood from branches of the internal iliac artery, the blood supply of the ovaries is by vessels (the *ovarian arteries*) which arise directly from the anterior aspect of the aorta itself just below the level of the renal arteries, that is, high up in the abdomen.

The proximity of the ovary to the ureter has important implications for the safety of the latter structure when the ovary is removed surgically.

The functional aspects of the ovaries are considered in the section on physiology.

The fallopian tubes

The uterine (or fallopian) tubes are normally about 10 cm in length and lie in the upper margin of the broad ligament extending from just above the ovary to the upper part of the uterus. The outer part (the *infundibulum*) is the largest being trumpet shaped with the edge of the opening into the pelvic cavity being extended into small, finger-like, projections call *fimbriae*.

Figure 2.4   **The female pelvic organs**

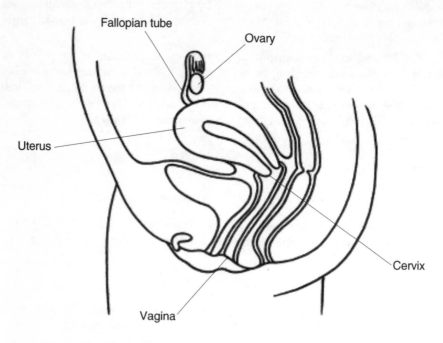

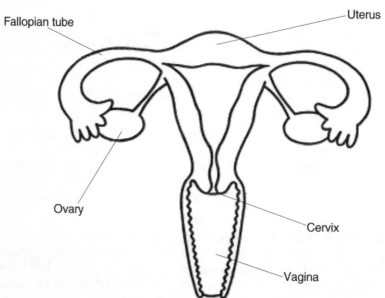

Simplified diagrams of this type are very helpful when explaining gynaecological conditions and procedures to patients

The infundibulum narrows medially to become the *ampulla* which constitutes a little more than half of the whole length of the tube. This, in turn, narrows further to become the *isthmus*. The outside diameter at this point is about 4–5 mm but the lumen is less than 1 mm. The tube then enters the cornual region of the uterus passing through the muscular wall as the *intramural* segment before opening into the uterine cavity at the *inner tubal ostium*.

The uterus

The normal, non-pregnant uterus is about the size and shape of a small pear, being some 75 mm long, 50 mm in breadth and 25 mm thick. It lies approximately centrally in the pelvis (though some deviation to one side is not uncommon) and is supported by the pelvic floor and by thickenings of the surrounding connective tissue. For descriptive purposes, it is divided into the *body* (or *corpus*) and *neck* (or *cervix*).

The fallopian tubes are attached to the part of the uterus called the *cornu* (or *cornual region*), the name being derived from the Latin for a horn. The part of the uterus above the site of insertion of the tubes is termed the *fundus*.

The cervix is perforated by the *cervical canal*, which is slightly wider in its mid-section than at each end. The upper part communicates with the endometrial cavity through the *internal cervical os*, whereas the lower part opens into the vagina at the *external os*. The part of the cervix which protrudes into the upper vagina (usually for a distance of about 12 cm) may be referred to as the *portio vaginalis*.

The uterine arteries run medially on each side of the cervix just above the level at which the ureters pass from back to front (see Figure 2.5). The anterior aspect of the mid-part of the cervix is intimately related to the posterior wall of the bladder.

In the pre-pubertal girl, the long axis of the uterus is approximately in line with the vagina (*axial*) but, in the sexually mature woman, the long axis is normally directed forwards (*anteverted* and pointing approximately towards the umbilicus) which, together with the usual slight forward curve (*anteflexion*), places the uterus almost at right angles to the vagina (see Figure 2.6). After the menopause, the uterus gradually reduces in size and tends to revert towards the axial position.

In about 15% of post-pubertal women, the uterus is tilted backwards (*retroverted*) and may also be bent posteriorly (*retroflexion*). Again, see Figure 2.6.

The anteverted position may not be explicitly recorded but, if it is, it will often be abbreviated to a/v. Retroversion, if correctly diagnosed, may be noted as r/v. Anteflexion and retroflexion are rarely noted and probably appreciated rarely, if at all, by British gynaecologists.

Figure 2.5   The uterine blood supply

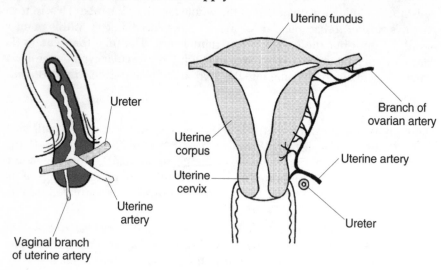

These diagrams show the close relationship between the uterine artery and the ureter as they pass lateral to the cervix. There is a significant risk of damaging the ureter when clamping and dividing the uterine artery during a hysterectomy

Figure 2.6   Uterine positions

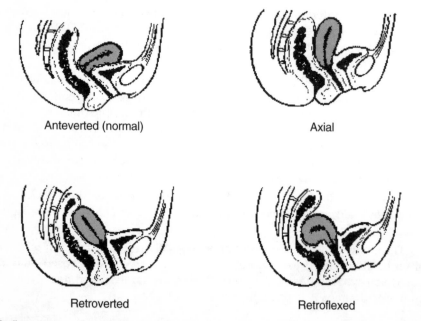

Median sections through the female pelvis, showing various positions which the uterus may adopt

The uterus is partly covered by *peritoneum* (sometimes called the *serosa* or *serosal layer*) but the wall consists largely of muscle with a thickness of about 2 cm. The inner cavity of the uterus (or *endometrial cavity*) is lined by a well defined layer called the *endometrium* which varies in thickness in response to the endocrine (hormonal) status of the individual. Superiorly, the cavity is in continuity with the lumen of the fallopian tubes and inferiorly becomes the canal of the cervix. In the normal, non-pregnant condition, the anterior and posterior surfaces of the endometrial cavity lie in apposition.

The vagina

The vagina extends downwards and forwards from the cervix to reach the exterior surface at the *vulva* where the *introitus* lies between the *labia minora*. The anterior wall measures about 75 mm in length but is extended superiorly by the cervix of the uterus so that the posterior wall is longer (about 90 mm). It is flattened antero-posteriorly so that the front and back walls normally lie in contact. Because the cervix protrudes into the vagina, it is surrounded by a circular recess which forms the anterior, posterior and lateral *vaginal fornices* (singular, *fornix*)

The bladder and urethra are situated deep to the anterior vaginal wall. The upper part of the posterior wall is covered by peritoneum and is separated from the rectum by the pouch of Douglas (see above). The middle section of the posterior wall is also related to the rectum with loose connective tissue in between whereas the lower part of the posterior wall is separated from the anal canal by a fibro-muscular structure called the *perineal body*.

The surface of the vaginal wall is thrown into small folds or *rugae*, which allow expansion, and is covered by non-keratinised, stratified squamous epithelium not greatly dissimilar to the external skin. In a virgin, the lower vagina is partially closed by the incomplete sheet of the *hymen*, represented after first coitus by *hymeneal tags*.

The external female genitalia

The rounded, hair-bearing area of skin over a pad of fat on the pubic symphysis is the *mons pubis*, behind which the *labia majora* and *minora* surrounding the vaginal *introitus* form the *vulva*. More posteriorly still, the *perineum* extends from the vaginal *fourchette* to the *anus*.

Note that the gynaecological description of the perineum does not correspond with the anatomical definition, which refers to the whole region bounded by the pubic symphysis anteriorly, the tip of the coccyx posteriorly and the ischial tuberosities on each side. The gynaecological use of the term roughly corresponds with the 'anal region' of the anatomical perineum.

The urinary tract

The ureters

The ureters drain urine from the medial aspect of the kidneys which are situated high on the posterior abdominal wall. They pass down the posterior wall on each side of the spine and a short distance from it before entering the pelvis by crossing in front of the sacro-iliac joints over the point at which the common iliac artery divides into the external and internal iliac arteries. They then run downwards and forwards passing the cervix uteri just above the lateral vaginal fornices (where they are crossed at right angles by the uterine arteries) to enter the lateral parts of the posterior aspect of the bladder.

As noted above, the ureters are at risk of surgical damage when the ovaries are removed. This risk is greatly increased if the ovary is plastered down in the ovarian fossa as may occur in the presence of endometriosis or after previous pelvic surgery. They may also sustain damage at hysterectomy when the injury usually occurs where they pass the cervix.

The (urinary) bladder

The bladder lies behind the symphysis pubis and adjoining parts of the pubic bone. Its size and shape depend on the volume of the contained urine. Posteriorly, it is related to the upper vagina and to part of the cervix. The ureters enter from behind and the urine leaves the bladder inferiorly by draining into the urethra.

The bladder may be damaged at laparoscopy (by the Veress needle or the trochar) and at laparotomy. Injury may also occur at hysterectomy and at Caesarean section because of the close relationship between the bladder and the anterior aspect of the *cervix uteri*.

The urethra

It is important to distinguish carefully between the *urethra* and the *ureter*, as they are anatomically quite distant.

The female urethra is about 40 mm long and 6 mm in diameter (the male urethra is almost five times longer). It leaves the bladder and runs down behind the pubic symphysis being closely applied to the anterior vaginal wall. It ends at the urethral meatus between the anterior ends of the labia minora.

The gastro-intestinal tract

The *sigmoid colon* enters the pelvis on the left side of the posterior wall and passes down to become the *rectum* which continues downwards behind the vagina to become the *anal canal* at the level of the pelvic floor.

Loops of small bowel are also usually present in the pelvis, lying in the pouch of Douglas.

PHYSIOLOGY

Physiology is the study of the processes underlying normal bodily functions. Pathology is the study of disease and its effect upon the body. Gynaecologists must therefore have detailed understanding of both the physiology and the pathology of the female reproductive system.

Basic genetics

At conception (the union of a sperm and an egg), a new individual is created. We all inherit many characteristics from each of our parents but these are mixed to produce a distinct individual.

The characteristics are transmitted in a highly controlled manner and will determine many of our adult characteristics, although much happens to us as we mature. For example, eye colour is inherited directly from our parents but we must learn to ride a bicycle since we are not born with the innate ability to do so.

Chromosomes, genes and DNA

Each cell in the body contains a nucleus and contained within that nucleus are the chromosomes. These chromosomes are made up of thousands of genes and the genes, in turn, consist of DNA (deoxyribonucleic acid). DNA is the basic building block of the genetic information at the cellular level.

The genes act as templates for the cellular production of many different proteins and these, in turn, can alter the form and function of tissue.

Human beings have 46 chromosomes in the nucleus of most of their cells, 23 inherited from the mother and 23 inherited from the father.

The gonads (testes in the male and ovaries in the female) are rather specialised and have only 23 chromosomes in some of their cells, these being the ova (eggs) in the female and the sperm in the male. When the egg and the sperm combine at conception, the number is restored to 46 (23 pairs) with a unique genetic identity.

One specific pair of chromosomes, the sex chromosomes, determines an individual's sex. At conception, the ovum will always provide an X chromosome and the sperm may supply either an X or a Y chromosome. XX produces a chromosomal female, whereas XY produces a male. Consequently, it is the chromosome content of the sperm which determines the genetic sex of the offspring.

Sexual differentiation

Chromosomal sex is determined by the presence or absence of a Y chromosome, as outlined above.

Gonadal sex is determined by whether or not the individual possesses ovaries or testes. A gonadal female has ovaries and a gonadal male has testes.

Phenotypic sex describes the body's sexual appearance and applies largely to the external genitalia. An individual with a penis and scrotum is phenotypically male, whereas one with a clitoris and labia is phenotypically female.

This may sound obvious but, because chromosomal males change from being phenotypically female to becoming male while in utero, the process is complicated and leaves room for error. For example, there is a condition called 'androgen insensitivity syndrome' (formerly known as 'testicular feminising syndrome'), where the chromosomal male fails to respond to the hormones that would normally cause the change from the phenotypical female form to male. These people are thus born apparently female with a clitoris and labia and often their condition is not discovered until adulthood, when they find they are unable to conceive a pregnancy. On investigation, it is found they have no ovaries and, in fact, have very underdeveloped testes in their abdomen; their sex chromosomes are XY, that is, they are a chromosomal male, but they will have been brought up as female.

The sexual physiology of the unborn

Until the sixth week of pregnancy, the foetus is phenotypically female but the gonads are undifferentiated and have the capacity to become either testes or ovaries. The chromosomes, however, will be either male (XY) or female (XX)

In the normal male embryo at the sixth week of pregnancy, the Y chromosome initiates the production of a protein called testicular differentiating factor. This causes the undifferentiated gonad to become a testicle which, in turn, begins to produce two hormones, MIF (mullerian inhibiting factor) and testosterone. These cause the foetus to become phenotypically male and, in so doing, also cause the re-absorption of the primitive female genital tract.

In the normal female, the absence of the Y chromosome causes the female form to persist and the gonad becomes an ovary, allowing the continued development of the female genital tract.

Childhood

During childhood, there is little difference in the hormone production between boys and girls but at puberty the two sexes diverge. Further discussion here is confined to the female physiology.

Puberty

Puberty is the sequence of events by which a child is transformed into an adult and becomes capable of reproduction. Several physical change are evident: breast development, axillary (armpit) and pubic hair growth, an increase in height commonly known as the 'growth spurt', and menarche, which is the onset of menstruation. The ovary will also be maturing and ovulation will commence but this has no obvious external manifestations since it does not necessarily coincide with menarche.

There is much variation in the timing of pubertal events. The first sign is usually breast bud development and an increase in height, followed by hair growth and then of menstruation. However, only about 50% of girls will follow this sequence. The whole process takes approximately two years, with menstruation usually beginning between ages 11 and 15 years.

The age at which puberty occurs is influenced by a number of factors, particularly that of body weight. Under-nourished girls are more likely to have a delayed menarche. The age of menarche has decreased in this century, probably because of the improvement in general health and nutrition.

The precise physiological processes that initiate puberty are unknown. Steroid hormones produced from the adrenal gland may be involved, particularly in the growth of the secondary sexual hair or telarche. A body weight of 48 kg or more is required to menstruate which explains why anorexic girls do not have menstrual bleeds. The menarche appears to be initiated in the hypothalamus which is located in the primitive part of the brain and produces a variety of 'releasing' hormones that act upon the pituitary gland (situated just below the brain) to release other hormones. The hypothalamic releasing hormone involved in the reproductive system is known as gonadotrophin releasing hormone (GnRH). During puberty, the hypothalamus gradually produces increasing amounts of GnRH which causes the release of the pituitary gonadotrophins (*trophin* – to grow) follicle stimulating hormone (FSH), and luteinising hormone (LH). In response to the gonadotrophins, the ovary begins to produce some ovarian hormones, gradually the female endocrine pattern will become established and cyclical ovulation and menstruation will occur. Initially, however, ovulation does not necessarily occur every month and, after the menarche, it usually takes two years or more for regular ovulation to become established.

The menstrual cycle

The menstrual cycle conventionally begins with the first day of vaginal bleeding and ends just before the next menstrual bleed starts. Most women have a cycle length of 28 days but the range is between 21 and 40 days. It is more common to have irregular menstrual cycles at the beginning and end of reproductive life.

The menstrual cycle depends upon the interaction of hormones produced in the hypothalamus, the pituitary gland and the ovary. The cycle consists of three distinct phases which are termed the follicular, ovulatory and luteal phases with reference to the events occurring in the ovary.

Follicular phase

In the follicular phase, the level of follicle stimulating hormone (FSH) from the pituitary increases. This initiates the growth and development of a cohort of eggs (between three and 20) within the ovary. Only one egg will usually be released at ovulation and the rest regress and die. The egg develops within a fluid-filled sac which is surrounded by a further layer of specialised cells, the whole structure being known as a follicle. The surrounding cells produce the hormone oestrogen (as oestradiol), the production of which gradually increases. This increase in oestradiol production raises the blood level of the hormone which is detected by the hypothalamus which then produces less GnRH (see above), thereby reducing the release of FSH and LH from the pituitary. This type of interactive system is widely encountered in physiological processes and is known as 'negative feedback'.

Figure 2.7   The pituitary-ovarian axis

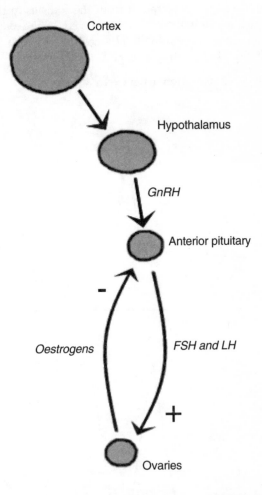

This greatly simplified illustration of the endocrine relationships shows the positive effect of FSH on ovarian function and the 'negative feedback' effect of the ovarian oestrogen on the pituitary

Ovulatory phase

As the production of oestradiol from the follicles in the ovary increases, the level of FSH, and initially of LH, is reduced. When ovulation is imminent, LH production ceases to be inhibited by oestradiol which now seems to cause the release of more LH creating a surge in the hormone.

Figure 2.8   Day of menstrual cycle

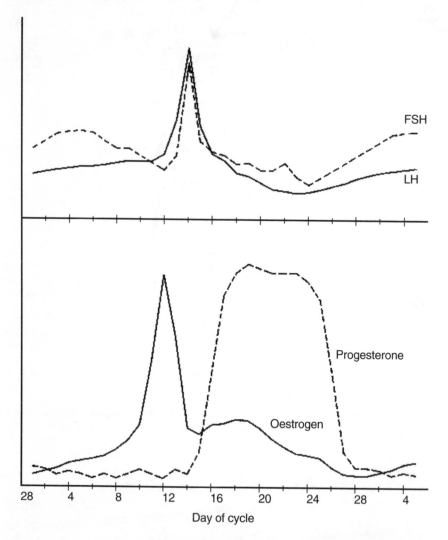

FSH

LH

Progesterone

Oestrogen

| 28 | 4 | 8 | 12 | 16 | 20 | 24 | 28 | 4 |

Day of cycle

The graphs illustrate the pattern of changes shown by the serum levels of FSH and LH (upper graphs) and oestrogen and progesterone (lower graphs) during a menstrual cycle in which conception does not occur. Note that the graphs for each hormone are at different scales and should not be taken to indicate actual levels.

Ovulation occurs 12–24 hours after the rise in LH. The exact mechanism of ovulation is not understood but the surface cells allow release of the egg into the pelvic cavity or, perhaps more commonly, into the overlying fallopian tube.

Luteal phase

Once ovulation has occurred, the number of follicular cells increases and they begin to produce the hormone progesterone. The serum level of this hormone is frequently measured as an indicator of ovulation; a level greater than about 10 nmol/l suggests that ovulation has taken place.

Pregnancy

During pregnancy, the female body undergoes enormous physiological changes in response to an increased hormonal production. The hormones are primarily produced by the placenta. Some of these are specific to pregnancy but the placenta also produces the female hormones oestrogen and progesterone which are present in far greater amounts during pregnancy than in the non-pregnant state.

The changes that occur in pregnancy are not restricted to the reproductive system but affect the whole body. It is beyond the scope of this book to do any more than outline the major changes that occur.

Very early in pregnancy, the amount of blood and other body fluids increases. This increase occurs before the uterus has enlarged sufficiently to need the extra blood supply and the additional blood is diverted to the skin contributing to the sense of warmth and well being that is frequently experienced.

The blood is also more 'sticky' than in a non-pregnant woman. A pregnant, or recently pregnant woman, is at least 10 times more likely to develop a blood clot (thrombus) in the deep veins of the leg (deep venous thrombosis or 'DVT') than at any other time during her lifetime. This is reflected in the fact that thrombosis and its sequelae are now the leading cause of deaths related to pregnancy.

The heart works harder during pregnancy and the blood pressure falls slightly. Elevation of the blood pressure in pregnancy is abnormal.

The rate of breathing is subconsciously increased often leading to a feeling of shortness of breath. This is exacerbated later in pregnancy as the pregnant uterus displaces the abdominal contents upwards against the diaphragm.

The digestive tract relaxes, leading to heartburn and indigestion. Gut movement is reduced, often leading to constipation. Fat is deposited in the body's fat stores.

The enlarging uterus presses upon the bladder and there is a dilatation of the urinary tract causing partial stasis of the urine and an increased incidence of urinary tract infections.

These changes subside at a variable rate as the pregnancy is completed. Some resolve within a few days but others take several weeks to return to the pre-pregnancy state. Lactation will further delay complete resolution.

Lactation

The production of breast milk (lactation) is the end result of a variety of influences. Pubertal breast development is initiated by oestrogen hormones but, during pregnancy, the breasts increase further in size in response to the high level of circulating oestrogen and, probably, also progesterone and human placental lactogen (HPL), both of these being produced by the placenta.

Prolactin (from the pituitary gland) is essential for lactation itself but its effect is largely suppressed until, after the birth of the infant, the maternal level of oestrogen falls allowing milk production to begin. Once initiated by the hormone changes, lactation is maintained by the continued suckling of the infant which stimulates the nerves endings in the nipples. The impulses are passed along the nerves to the hypothalamus and thence to the pituitary gland. This gland releases a hormone called oxytocin which acts upon the small muscles surrounding the milk ducts in the breasts causing muscular contraction and release of the milk (the 'let-down' reflex).

The menstrual cycle is generally suppressed during lactation. However, ovarian suppression decreases with the passage of time even if lactation continues so that the possibility of ovulation and, hence, the chance of another pregnancy arises. Consequently, lactation should not be relied upon as contraception.

The menopause

The term 'menopause' refers to the cessation of menstrual bleeding and 'climacteric' identifies the period of time before and after this occurs. The two words are often, though incorrectly, used synonymously.

With advancing years, the ovary has fewer primitive eggs and fewer developing follicles; hence, less oestrogen is produced. The GnRH (from the hypothalamus) increases in an attempt to drive the ovaries but to no avail; the FSH and LH levels increase but the oestrogen hormones are low.

Effects of the menopause/climacteric

These may be considered in two different categories.

First, there are the obvious symptoms that may be experienced by any woman in the climacteric. They include facial flushing (which may be extremely embarrassing), night sweats, irritability and an inability to concentrate. Other symptoms are related to thinning of the epithelium of the uro-genital tract and include bladder weakness and dyspareunia (discomfort during sexual intercourse). All these symptoms will generally resolve but one quarter of women will continue to experience them in varying degrees for more than five years.

The second group of problems are also due to the lack of oestrogen but do not necessarily cause symptoms; nevertheless, they are vastly more important in terms of the general health of an increasingly ageing population. The major factors are cardiovascular disease and osteoporosis (de-mineralisation of the bones). Their importance lies in the fact that they are responsible for a good deal of the ill health and death in the post-menopausal population. Cardiovascular disease includes heart attacks and strokes. Before the menopause, it is uncommon for women to suffer either a heart attack or a stroke but, after the cessation of ovarian activity, the female incidence of these conditions rises and soon matches that of men. The other important health problem in the older post-menopausal woman is that of fragile bones or osteoporosis and there is an associated rise in the incidence of fractures. These are often incapacitating and, if a large bone such as the femur is involved, may prove fatal.

Hormone replacement therapy (HRT)

Hormone replacement therapy aims to replace the ovarian hormones that are no longer produced after the menopause. The most important hormone is oestrogen but, unless the woman has already undergone a hysterectomy, progesterone should also be administered to prevent over-stimulation of the uterine lining, a condition which is associated with an increased risk of endometrial carcinoma. The addition of progesterone for two weeks in each month usually causes the woman to have regular monthly bleeding. Many women are happy to tolerate this, certainly for a few years, but women who choose to have HRT for longer than about five years often desire an end to the inconvenience of vaginal bleeds. Newer preparations provide a small continuous dose of progesterone designed to minimise the chance of bleeding. HRT can be administered by tablet, patch, gels or implants. Some preparations may have advantages for particular women but the choice is usually determined by the woman's preference.

HRT commenced at the menopause and continued for five years will reduce the chance of fractures by approximately 50%.

Contra-indications and side effects

Much of the practice of medicine consists of the assessment of the benefits and risks of a possible line of treatment in order to arrive at a balanced decision; the administration of hormone replacement therapy is no exception.

Many women experience no untoward symptoms at the climacteric and, for many more, any symptoms are minor and transient. Unfortunately, a significant proportion may be subject to episodes of vasomotor instability ('hot flushes'), disturbances of sleep patterns and emotional lability. All these symptoms respond well to HRT, the hot flushes sometimes ceasing within 36 hours of starting therapy though other symptoms usually take longer to improve.

The relief of climacteric symptoms may require HRT for a few months or up to three or four years but many women now continue on the therapy for the long term benefits of the reduced incidence of heart disease, cerebro-vascular accidents ('strokes') and osteoporosis. This may be particularly appropriate if there is a family history of any of these conditions.

In contrast, HRT is contra-indicated for women who are known or suspected to be suffering from carcinoma of the breast or from oestrogen dependent malignancies in other sites. It is also contra-indicated in the presence of some severe cardiac or renal diseases or if hepatic disease has interfered with liver function.

High doses of oestrogen, such as in some oral contraceptives, have been implicated in the causation of veneous thrombosis. The lower, replacement doses associated with HRT were formerly thought to have no such effect but recent analysis of the published studies suggests that they may also increase the thrombosis rate, though to a much smaller extent. The current view is that the risk of thrombosis in women not taking HRT is about one in 10,000 per year and that HRT increases this to about three in 10,000 per year. Most of these cases respond to treatment but a few prove fatal, the death rate being estimated at one in one million per year for non-HRT women and three in one million per year on HRT. A history of deep venous thrombosis or of thrombo-embolism is usually regarded as a contraindication to the use of oestrogen supplements.

On first starting HRT, many women will experience cyclical breast tenderness. In the majority of cases, this will improve after the first two or three months of treatment but sometimes it persists and the symptom may occasionally develop in women who have been taking HRT for several years. It is thought to be the commonest reason for women to discontinue treatment, often without reference to medical advice. Many cases resolve if the HRT preparation is changed.

Some women, particularly those who have suffered from pre-menstrual symptoms during their natural cycle, may complain of HRT-induced PMS. Again, a change of preparation may be effective.

Headaches can be associated with HRT and may be sufficiently severe and frequent to cause cessation of treatment. In a few instances, true migraine attacks may be precipitated.

The bleeding associated with combined oestrogen/progestogen HRT may be heavy and scanty but irregular bleeding may occur with the so called 'non-bleeding' HRT. Many women attribute weight gain to HRT and there may certainly be an alteration in dietary needs but any increase in body weight seems to be related to an incorrect dose of oestrogen since, contrary to expectations, an increased dose may be followed by a return to normal weight.

Oestrogens were thought to cause elevation of the blood pressure but a large US study some years ago demonstrated that mild hypertension could actually improve on HRT; severe hypertension remains as a contra-indication.

The role of unopposed oestrogen in the development of endometrial hyperplasia and possibly carcinoma has already been mentioned above, and the original oestrogen-only preparations are contra-indicated in women who retain their uterus (though a few, who find the side effects of the combined preparations to be unacceptable but who value the oestrogen effects, may choose to take the risk).

The possible association between HRT and an increased risk of breast cancer has been a subject of discussion and disagreement for many years. The question has been resolved, at least for the present, by the recent publication of a meta-analysis of the available data which concluded that the risk is probably doubled if HRT is taken for longer than about eight years. Cancer in women on HRT seems to be more amenable to treatment but the mechanism for this is, as yet, unexplained. It has been suggested that women on therapy are more likely to attend for regular medical review with the result that the disease is detected sooner than would otherwise be the case.

In any discussion with patients, it is important to realise that the increased incidence of breast cancer is less than the decreased mortality from heart disease and strokes. Women wishing to remain on long-term HRT should have regular mammography, perhaps yearly if there is a family history of breast cancer or 2–3 yearly otherwise.

Progestogen HRT

In recent years, the use of progestogens derived from plant extract (notably the yam), have been promoted as alternatives to conventional HRT. In some women, they are certainly effective in relieving climacteric symptoms but their long term effects remain to be established. They do offer a useful option for women who are unable or unwilling to take oestrogens.

CHAPTER 3

COMMON OPERATIVE PROCEDURES IN GYNAECOLOGY

In this book, important operative points are generally mentioned along with the conditions with which they are associated but there are some surgical procedures which are employed so frequently in gynaecology that they merit separate consideration. These are *dilatation and curettage* (D & C), *hysteroscopy*, *laparoscopy* and *hysterectomy*. In addition, this chapter also deals with commonly used techniques for opening the abdominal cavity.

The procedures to be described are usually performed under general anaesthesia and this itself carries small but significant hazards. Since this volume is concerned with gynaecology, these risks are not considered in detail here but this fact should not be taken to imply that they are unimportant.

The anaesthetist is usually responsible for the safety of the patient in the operating theatre and, when electrosurgical equipment is to be used (for example, diathermy cauterisation), there is the special consideration that it is essential that no part of the anaesthetised patient is in contact with any metallic part of the operating table or its attachments. If the patient is not properly insulated by suitable rubber or plastic padding, an otherwise insignificant fault in the electrical equipment could result in a serious burn at the point of contact. The courts have, on occasion, applied the principle of *res ipse loquitur* to such burns and may place the burden of proof on the defendant to show that the injury was not due to negligence.

THE D & C

The term D & C is the widely accepted abbreviation for dilatation and curettage in which the cervical canal is stretched (dilated) and instruments then introduced into the uterine cavity to scrape (curette) the lining. Patients often refer to this as a 'scrape' or, sometimes, as 'cleaning the womb'. The procedure is similar to the commonly used method of surgical termination of pregnancy but, because there are differences both in the instruments used and in the risks involved, the latter is discussed separately (Chapter 13).

The D & C is undoubtedly the most frequent operative procedure undertaken by gynaecologists, though, in recent years, it has been partially replaced by other, more newly developed techniques.

Indications

The indications for performing a D & C fall into two groups, diagnostic and therapeutic.

Diagnostic

The majority of D & Cs are performed as part of the investigation of gynaecological problems since, at least until the advent of hysteroscopy, it was the only way in which the cavity of the uterus could be satisfactorily explored. Unfortunately, gynaecologists often fail to explain to the patient that the procedure is not necessarily expected to cure their symptoms and, in consequence, the woman may be understandably aggrieved when, having undergone a D & C, her symptoms persist unaltered.

The term 'dysfunctional uterine bleeding' is unsatisfactory, being essentially descriptive and unrelated to any particular pathological process. Furthermore, by providing a convenient label, it may impede the search for a true diagnosis. However, it is convenient to use it here as, prior to the D & C, the precise diagnosis will usually be unknown, the purpose of the curettage being to obtain a sample of the endometrium for histopathological examination, following which, appropriate management can be planned. In some cases, the curettage may be followed by an improvement in the symptoms for several months but the effect is almost always only temporary and appropriate follow-up arrangements should be made.

Menorrhagia is a very common presenting symptom in every general gynaecological clinic and is often investigated by an initial D & C. In about one-third of all cases, there will be a reduction in the menstrual loss but this is likely to be transient. In those cases where heavy periods are due to some anatomical factor, such as uterine fibromyomata, no improvement can be expected and the purpose of the D & C is to exclude other pathology before planning the definitive management.

The possible causes of post-menopausal vaginal bleeding (PMB) are discussed in Chapter 5, but the most significant of these *and the one that must be excluded in every case* is a carcinoma of the endometrium. The only safe rule to follow is that every case of PMB must be investigated by D & C (or by one of the more recent techniques discussed later in this chapter); this should apply even if an obvious alternative cause for the bleeding is present. The author has recently been invited to comment on the case of a 56 year old woman who presented to her general practitioner with post-menopausal bleeding which was attributed to her hormone replacement therapy; in consequence, she was not referred for further investigation until 18 months later, when a D & C revealed her to have an advanced endometrial cancer.

Intermenstrual bleeding may also be due to pathology within the uterine cavity and, in some of these, the D & C may be both diagnostic and therapeutic. For example, some intermenstrual bleeding will be due to endometrial polypi and their removal by curettage may then be curative.

Therapeutic

Dysmenorrhoea may occasionally be treated by dilatation of the cervix (not necessarily followed by curettage). In the past, this was done quite frequently and was based on the assumption that the pain was the result of poor drainage of menstrual fluids due to a narrow cervical canal causing a rise in pressure within the uterine cavity. The theory is unfashionable at present and some authorities would deny that this indication is ever valid, though others would admit that it might have a place in a few cases, especially if the symptoms follow some other surgical procedure on the cervix, such as a cone biopsy.

The removal of endometrial polypi has already been mentioned but other intra-uterine conditions may also be treated by the curettage. Occasionally, small pieces of placental tissue may remain within the uterus after the delivery of a baby. Usually, these fragments are evacuated naturally with the first menstrual period after the delivery but, occasionally, they may remain in utero, forming a placental polyp and causing irregular bleeding which may sometimes be heavy. Removal by curettage is simple and effective. Not long ago, the author removed a placental fragment that had been present and causing symptoms for so long that it had undergone calcification.

The different types of abortion (miscarriage of pregnancy) are discussed in the appropriate section of this book but many of these will need treatment by the evacuation of retained products of conception, usually abbreviated to 'evacuation', 'evac' or 'ERPC'. The procedure in such cases is essentially the same as for a D & C on the non-pregnant uterus but the risks of haemorrhage and perforation are more akin to those associated with the surgical termination of pregnancy.

The procedure

In most women, the cervix of the uterus is surprisingly insensitive and may be grasped with sharp instruments, frozen or even cauterised with red-hot wires with very little discomfort to the patient. In contrast, it is extremely sensitive to dilatation of its canal and any attempt to do so in the conscious patient usually causes severe pain and may result in profound neurogenic shock (this was frequently the cause of death in cases of 'back street' abortions). It is possible to carry out modest dilatation under local analgesia but much more common for a general anaesthetic to be given. The development of sedo-analgesia (the so called 'twilight sleep') in recent years does offer an alternative, especially if some local anaesthetic is also injected on either side of the cervix before the dilatation begins.

Following the induction of general anaesthesia, the patient will normally be placed into the 'lithotomy position' in which her hips and knees are flexed to 90° or slightly more and her thighs are abducted. This position of the legs is usually maintained by placing her feet in double webbing 'stirrups' which are supported by poles attached to the side of the operating table but other equipment is sometimes preferred, usually some variation of the 'Lloyd-Davies supports'.

Most women are able to adopt this position without difficulty but the presence of osteo-arthritic changes in the hips or knees may limit movement of these joints and general anaesthesia will abolish the muscle spasm which would, in the conscious patient, protect the affected joint from damage. The anaesthetist cannot take the proper precautions to safeguard the patient unless adequately forewarned by the gynaecological team (who will have been responsible for the pre-operative clinical history and examination). Any relevant non-gynaecological information must therefore be clearly recorded in the notes and is also best included as an additional comment (for example, 'Stiff right hip') on the operation list supplied to the operating theatre. This is particularly important in the case of a D & C which, being classified as a 'minor' procedure, is often delegated to one of the more junior members of the gynaecological team who may well not have met the patient pre-operatively.

The lithotomy position may also impose some strain on the joints of the lower spine, especially if the patient is positioned too far down the operating table, so that her buttocks are unsupported.

After positioning of the patient, the surgeon (now 'scrubbed-up' and wearing a sterile gown and gloves) should inspect the vulva for any apparent abnormalities. The presence of any vaginal discharge should be noted and a swab may be taken for bacteriological examination if necessary.

The lower part of the mons pubis, the vulva and the perineum are then cleaned with a gauze or sponge (usually held in sponge-holding forceps) soaked in a water-based antiseptic solution. A second swab is then used to cleanse the vagina using the same solution. Antiseptic solutions containing surgical spirit should not be used in the vagina; this is especially true if the use of any diathermy is contemplated as severe vaginal burns have resulted from ignition of residual pools of the spirit. The lower part of the patient's body (usually including the legs) is then covered with sterile towels, leaving the vulva exposed.

The surgeon then performs a bimanual examination, the purpose of which is primarily to determine the size and position of the uterus, though any other palpable abnormalities should also be noted (for example, irregularities of the cervix, pelvic masses, etc). The information should be documented in the operation note. Omission of this assessment increases the risk of subsequent perforation of the uterine wall by the surgical instruments.

A speculum is introduced into the vagina and positioned so that the best possible view of the cervix is obtained, following which, the anterior lip of the cervix is grasped with tenaculum or Volsellum forceps and gently drawn downwards to straighten out the curvature of the cervico-uterine canal and also to steady the uterus.

The length of the uterine cavity may then be measured by introducing a uterine sound through the cervical canal and advancing it gently until the tip of the instrument is felt to have reached the fundus of the uterus. Undue force in this manoeuvre may result in perforation of the uterine wall, especially if the operator is unsure of the approximate length of the cavity or its probable direction (hence the need for the preliminary bimanual assessment). In the case of a recently pregnant uterus (for example, if the D & C is being performed after an abortion or recent delivery), the increased vascularity of the uterine wall renders it very soft and it may be difficult or impossible to feel when the top of the cavity has been reached; in such cases, therefore, it may be wiser to omit the use of the sound altogether. Difficulties may also be encountered if the cervical canal is very tight, when it may be impossible to introduce the sound (the rounded tip of which has a diameter of about 3 mm) and it may be necessary to use a very small dilator; such cases should be left to experienced gynaecological surgeons if the risk of uterine perforation and the creation of false passages is to be minimised.

The purpose of the uterine sound is to establish not only the length but also the direction of the uterine cavity in preparation for the subsequent introduction of the cervical dilators. Various patterns of dilators have been described but the type most commonly used is that attributed to Hegar. These are manufactured in single and double-ended versions and are available in sizes that increase by 1 mm or by 0.5 mm. For most purposes, the 1 mm increments are satisfactory but, if the dilatation proves unusually difficult, 0.5 mm increments may help to prevent damage to the cervical tissues. A dilatation of, for example, 9 mm is often recorded as 'Hegar 9' (or sometimes 'H 9'). The introduction of the dilators should be accompanied by counter-traction on the tenaculum forceps to draw the cervix slightly downwards thereby steadying it and reducing the natural curve in its canal.

Over dilatation of the cervix, especially if hurried or forcible, may cause permanent damage, though this may not be apparent at the time. Some experience is required to judge how far dilatation may safely be taken but it should never be more than is required for the safe introduction of subsequent instruments and, as a general guide, should not exceed 9 mm for the non-pregnant cervix. The softer cervix of pregnancy may usually be dilated as far as 14 mm without damage. Despite the need to avoid over dilatation, insufficient enlargement of the cervical canal can also cause problems because of the increased resistance to the subsequent introduction of other instruments, with the result that they may enter the uterine cavity in an uncontrolled manner and themselves cause damage to the uterine wall.

Once dilatation of the cervix has been completed, it is then usual to introduce polyp forceps into the uterine cavity. This instrument is designed to grasp any polypi or other debris that may be present within the uterine cavity so that, if small enough or sufficiently compressible, it may be drawn out through the cervical canal.

A suitable curette is then selected, the size of which (like the polyp forceps which preceded it) is necessarily limited by the extent of the cervical dilatation. It is, however, important not to use instruments which are of too small a size, since this will again be associated with a risk of uterine perforation. Apart from being manufactured in various sizes, uterine curettes may be blunt or sharp edged and some gynaecologists claim that, when dealing with the softened (and therefore more easily damaged) wall of the recently pregnant uterus, it is safer to use the blunt variety. The authors do not subscribe to this view, believing that it is safer to use a sharp curette with due care than to indulge in over enthusiastic curettage with a blunt instrument in the mistaken belief that no harm can result. During the curettage, any fragments of tissue which are obtained should be inspected with the naked eye (after removing any associated blood clot) before being placed in a preservative solution (usually 10% formaldehyde in water) prior to being sent to the laboratory for histopathological examination. Occasionally, it may also be necessary to send a specimen dry or in 'normal' (also called 'physiological') saline (0.9% sodium chloride in water) if bacteriological examination is indicated.

On conclusion of the curettage, the tenaculum forceps which have been grasping the cervix are removed and the vagina is mopped out with a gauze swab, taking care to recover any fragments of endometrium which may be mixed with the blood which will be present. The cervix should then be inspected to determine whether there is any continuing bleeding emerging from the cervical canal; if so, it will usually stop if the surgeon, having removed the vaginal speculum, places two fingers in the vagina and the other hand flat on the patient's lower abdomen, then firmly compressing the uterus for about 60 seconds. If this fails to control significant haemorrhage, it may be that the uterine cavity is not yet empty or that its wall has been perforated.

Troublesome bleeding may occur from the site of application of the Volsellum forceps; this may require the insertion of a haemostatic suture.

Once the surgeon is satisfied that any significant blood loss has ceased, the sterile towels are removed, the patient's legs taken down from the lithotomy position and the anaesthetic discontinued. In uncomplicated cases, the whole procedure will probably take no longer than about 10 minutes and subsequent recovery of consciousness is rapid. Post-operative pain, if present at all, is limited to minor lower abdominal discomfort, which soon passes off.

Many patients are now discharged from hospital within a few hours of the procedure but, before leaving, should be warned to return in the event of increased vaginal bleeding or significant abdominal pain.

Hazards of the procedure

Apart from the risks of anaesthesia and of positioning the patient, the major hazard of a dilatation and curettage is of perforation of the uterine wall. This arises because the cervical canal and uterine cavity have a variable direction and degree of curvature. Although the instruments (uterine sound, dilators and curette) are also curved, they are not flexible and, if incorrectly introduced, may create a false passage within the uterine wall or even penetrate the wall entirely. This is especially so if the natural curve of the cavity is presumed to be forwards (the usual case) when the uterus is retroverted and retroflexed, in which case, the actual curve will be backwards.

Figure 3.1   Uterine perforation

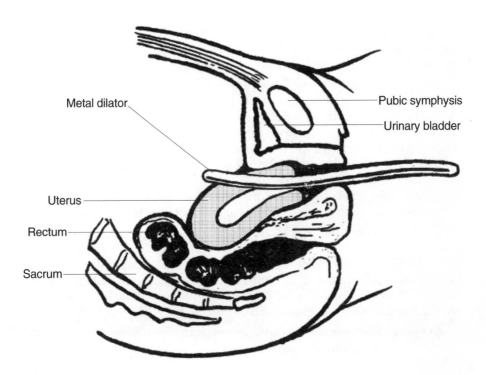

Median section through a female pelvis, showing a retroverted uterus with a perforation of the anterior wall by a metal dilator

Minor perforations probably occur fairly frequently and are of little significance but their real importance lies in the fact that there may be associated damage to other intra-abdominal structures, in particular, major blood vessels or loops of bowel resulting in post-operative internal bleeding or sepsis.

Provided all reasonable precautions have been taken, the creation of a perforation is not, of itself, evidence of negligence. It is, however, essential that, if a perforation is suspected, the operation is discontinued and consideration is given to the possible need for a laparoscopy (or laparotomy) to inspect the damage. Furthermore, the situation should be fully explained to the patient when she has regained consciousness and she should be kept under observation in hospital if necessary or, at the very least, warned to return immediately in the event of any untoward symptoms. Antibiotic therapy may be indicated, especially in the event of possible damage to the bowel.

Uterine perforation is much more common when the uterine wall has been softened by the presence of a pregnancy (either current or in the recent past) and there are also other hazards in this situation which are described in the discussion of the surgical termination of pregnancy.

It has already been pointed out that dilatation of the cervix beyond 9 mm (14 mm in pregnancy) should normally be avoided. The reason for this is that excessive dilatation, though not necessarily causing any visible tear, may result in rupture of the muscle fibres within the substance of the cervix. Such internal damage may give rise to cervical incompetence when, in a subsequent pregnancy, the cervix opens inappropriately early with miscarriage or premature delivery of the foetus. This can happen at any stage of the pregnancy after about 12 weeks but is most common at 16–18 weeks, when the foetus is still incapable of independent, extra-uterine life.

Cervical incompetence was quite frequently encountered in the years following the legalisation of the termination of pregnancy in the UK by the Abortion Act 1967, but, since recognition of the need to avoid over dilatation, its incidence has decreased. In some units, there has recently been a trend towards the re-introduction of later surgical terminations, the long-term effects of which remain to be assessed.

Cervical incompetence may also follow high cervical cone biopsies and termination of pregnancy by prostaglandin.

The operation notes

The procedure has here been described in considerable detail but it would not be usual to include all this information in the clinical record of the operation. A typical operation note might read as follows:

DATE: 4-1-99
SURGEON: Mr A Smith
ANAESTHETIST: Dr B Jones
PROCEDURE: D & C

V & V: nad

Cx: nad

Ut: n/s a/v m

Ad: nad

PoD: nad

Cavity 8 cm

Cx dilated to H 8

Sharp curettage   smooth cavity normal looking
curettings (histology)

Minimal blood loss

The five lines recording the initial examination indicate that no significant abnormality was detected (nad) in the vulva and vagina (V & V), cervix (Cx), adnexal regions (Ad) or pouch of Douglas (PoD) and that the uterus (Ut) was of normal size (n/s), in an anteverted position (a/v) and normally mobile (m).

The operation note must, of course, be signed.

HYSTEROSCOPY

A significant feature of gynaecology in the UK in recent years has been the increased availability and use of the hysteroscope. This instrument, which is designed to enable the surgeon to visually inspect the uterine cavity, was first developed in Germany and France. Although a few British gynaecologists, including the author, were using early versions of the instrument almost 20 years ago, it was not until technical developments in optical systems and light sources improved the quality of the view that the procedure became more widely adopted. These improvements have been accompanied by electronic advances which have produced small, light camera systems which may be attached to the basic instrument allowing the procedures to be viewed on screen and to be recorded on videotape and as still photographs.

The hysteroscopes themselves have become narrower and, at the time of writing, are commercially available as small as 2 mm in diameter (see below), though the most common sizes are between 5 mm and 7 mm. The cervical dilatation required for their introduction into the uterine cavity is no greater than that needed for a routine D & C.

Indications

When a pathological change in the endometrium is generalised or, at least, fairly widespread, the diagnostic reliability of the D & C is good. For localised lesions of the uterine cavity, however, the detection rate can depend as much on luck as on the skill of the operator. This situation is vastly improved by the use of a hysteroscope to inspect the endometrium. In addition, recent technical advances have greatly advanced the therapeutic capabilities of the instrument.

Diagnostic

The diagnostic indications for the use of the hysteroscope are essentially the same as for a D & C. At present, not all gynaecological units have the required equipment but, in those which do, there are few occasions when visual inspection of the uterine cavity should not precede a curettage. Exceptions are when the curettage is performed after a miscarriage or when there is active bleeding in progress, which will obscure the hysteroscopic view.

Therapeutic

In addition to its value as a diagnostic tool, the hysteroscope can also be used to perform some types of surgical treatment within the uterine cavity. As with the D & C, though much more reliably, polypi can be removed but so, too, can some fibroids, as the possibilities for treatment with the hysteroscope are wider than when the curette was used blindly.

One of the most significant advances has been the opportunity of treating the common condition of menorrhagia by endometrial ablation (coagulation or resection). When first introduced, these techniques generated a great deal of enthusiasm since they offered an alternative to a hysterectomy. Not only did the new methods avoid an abdominal incision and the psychological factors associated with a hysterectomy but they also offered a much shorter stay in hospital (most operative hysteroscopies being done as day cases or, at the most, with overnight stay) and an early return to all normal activities. Latterly there has been a shift of opinion as the long-term effects have become apparent, in particular the incidence of 'failure' as evidenced by the return of heavy periods. This is not to suggest that the hysteroscopic treatments are unsatisfactory but merely that they are now finding their rightful place in the gynaecological armourmentarium.

The procedure

After any necessary dilatation of the cervix, the hysteroscope must be passed into the uterine cavity with some care if perforation is to be avoided as, unlike most of the other instruments which are curved to follow the line of the cervical canal, the majority of hysteroscopes are rigid and have no curve. In some cases, the author has found it possible to enter the uterine cavity under direct hysteroscopic vision when it had proved impossible to introduce either a uterine sound or a cervical dilator but this manoeuvre is made more difficult by the fact that the viewing axis is usually at an angle of about 30° to the long axis of the instrument.

In order to distend the uterine cavity (and to flush away any blood), fluid is usually introduced into the cavity by a side tube running beside the optical part of the hysteroscope. As some of the fluid will inevitably enter the bloodstream, it must be chosen with regard to its physiological characteristics as well as to its physical properties. For diagnostic purposes or for laser ablation of the endometrium, the fluid will usually be 0.9% saline, though 5% dextrose, dextrose-saline and Ringer lactate solution have also been used successfully. A special solution (Hyskon), a 32% solution of dextran 70 in 10% dextrose, is available. This has excellent optical properties and does not mix with blood but instruments must be thoroughly washed immediately after use to prevent crystallisation within the fluid channels. If electrodiathermy is required (endometrial resection or roller ball coagulation), electroconductive solutions are useless and 1.5% glycine should be substituted.

In order to avoid missing any significant features, the uterine must be inspected systematically. The usual method is to begin at the fundus taking care to identify both tubal ostia. The uterine walls are then checked as the hysteroscope is slowly withdrawn, finally viewing the region of the internal cervical os and the cervical canal itself.

Operative hysteroscopy

The same optical system is usually used but it is introduced into the uterine cavity within a larger sheath (the diameter of which would be typically 10 mm), thereby enabling specially designed instruments to be passed alongside. By this means, it is possible to take biopsies of any intra-uterine lesions, to destroy the endometrial lining of the uterus by electro-coagulation using a 'roller ball' or to remove it by electro-resection, or to excise polypi or moderate sized fibroids.

Although hysteroscopic surgical techniques are themselves quite simple, it is essential, before attempting them, that the operator has acquired good hand/eye co-ordination by experience with the diagnostic procedures and, ideally, by practising on the specially designed training models which are now available. Neglect of this basic tuition has caused a number of medico-legal problems, mainly due to the inadvertent, and sometimes unrecognised, perforation of the uterine wall and, as a consequence, some units now insist that gynaecological surgeons provide documentary evidence of having attended a course in this type of procedure before they may operate on patients.

Hazards of the procedure

Hysteroscopy, being essentially an extension of the older D & C, is associated with the same hazards. As has already been pointed out, the fact that the hysteroscope itself is both straight and rigid makes it somewhat more difficult to follow the normal curve of the cervical canal and uterine cavity. Extra care must therefore be taken if perforation of the uterine wall is to be avoided.

Operative hysteroscopy carries additional risks as over enthusiastic electro-cautery may result in full thickness damage to the wall with subsequent ischaemic necrosis and sloughing of the tissues while poorly controlled electro-resection may cut through the wall. Even correctly performed operations will result in the presence of tissue fragments which, if not removed from the uterine cavity, can provide a focus for intra-uterine infection which, if not diagnosed and actively treated, may lead on to a more generalised pelvic infection.

Operative techniques, especially those involving large areas of the endometrial surface, may also result in troublesome haemorrhage. In addition, unless both tubes are obstructed, some of the fluid used to distend the uterine cavity will find its way into the peritoneal cavity and it may also enter the patient's blood stream via damaged vessels in the uterine wall. The absorption of small quantities of these fluids is usually well tolerated but large quantities may cause a significant fall in the patient's body temperature and can result in circulatory overload leading to pulmonary and cerebral oedema, convulsions, coma and death. If the fluid in use is 5% dextrose or glycine, the effect is exaggerated by a dilutional hyponatraemia. In all cases therefore, it is essential that the fluid balance is carefully monitored.

The operation notes

The operation note for a hysteroscopy will follow a similar pattern to that already described for a D & C except that the hysteroscopic appearances must be included. A simple diagram may provide a useful supplement to the verbal description but visual records in the form of still photographs or videotape are even better.

LAPAROSCOPY

Like the hysteroscope, the laparoscope was first developed on the Continent and it was only later, in the 1960s, that it began to be widely used by gynaecologists in the UK. Since then, its use has also been taken up by general surgeons and it has led to an enthusiastic following for 'key-hole surgery'.

Indications

Diagnostic

Laparoscopy provides a simple and reasonably safe method of visually inspecting the pelvic organs and some of the other intra-abdominal organs such as the liver and gall bladder. The appendix can often be seen though structures on and in the posterior abdominal wall such as the kidneys are hidden by the loops of small and large bowel. The technique is therefore of considerable value in the investigation of a wide range of problems being particularly valuable in the assessment of pelvic pain, both chronic and acute, of tubal causes for infertility and in cases of suspected ectopic pregnancy.

Therapeutic

There has been a vast proliferation of therapeutic indications for gynaecological laparoscopy in recent years along with a corresponding proliferation of specially designed instruments ranging from knives, needles and scissors, through electrosurgical instruments of various kinds to the laparoscopically guided application of laser beams. These developments have both facilitated and been stimulated by a vast increase in the range of procedures which can be carried out endoscopically.

Until the mid 1980s, laparoscopic surgery was generally limited to the electrocauterisation of localised lesions (particularly small endometrial deposits), the division of adhesions and the performance of procedures designed to obstruct the fallopian tubes for elective sterilisation. To these have now been added myomectomy, ovarian cystectomy, and tubal surgery for the correction of obstruction and for the removal of ectopic pregnancy as well as laparoscopically assisted vaginal hysterectomy.

The techniques employed in these operations are significantly different from those used in traditional gynaecological surgery and it is, therefore, essential that the aspiring laparoscopic surgeon has specific training and supervised experience. Neglect of this precaution has resulted in these newer procedures giving rise to a disproportionate number of medico-legal claims in recent years but, because of their specialised nature, they will not be discussed in detail in this volume.

The procedure

Following the induction of general anaesthesia, the patient is placed on the operating table. During gynaecological laparoscopies, both abdominal and vaginal access is usually required and the patient's legs are therefore normally flexed and abducted at the hips and flexed at the knees, being supported in a similar way to that used for the D & C, though, for laparoscopies, the hip flexion is usually limited to about 45°. The vulva and vagina are then cleansed with a water-based antiseptic solution and sterile towels placed to cover the unprepared areas. Preparation of the skin of the abdominal wall is often done simultaneously though this may be postponed until the vaginal preparations are completed.

The bladder is then usually emptied by passing a catheter into the urethra though some surgeons are content to rely on the patient having emptied her bladder shortly before coming to the operating theatre.

In order to facilitate proper inspection of the pelvic cavity, it is usually necessary to alter the position of the uterus and, except in the presence of an intra-uterine pregnancy, the anterior lip of the uterine cervix is grasped with tenaculum forceps and a suitable instrument introduced into the uterine cavity. Commonly, this is a hollow metal instrument of the type described by Provis or Spackman but other designs have been produced by specialised instrument manufacturers.

The abdominal wall must be cleansed to well above the umbilicus extending down to the groins as it may be necessary to introduce instruments at various sites on the abdomen without jeopardising the sterile precautions. Sterile towels are then placed to cover all but the essential operative area and some degree of head-down tilt is then usually applied to the operating table.

It is important to realise that, in the normal abdominal cavity, the contained structures are separated from one another by only a thin film of fluid. In order to obtain a view of the organs, it is necessary to create space between them artificially; this is done by the introduction of a gas into the abdomen. The gas usually used is carbon dioxide which has the advantages of being readily available and inexpensive, but does not support combustion (electrocautery may therefore be used) and is rapidly absorbed into the blood stream whence it leaves the body by the normal gas exchanges in the lungs.

The passage of un-physiological amounts of carbon dioxide into the blood does have an acidifying effect which, in the normal patient, can be counteracted by a small increase in the ventilation rate during the procedure. Because the effect persists for a short while after the operation is over, however, it may occasionally cause cardiac irregularities in the recovery phase when spontaneous respiration is often reduced. The acidaemia may also provoke a sickle cell crisis in susceptible patients and in such individuals nitrous oxide gas is sometimes used though electrocautery cannot then be employed as nitrous oxide does support combustion.

In order to introduce the gas, a needle must be inserted into the abdominal cavity and the site usually selected is at the lower border of the umbilicus. Not only is the abdominal wall thinner here than elsewhere but it is normally also the site subsequently used for the insertion of the laparoscopic trochar itself. There are dangers associated with the use of this site (see 'Hazards of the procedure', below) and insertion of the needle in the midline 3–4 cm below the umbilicus has been advocated as being safer.

The needle used is one described by Veress or a variation thereof. This is about 12 cm long (17 cm overall, with longer needles available for use in obese patients) with a diameter of about 2 mm. The needle has a rounded tip with a side hole for the passage of the gas but this part is spring loaded within the outer, sharp pointed needle so that, when sufficient resistance is encountered, the blunt tip will be pushed back into the outer sheath by further advancement of the needle, allowing the tissue to be perforated. Theoretically, at least, mobile structures such as loops of bowel will offer insufficient resistance and will be pushed out of the way thereby avoiding puncture. Various techniques have been described to confirm that the tip of the needle is correctly sited within the abdominal cavity but none is consistently more reliable than the 'feel' of the needle in the hands of an experienced laparoscopist.

When the needle is considered to have been correctly placed, it is connected to a gas source by a sterile, flexible tube. In the early days of laparoscopy, various improvisations were in use but for the past twenty years or so the gas has been supplied by a mechanism which limits both the pressure and the flow rate to pre-set values, usually also with a measure of the total amount of gas which has been insufflated. During insufflation, it is important that the operator observes the abdomen for symmetrical distension.

Once sufficient gas has been introduced to distend the peritoneal cavity, the Veress needle is removed, the skin is incised with a scalpel at the umbilical margin and the laparoscopic trochar and canula are inserted. The trochar is then removed to allow the passage of the laparoscopic telescope down the canula. The telescope can be used for direct vision but it is now common practice in many units to attach a small colour television camera to the proximal end of the telescope so that the view can be seen on a television screen; as well as being of interest and instruction for the other members of the operating team, this enables videotape recordings and still photographs to be made.

On insertion of the telescope, the surface of the immediately adjacent structures should be inspected to exclude any apparent damage and the instrument can then be directed towards the pelvis, where the view may be improved by manipulation of the uterus using the instrument previously inserted for the purpose, increasing the head-down tilt of the operating table to allow gravity to move loops of small bowel away and, if necessary, by the introduction of other instruments at other sites on the abdominal wall in order to manipulate other structures. Proper examination of the pelvic side walls requires the additional use of a telescope with a field of view at an angle to its longitudinal axis, though these are not available in all units.

If patency of the tubes is to be assessed (in the investigation of fertility), a diluted solution of methylene blue is then introduced into the uterine cavity under gentle pressure and the tubes are observed for evidence of the blue dye as it first fills the tube and then spills out of the fimbrial end.

Before finally concluding the procedure, the laparoscope should be rotated to allow inspection of the upper abdominal structures.

The telescope is then withdrawn and the trumpet valve on the canula is opened to allow the escape of as much of the gas as possible before the canula to is taken out. The skin incision is then closed in whatever manner is considered appropriate (usually by suturing). Finally, any instruments left in the vagina must be removed.

Hazards of the procedure

A few years ago, laparoscopy was beginning to develop a reputation for being a hazardous procedure with a high complication rate. This was because the laparoscope had suddenly been 'discovered' by a large number of gynaecologists who adopted it with an enthusiasm which was not matched by adequate training in its use. To some extent, this was the fault of the equipment manufacturers who actively promoted the instrument, doubtless seeing it is an untapped source of revenue, but they soon appreciated the dangers, both clinical and financial, and are now the willing sponsors of numerous training courses throughout the country.

The design of the Veress needle is intended to minimise the chance of accidental injury to the intra-abdominal viscera but such injuries are occasionally inevitable. Even with the correct placement of the needle, perforation of the bowel wall will occasionally occur, especially if, unbeknown to the surgeon, loops of bowel are adherent to the anterior abdominal wall close to the point of insertion of the needle. An unnoticed umbilical hernia may cause problems.

If bowel damage is suspected (the author, on withdrawing a Veress needle recently, found faecal material at the tip) a careful inspection of all visible bowel should be performed as soon as the laparoscope has been introduced. If no major damage or leakage of bowel contents is seen (in most cases, the site of the damage will not be found), no special treatment is indicated, though a course of antibiotic may be advisable and it is essential to inform the patient of the suspected injury before she is discharged from hospital. She should be warned to return immediately should she develop any signs that might indicate a peritonitis, for example, a pyrexia or significant abdominal pain.

Poor technique with the Veress needle may result in damage to any of the major blood vessels in the abdomen. Injuries to the abdominal aorta and to the inferior vena cava have been described, as well as damage to the common iliac arteries and veins. Bleeding from these vessels may be retained behind the peritoneum of the posterior abdominal wall so that it is not apparent when the laparoscope is introduced but the patient may collapse from hypovolaemia sometime later.

Bladder damage may occur but it is usually not serious.

If the insufflation gas is introduced down a misplaced needle, additional hazards are encountered. Insufflation of the bowel is not, in itself, unduly serious but it may cause further tearing of the bowel wall at the site of the perforation. Rapid insufflation of gas into a blood vessel, however, may cause gas embolism with infarction of tissues or potentially fatal effects in the case of embolism to the lungs. For this reason, the initial insufflation rate should be low until the operator is reasonably certain that all is well.

Over-inflation of the abdomen may cause anaesthetic problems by restricting the excursions of the diaphragm but this risk has been largely eliminated by improvements in the insufflation equipment which now limits the maximum pressure which can be achieved

The creation of a satisfactory pneumoperitoneum minimises the risks associated with the introduction of the laparoscopic trochar itself but, should any of the intra-abdominal structures be injured with this instrument, its greater size compared with the Veress needle means that any damage is much more likely to be significant. The structures already described are again at risk.

The insertion of additional portals should be performed under direct (laparoscopic) vision to avoid intra-abdominal injuries but, if the site is low in the midline, a patent urachus may be encountered and, if, as is more usual, the site is more lateral, blood vessels in the anterior abdominal wall may give rise to troublesome bleeding.

Any operative procedures performed laparoscopically may cause accidental injury. When direct damage is inflicted, for example, by a misplaced cut with scissors, it will usually be immediately apparent. Heat injury at the time of diathermy, whether for haemostasis or for coagulation of the tubes at sterilisation, may be much more difficult to detect. The damage may result from the careless application of a hot instrument to nearby structures or may result from the conduction of the diathermy current. Laser surgery may cause damage to structures behind the target point.

Removal of the entry ports is usually straightforward but abdominal wall vessels may continue to bleed. The re-absorption of carbon dioxide gas from the abdominal cavity may cause cardiac arrhythmias and its role in the precipitation of a sickle cell crisis has already been mentioned. The skin incisions may become infected.

HYSTERECTOMY

The operation of hysterectomy carries with it considerable emotional overtones and it is perhaps not surprising that it is associated with a number of myths and misunderstandings. In recent years, there has also been some criticism of gynaecologists for advising hysterectomy too frequently and, whilst there may well be some justification for this, it has had the undesirable effect of increasing many women's anxiety and causing a few to refuse the offer of an operation from which they would undoubtedly have benefited.

Many units are now introducing pre-operative counselling for this and some other gynaecological procedures often recruiting patients who have already undergone the procedures to give explanations and reassurance to other women.

Types of hysterectomy

Many patients interpret the operation of hysterectomy as meaning that their entire gynaecological apparatus will be removed and some may even believe that sexual intercourse will not then be possible. It is therefore important that the gynaecologist explains exactly what structures are to be removed and how the patient's future life will be affected.

The route by which the hysterectomy is performed may be abdominal or vaginal. The former is more common in the UK, though increasing numbers of vaginal hysterectomies are now being performed. The abdominal hysterectomy involves an incision of the anterior abdominal wall which in the past was usually made in the midline longitudinal axis and extended from just below the umbilicus to a short distance above the symphysis pubis. This incision is still used when the uterus is greatly enlarged, when good exposure is required and, sometimes, if the patient is obese but, since the 1960s, increasing use has been made of the supra-pubic transverse incision often ascribed to Pfannenstiel, a German gynaecologist who described the technique in 1900 (though the method used today usually differs slightly from his original description).

The vaginal route has long been more popular on the Continent and has the advantage that the patient receives no abdominal scar and the hospital stay is usually shorter, an important consideration in the present cost conscious climate. The classical vaginal operation is made much more difficult if the uterus is large or if it is tethered to adjacent structures but this may, at least in part, be overcome by the use of the 'laparoscopically assisted vaginal hysterectomy' a recently introduced technique which requires specialist training and which is still not included in the expertise of the majority of gynaecologists.

The author has also been asked whether he intents to remove the uterus by the 'vacuum method' but has yet to discover exactly what patients mean by this!

Sub-total abdominal hysterectomy

This operation removes the body of the uterus and the upper part (one third to half) of the cervix. It was often the operation of choice until the 1950s as it avoids separation of the bladder from the front of the cervix and greatly reduces the risk of damage to the ureters. Unfortunately, the residual cervix remains susceptible to all the usual diseases of cervical tissue, including cancer, and the resulting 'stump carcinoma', whilst no more common than in the intact uterus, is associated with a much worse prognosis. For this reason, the operation was largely abandoned in favour of the total hysterectomy but it has seen a limited return to popularity in recent years because of the belief that the enjoyment of sexual intercourse may be adversely affected by removal of the cervix. Whilst it is certainly true that some women do experience sensation when their cervix is touched, the evidence that this is a factor in coital pleasure is limited.

The sub-total operation may be useful when extensive disease (particularly endometriosis) has rendered pelvic dissection more than usually difficult and dangerous.

A few patients continue to menstruate after the sub-total operation (though the monthly bleed is much reduced in amount), an annoyance which can be avoided by the destruction of the lining of the residual cervix by electrocautery at the time of the operation.

Total abdominal hysterectomy (TAH)

This is currently the most widely practised type of hysterectomy in this country. The body of the uterus and the whole of the cervix are excised and the open vault of the vagina is then either closed by sutures or, less frequently, left to heal by granulation. It should be noted that neither the sub-total nor the total operation includes removal of either the tubes or the ovaries.

Hysterectomy with right/left/bilateral salpingectomy

This implies that one (or, in the case of bilateral, both) of the tubes are removed. Because of the close approximation of the tubes and ovaries, it is usual to leave both of these structures in situ unless there is some specific reason to do otherwise. Fortunately, diseases of the fallopian tubes are rare but the author has seen one case of a post-hysterectomy hydrosalpinx which caused an intermittent, watery vaginal discharge and which had to be removed by a second operation. Provided the blood supply to the ovary is not endangered, there may be some small benefit in removing the tubes.

Hysterectomy with right/left/bilateral salpingo-oophorectomy

This involves the removal of the whole of the uterus and also one or both tubes and ovaries. The bilateral operation is the one which is commonly (but incorrectly) assumed when a 'hysterectomy' is mentioned. It is often abbreviated to TAH & BSO.

The removal of the ovaries has an important influence on the endocrine status of the pre-menopausal patient, since she will have, in effect, undergone the menopause in minutes rather than months. For this reason, unless contraindicated by the clinical circumstances, such patients may be given hormone replacement therapy.

Extended hysterectomy

This is a TAH & BSO with the addition of the removal of other structures such as a cuff of the upper vagina and lymph nodes from the pelvic side wall. This operation is undertaken only for malignant disease. It may be referred to as a 'Wertheim' hysterectomy, after the Viennese Professor of Gynaecology, Ernst Wertheim (1864–1920), who described the radical operation for cervical cancer.

The vaginal operation

The vaginal hysterectomy has long been chosen for patients who need the removal of the uterus but who also have a vaginal prolapse in need of repair indeed, the hysterectomy may, in some cases, be advised solely because it offers the opportunity of a better repair.

Access to the uterine supports is obtained by incision into the upper vaginal wall, the uterus is drawn down by traction on the cervix and the supports are clamped, divided and ligated. After removal of the uterus, it is important that all significant bleeding is controlled. The pelvic peritoneum is usually closed from below and the divided uterine supports brought together in the midline before the vaginal wall is repaired. Failure to deal with bleeding may give rise to a pelvic haematoma which may then become infected resulting in the important complication of a pelvic abscess.

The reasonably competent gynaecological surgeon will be able to remove any uterus by the abdominal route (though the degree of difficulty will vary with the clinical situation) but this is not necessarily true of the vaginal route. It is therefore essential that cases for this operation be properly selected. In patients with severe degrees of vaginal prolapse, the operation is likely to be easy, whereas, if the uterus is bound to the surrounding tissues by adhesions or grossly enlarged by fibroids, it may be more appropriate to choose the abdominal approach. Proper pre-operative assessment with due regard to the surgeon's own expertise and experience is therefore essential.

Schauta's operation

This is the vaginal equivalent of the extended abdominal hysterectomy (though without including the pelvic lymph nodes) and commemorates the name of Friedrich Schauta (1849–1919), who, like Wertheim, was a professor in Vienna. The operation was devised as an alternative treatment of cancer of the cervix but has not been widely adopted in Britain, where most gynaecologists have favoured the abdominal route.

The abdominal operation

The operative details will vary depending on which type of hysterectomy is being performed as well as on the preferences and training of the individual surgeon and the clinical features of the case. Consequently, it is not possible to detail every variation and the description which follows is a generalised version which assumes that the anatomical situation is normal.

When the patient has been anaesthetised and placed on the operating table, the bladder is catheterised. One of the hazards of opening that part of the abdominal wall just above the symphysis pubis is that, in doing so, the bladder may be damaged; this risk is reduced if the bladder is empty. The skin of the anterior abdominal wall is cleansed with a suitable antiseptic solution and sterile towels are placed in position around the proposed site of the incision.

In the past, hysterectomies were usually performed through a longitudinal sub-umbilical midline incision extending from a short distance below the umbilicus to just above the symphysis pubis but, since about the 1960s, the supra-pubic transverse incision has become the more common. This is placed just below the upper margin of the pubic hair (which is shaved pre-operatively) and is slightly curved to run parallel to the natural skin folds. Unlike the longitudinal incision, the edges of the transverse incision tend to fall together so that, when the wound is sutured, the skin is not under tension and consequently heals better. The transverse incision also causes the patient less discomfort (aiding the desirable early mobilisation post-operatively) and it is cosmetically much preferred.

The wound is deepened through the subcutaneous fat and, in the longitudinal incision, the fibrous band joining the medial edges of the sheath of the rectus abdominis muscle. In the transverse incision, only the anterior layers of the rectus sheath are incised and the underlying muscles are then separated (there is no true posterior or deep sheath at this level).

The parietal peritoneum is then opened. This must be done with care, as the peritoneal cavity is only a potential space until air is admitted. Consequently, the wall of the underlying bowel (usually a loop of the small bowel) may easily be damaged if care is not taken. It is also possible to damage the bladder if that organ is situated abnormally high on the under aspect of the anterior abdominal wall or if the peritoneum is opened too close to the symphysis pubis. The usual method is to pick up the peritoneum with two artery clips placed with their tips about one centimetre apart and to then make a small nick in the peritoneum with a scalpel to allow the ingress of air. This causes the bowel to fall away (provided it is not adherent) and the opening can then be enlarged.

The edges of the wound are held apart by a self-retaining retractor (of which various patterns are available) and the loops of bowel in the pelvis are lifted out of the way. A few degrees of head-down tilt may be sufficient to prevent the bowel from returning to obscure the view but more commonly it is necessary to hold it out of the pelvis by the use of one or more moist gauze packs. These packs, like all gauze swabs in use while the abdominal cavity is open, must have a radio-opaque thread woven into the material and usually also have a long linen tape firmly sewn to one corner. The other end of the tape remains outside the abdomen (often with a spare instrument such as a small artery clip attached) as a safeguard against inadvertently leaving the pack inside the abdominal cavity when it is later closed.

Two clamps are then applied across the tube and ovarian ligament on one side and these structures are divided between the instruments (the clamps will be applied lateral to the tubes and ovaries if these structures are also being removed). The tissue contained within the more lateral of the two clamps is then ligated with an absorbable suture. The round ligaments may be included or may be clamped, divided and ligated separately. The same procedure is carried out on the other side. The peritoneum of the utero-vesical fold is then opened and the bladder pushed down from the anterior aspect of the cervix after which the tissues on either side of the uterus can be divided.

The uterine artery and vein run in the lower part of the fold of peritoneum called the broad ligament and, a short distance below on either side of the cervix, the ureter passes forwards to enter the bladder. Care must therefore be exercised at this point if both haemorrhage and ureteric damage are to be avoided when the vessels are clamped, divided and ligated. The prior downward dislocation of the bladder offers some protection in this respect, since it usually carries the ureters down with it.

It is the author's practice to clamp and divide the utero-sacral ligaments as individual structures, though many surgeons include them as part of the vaginal wall when this is divided subsequently.

The lateral vaginal angles are then clamped as a branch of the uterine vessels runs downwards here to supply the upper vagina and may give rise to troublesome haemorrhage if not secured. The upper vagina can then be opened, usually through the anterior fornix, and the incision carried round to free the uterus, allowing its removal.

In the past, it was common practice to oversew the vaginal edge to prevent haemorrhage, leaving the passage open for the drainage of blood and serum from the pelvis. This greatly reduced the chance of a pelvic haematoma with the attendant risk of a pelvic abscess. Though a pelvic abscess remains a serious (though, fortunately, rare) complication, its dangers were reduced with the introduction of antibiotics and most surgeons now close the vaginal vault with sutures. The author then also closes the pelvic peritoneum, though there has been a trend away from doing so in recent years, many surgeons claiming that it is unnecessary.

After ensuring that all bleeding has been controlled and that all packs, swabs, instruments and needles have been removed from the abdominal cavity, the abdominal wall is closed by suturing of the layers and a suitable dressing applied to the wound.

Before the abdominal wall is sutured and again afterwards, the scrub nurse will count the swabs, instruments and needles to ensure that all those used have been returned to her. By agreement between the medical defence societies and the Royal College of Nursing, it is considered a joint responsibility of the surgeon and the scrub nurse to ensure that nothing is inadvertently left in the abdominal cavity or the wound. Very occasionally, the clinical situation may demand that the usual safeguards be ignored, in which case it is essential that a detailed statement to that effect is recorded in the patient's notes.

Before the anaesthetic is finally discontinued and the patient leaves the operating table, some surgeons swab out the vagina to remove any blood or blood clots, considering that, if this is not done, the subsequent post-operative loss from the vagina may be mistaken for fresh haemorrhage.

The operation notes

A typical operation note might read as follows (see over):

DATE:	4-1-99
SURGEON:	Mr A Smith
ASSISTANT:	Dr M Casey
ANAESTHETIST:	Dr B Jones
OPERATION:	TAH with conservation of both ovaries
Incision:	Supra-pubic transverse
Findings:	Normal uterus apart from a small sub-serous fibroid on anterior surface
	Normal tubes and ovaries
	No pelvic adhesions or endometriosis
Procedure:	Ovarian and uterine pedicles clamped, divided and ligated
	Vagina opened and uterus excised
	Some bleeding from right vaginal angle
Closure:	Vaginal vault closed with interrupted sutures
	Abdominal wall closed in layers after all haemorrhage secured.
	Sub-cuticular 4/0 polyglycolic acid suture to skin
Drains:	None
Estimated blood loss:	150 ml

The fact that neither ovary was removed is specifically stated, the initial findings are recorded and the complication encountered is noted. Although there is no detailed account of the exact sutures used at each stage, there is a specific record of the way in which the skin was closed, as the ward staff will need to know whether any sutures, clips or staples need to be removed.

As always, the operation note must be signed.

CHAPTER 4

DEVELOPMENTAL ANOMALIES

Examination of the early human embryo reveals the presence of two longitudinal structures on each side of the midline of the posterior wall of the primitive internal cavity. These structures are the mesonephric (Wolffian) and paramesonephric (Mullerian) ducts. In the male embryo, the former develops into part of the genital system and the Mullerian duct regresses whereas, in the female, the reverse happens. The details of these changes, though of considerable interest to the embryologist, are of little clinical importance but, in considering the developmental anomalies of the female genital organs, it is helpful to realise that they form by partial fusion of two separate tubes. Anomalies can result from incomplete development or incomplete fusion. It should also be remembered that the lower part of the vagina forms by an invagination of the external skin and anomalies of this region therefore occur independently.

OVARIAN ABNORMALITIES

The ovaries develop from the undifferentiated gonad which is present in the early embryo on the posterior abdominal wall close to the developing kidneys. In some cases, this development fails and the ovary on one or both sides is hypoplastic ('streak ovaries') or even absent. Menstruation may not occur or may cease early ('primary ovarian failure' or 'premature menopause'), and circulating oestradiol levels will be low.

Many of these cases are associated with chromosome abnormalities and cytogenetic studies should always be performed.

It is usually advisable to recommend oestrogen replacement therapy (combined with progestogen), as these women are otherwise prone to develop osteoporosis in later life.

TUBAL ABNORMALITIES

One or both tubes may be absent or present only as a fibrous cord. Bilateral absence of the tubes obviously precludes a normal conception but unilateral absence may be associated with apparently normal fertility.

Many years ago, one of the authors admitted a patient for elective sterilisation after the birth of her sixth child. She had undergone no previous surgery but, when she was laparoscoped (to perform the sterilisation), she was found to have only ever had one tube.

Most (but not all) cases of tubal maldevelopment are associated with abnormalities of the uterus.

UTERINE ABNORMALITIES

Failure of development

As with any other organ, not all (normal) uteri are the same size. In addition to this genetically determined difference, the uterus also varies in size depending on the level of circulating oestrogen (hence its shrinkage after the menopause in the absence of HRT). It is probable that minor degrees of uterine hypoplasia therefore remain undetected but more severe cases may be associated with recurrent miscarriage. Pre-conception priming with exogenous oestrogen has been tried but is of doubtful value.

In rare cases, the uterus may be entirely absent or represented by a firm nodule of solid tissue. Such cases are amenorrhoeic and infertile. Chromosome studies may demonstrate an abnormality.

If the ovaries, tubes and uterus are all absent the possibility of testicular feminising syndrome should be considered (see Chapter 2).

Failure of fusion

In order to form the normal uterus, cervix and upper vagina, the two Mullerian ducts must fuse together and the tissue of their fused walls must break down. The adult tubes, of course, remain separate and are derived only from the Mullerian duct on the same side.

Arrest of this process may occur at any stage, so that abnormalities in the adult vary from the fairly common 'Y' shaped uterine cavity to uterus didelphys and double vagina (see Figure 4.1).

Minor abnormalities cause little or no clinical problem and may be chance findings on investigation for some other reason. More surprisingly, the severe anomalies are also, frequently, of little significance and even women with completely separate uterine horns may be normally fertile, though the risk of premature labour and of the need for delivery by Caesarean section is increased.

Moderate conditions, such as the septate and sub-septate uterus, are more likely to be associated with recurrent abortion and also with malpresentation of the foetus, which often adopts a transverse lie (with one foetal pole in each uterine horn) near term.

Figure 4.1   Developmental Anomalies

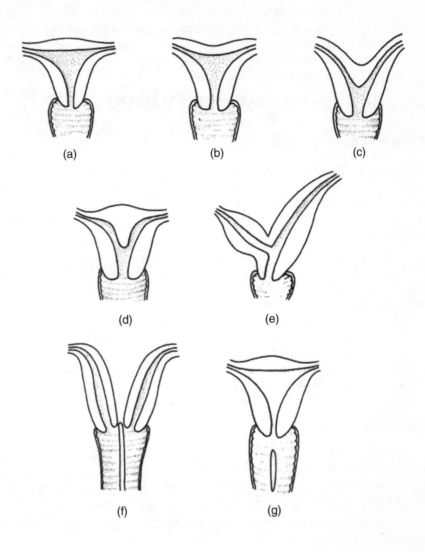

Various fusion abnormalities of the uterus and vagina: (a) normal appearances; (b) arcuate fundus, with little effect on the shape of the cavity; (c) bicornate uterus; (d) sub-septate uterus with normal outline; (e) rudimentary horn; (f) uterus didelphys; (g) normal uterus with partial vaginal septum. (Illustration reproduced from Dewhurst, CJ, *Integrated Obstetrics and Gynaecology for Postgraduates,* 1972, Oxford: Blackwell Scientific, p 8, fig 1.9.)

The combination of incomplete fusion and unilateral arrested development produces the rudimentary horn. The poorly developed horn may be incapable of containing a growing conception and may rupture. The symptoms resemble those of the ruptured tubal ectopic pregnancy but tend to occur at a later gestational age (usually 12–14 weeks) and the intra-peritoneal haemorrhage is greater with the rapid onset of hypovolaemic shock.

VAGINAL ABNORMALITIES

Failure of development

Vaginal agenesis is usually associated with absence of the uterus. If this is not the case, the onset of menstruation will cause the uterus to become distended by the retained menstrual blood (haematocolpos).

Chromosomal anomalies may be present and abnormalities of the renal tract are common (see below).

Surgical correction can be performed by dissecting a space between the bladder and rectum. The space is then lined by a split skin graft from the thigh. Unfortunately, the graft tends to contract unless regular sexual intercourse occurs or vaginal dilators are used. This procedure was originally described by McIndoe and Read, after whom it is named, but, more recently, the Williams operation was described, in which a 'U' shaped incision is made in the vulval skin which is then sutured to form a tube, opened anteriorly and covered by a second layer of skin. Despite the abnormal direction of the new 'vagina', it may be functionally very satisfactory.

Failure of fusion

A partial or complete septum may remain in the vagina. The septum is usually flexible and may be unnoticed by the woman or her sexual partner. Problems can occur at vaginal delivery when rupture of the septum may cause severe haemorrhage. Surgical division is usually easy.

The imperforate hymen is described in Chapter 5.

WOLFFIAN DUCT REMNANTS

Wolffian duct tissue may fail to completely regress and may become cystic, forming fimbrial cysts, broad ligament cysts and para-cervical and para-vaginal cysts.

Fimbrial cysts are common and rarely exceed 20 mm in diameter. Being smooth, mobile and often pedunculated, they may undergo torsion. They are rarely of clinical significance but on pre-operative investigation, are often mistaken for ovarian cysts and are therefore removed surgically even though the correct diagnosis is recognised at operation.

Broad ligament cysts are similar to follicular cysts in appearance but lie within the layers of the broad ligament. They may occasionally grow to a diameter of 10 cm or more.

Para-cervical and para-vaginal cysts may be palpable in the lateral vaginal fornix or beneath the skin of the vaginal wall. They may cause discomfort during sexual intercourse. Surgical removal must be undertaken with caution as the cystic cavity may extend for a considerable distance and both the ureter and the uterine vessels may be at risk.

URINARY TRACT ANOMALIES

The development and growth of the genital tract is closely associated with that of the urinary system. Developmental anomalies of both systems may be present and the discovery of a genital anomaly is an indication for further investigation of the urinary tract by ultrasonic scanning and radiological techniques. Renal agenesis, unilateral or bilateral renal and/or ureteric reduplication and the pelvic kidney may be found.

CHAPTER 5

MENSTRUAL DISORDERS

Amongst the most common of reasons for consulting a gynaecologist are problems with the menstrual periods. The bleeding may be too heavy (menorrhagia), too painful (dysmenorrhoea), too frequent (polymenorrhoea), too light or infrequent (oligomenorrhoea), or absent (amenorrhoea).

Apart from cyclical bleeding, vaginal bleeding may also occur at other times. This may be between the periods (intermenstrual bleeding or IMB), after sexual intercourse (post-coital bleeding or PCB) or bleeding after the normal cycle has stopped at the menopause (post-menopausal bleeding or PMB).

Apart from disordered bleeding, the other important cyclical problem is the pre-menstrual syndrome, which is discussed separately.

CYCLICAL PROBLEMS

Menorrhagia

Menorrhagia (heavy menstrual bleeding) is defined as the loss of 80 ml or more of blood during each period bleed. Although of some value in research, this definition is clinically unsatisfactory both because the menstrual loss is almost never measured and also because women have remarkably different tolerances to menstruation. It is not unusual to diagnose anaemia due to menorrhagia in a woman who perceives her periods to be normal and just as common to be consulted by a woman who complains of 'heavy periods' but who needs to use only one pack of sanitary protection for each monthly bleed. If a woman does not have excessive menstrual loss, any treatment aimed at reducing the bleeding is unlikely to help her.

Detailed questioning may go some way to establishing the amount of bleeding and whether it is interfering with the woman's life. The duration of the bleeding may also be important in this respect, especially in communities where sexual intercourse does not take place during the bleeding – orthodox Jews are proscribed from having coitus until five days after the last trace of blood. Enquiry may be made regarding type of sanitary protection needed (for example, 'regular', 'super-plus', etc) and how frequently the protection must be changed. The woman should also be asked about the passage of clots of blood and whether the bleeding may flood through the sanitary protection. Women with severe menorrhagia may have to resort to the use of hand towels or items of bed linen in place of commercial sanitary towels or tampons during the heaviest flow.

Menorrhagia is often associated with the presence of fibroids in the uterus, the condition of adenomyosis (endometriosis of the myometrium) and with the common but diagnostically unsatisfactory condition known as dysfunctional uterine bleeding, sometimes abbreviated to DUB.

Occasionally, general medical conditions can cause heavy cyclical bleeding. These include thyroid gland dysfunction, usually an underactive thyroid (hypothyroidism), or disordered blood clotting. The latter are rare but must be considered because of their important implications in the event of injury and during childbirth; specific tests in a haematological laboratory may be required to establish the diagnosis.

Examination

Any woman complaining of menorrhagia or, indeed, any other abnormal vaginal bleeding, should be examined clinically. Before the gynaecological examination is carried out, a brief but reasonably thorough general examination should be performed. Anaemia may be suspected if there is pallor of the palms of the hands, nail beds or of the conjunctiva of the eyes, whilst exophthalmos or a goitre may suggest thyroid dysfunction.

Abdominal examination must be performed to detect the presence of any masses or tenderness.

A vaginal examination then allows assessment of the uterus with particular attention being paid to its size. Other pelvic abnormalities, such as ovarian cysts, must also be excluded.

Investigation

Laboratory estimation of the haemoglobin level (or, more commonly, a full blood count) is required to detect anaemia, since clinical judgement is notoriously unreliable. The wife of a gynaecological colleague managed to reduce her haemoglobin to less than 5 g/dl (one-third of normal) by menorrhagia due to fibroids before the anaemia was noticed!

Early thyroid dysfunction is often clinically undetectable and its exclusion may require laboratory estimation of the thyroid hormone levels in a blood sample.

The presence of uterine enlargement or other pelvic mass may indicate a need for an ultrasonic scan. This investigation is often overused, probably because of its presumed safety, and is certainly not mandatory in all cases of menorrhagia. Fibroids, endometrial polypi and malignant tumours can be identified but it is probably inadvisable to rely on a scan unless supplemented by some form of endometrial biopsy (see below).

A woman over the age of 40 years complaining of heavy menstrual bleeding should have her uterine cavity explored and this is also advisable if the uterus is found to be enlarged clinically at any age. Formerly, the usual procedure was a D & C but it is now preferable to perform a hysteroscopy (see Chapter 3). Hysteroscopes are now available which are small enough to allow the procedure to be performed in the outpatient clinic without an anaesthetic.

The endometrium can be sampled for histological examination not only at D & C or hysteroscopy but also by the application of mechanical suction to a small metal or plastic tube passed through the cervix into the uterine cavity. This does cause some discomfort to the patient but is well tolerated by the majority of women. Enthusiasts for the method have claimed that the diagnostic accuracy is as good as for a D & C but independent studies suggest that reliability is lower though it may be useful if combined with ultrasonic scanning.

Treatment

The options for treatment can be divided into two categories: medical (implying the use of drug therapy) and surgical (operative).

Occasionally, a hysterectomy may be offered as the first choice but, more commonly, medical treatment is suggested initially, especially if the uterus is not obviously enlarged by fibroids. Unfortunately, this sometimes results in women being obliged to suffer several more years of conservative treatment of variable and often short term efficacy before having the surgery that they would have happily accepted much earlier.

Medical treatment

Non-steroidal anti-inflammatory drugs

In the initial treatment of menorrhagia, the most commonly prescribed drugs are of the non-steroidal anti-inflammatory group (abbreviated to NSAID). These preparations are related to aspirin and have the effect of reducing prostaglandin production by the endometrial lining. There are a large number of different preparations in widespread use for a variety of indications, the most popular in gynaecological practice probably being mefenamic acid. As well as reducing menstrual blood flow, they also have analgesic actions. To be effective they must be taken regularly during the menstrual flow.

Progestogens

Progestogens are substances which are largely converted to the hormone progesterone by the patient's metabolic processes. They are frequently used to regulate and control menstrual bleeding and are most effective in those women who have been shown to have anovulatory (and, therefore, progesterone deficient) menstrual cycles. Common examples of progestogens are norethisterone and medroxyprogesterone acetate (sometimes abbreviated to NET and MPA).

Tranexamic acid

Tranexamic acid has been widely used in Scandinavian countries and is becoming increasingly popular in the UK. It is taken during the menstrual flow, having its effect by promoting blood clotting. It is generally very well tolerated, having few side effects, but should not be given to women who have a history of deep venous thrombosis or of pulmonary embolism.

Ethamsylate

This stabilises the small blood vessels thereby reducing the bleeding from the uterine lining. Like tranexamic acid, it has few side effects and need only be taken during the menstrual period.

LHRH analogues

These preparations abolish the menstrual cycle by causing a reversible 'menopause'. They decrease bone mineralisation and should not be administered for longer than about six months but may be useful to arrest cyclical bleeding as a temporary measure whilst an anaemia is corrected prior to definitive surgical treatment.

Danazol

Danazol, a steroid derivative, can be used to treat menorrhagia though it is rarely used as a first line treatment. It is frequently effective but its use is limited by its side effects (see Chapter 7).

Progesterone releasing intrauterine contraceptive devices

Developed as contraceptive devices, these were found to reduce or abolish menstrual blood loss. In many patients, the bleeding is heavier or prolonged for the first three or four months after insertion of the device but the loss then decreases, sometimes stopping altogether. They are discussed in greater detail in Chapter 10.

Surgical treatment

Hysterectomy and the alternatives

For many years, the surgical treatment of menorrhagia, even in the absence of fibroids or other obvious pathology, was limited to a hysterectomy, either with or without removal of the ovaries. It was then realised that removal of the uterine lining, the endometrium, would be sufficient to abolish the bleeding and various techniques were devised which can be collectively described as 'endometrial ablation'. These include destruction of the endometrium by heat (thermo-coagulation), by cold (cryo-coagulation) or by laser evaporation under direct vision at hysteroscopy. Hysteroscopy also permits diathermy coagulation often applied by a device known as a 'roller ball' or the cutting away of the endometrial layer (endometrial resection), sometimes referred to as TCRE (trans-cervical resection of the endometrium). Like the hysterectomy, these methods normally remove fertility, though it may be advisable to recommend the use of contraception to avoid the small risk of an unwanted pregnancy.

Despite these new developments (most of which require specialised instruments and training in their use), the hysterectomy continues to hold an important place in the range of surgical treatments, not least because it is the only one which can be guaranteed to stop the bleeding. The operation may be performed abdominally or vaginally, the latter becoming more popular since the introduction of the laparoscopically assisted vaginal hysterectomy (LAVH), which reduces the length of the in-patient stay and post-operative recovery.

Myomectomy

If menorrhagia is associated with the presence of fibroids, the removal of the tumours by the operation of myomectomy may, but does not always, reduce the cyclical bleeding. Fibroids which distort the uterine cavity are the most likely to cause heavy bleeding and may be best removed at hysteroscopy. Other treatments of fibroids, including laser evaporation and vascular embolisation, are currently being assessed.

Pre-operative assessment

The increased range of surgical options has made it more important than ever that the appropriate operation is selected for the individual patient. The pre-operative discussion should take into consideration the patient's own wishes as well as the strictly medical factors. For example, as a generalisation, fibroids are best treated by a hysterectomy, since a myomectomy may be technically more difficult, post-operative complications may be more common and more fibroids may grow if the uterus is retained. If the woman wishes to keep the options of fertility, however, a myomectomy may be the correct choice, despite its disadvantages.

All the methods of endometrial ablation have significant failure rates and even surgeons experienced in the techniques are likely to have total success in only about 80% to 85% of cases (though reduction of the bleeding in a further 5% to 10% may be sufficient to satisfy the patient). Nevertheless, the lesser disruption of daily life when compared with a conventional hysterectomy may make ablation more acceptable in some cases.

Dysmenorrhoea

Cases of dysmenorrhoea are usually classified into 'primary' and 'secondary', the latter being associated with other pathology.

Primary dysmenorrhoea appears to occur almost exclusively in ovulatory cycles so that the first menstrual bleeds after the menarche, often being anovulatory, may be painless. The pain is often described as being 'cramping' or 'colicky' and seems to be associated with the excessive release of natural prostaglandins, which may also cause nausea, vomiting and diarrhoea.

Treatment with drugs having an anti-prostaglandin effect may be effective. This includes aspirin, accounting for much of its 'over the counter' sales in the past, though more potent anti-prostaglandins are now available. Oral contraceptive tablets are also effective, since they render the cycles anovulatory and may be a good choice if the woman does not wish to conceive.

The management of secondary dysmenorrhoea relies on treatment of the underlying condition, the most important of which is endometriosis (and adenomyosis), which is dealt with separately in this volume. Chronic pelvic inflammation from other causes, usually infection, may be more severe at the time of the periods and may therefore present as dysmenorrhoea. Occasionally, stenosis of the cervical canal following surgery (for example, a cone biopsy) may impede the drainage of menstrual blood from the uterine cavity and the consequent uterine contractions may be very painful.

Conventional gynaecological teaching insists that retroversion and retroflexion of the uterus never cause dysmenorrhoea but are merely variations of the normal. Although this is certainly true for the majority of retroversions, the senior author well remembers being consulted by a patient in her early 20s who had suffered from incapacitating dysmenorrhoea for many years. She had previously sought help from three other (highly reputable) gynaecologists, all of whom had identified the retroflexion of her uterus and told her that it was of no significance. Correction of the uterine position and the insertion of a Hodge pessary resulted in the complete relief of her symptoms. Fortunately, she was one of the small number of patients in whom the uterus remained in its new position even when the pessary was removed after four months. It may be that the backwards displacement of the uterus sometimes results in 'kinking' of the cervical canal which is thereby partially obstructed and it is unfortunate that uncritical acceptance of the 'official' view may be condemning a number of women to the suffering of avoidable pain.

Polymenorrhoea

The normal range of cycle duration is usually taken to be 21 to 40 days. The complaint of abnormally frequent menstrual bleeds is quite common but careful history taking will often elicit the fact that this is a misinterpretation of the true situation.

The normal range

Some women will have a normal, regular cycle as short as 23 days. They can be reassured that this is of no significance so long as the bleeding is not excessively heavy (frequent periods often tend to be rather light). If the woman wishes to conceive, it may be worth pointing out that ovulation usually occurs about 14 days before the next period which, in a 23 days cycle, means day 9 or perhaps 10 of the cycle.

The altered cycle

A woman who has previously been used to having a very regular cycle of perhaps 29 days will sometimes seek advice if her periodic bleeding changes to a cycle of 26 days. Providing the bleeds themselves remain normal, it is very unlikely that there is any pathological significance to the change and all that is required is reassurance that the new pattern is still within the normal range.

'Twice in a month'

Women will sometimes complain of having had two periods in a month. The actual dates on which the bleeds began should be ascertained and, in many cases, the answers will be something like 'I bled on the 2nd of July and again on the 30th'. Reference to a calendar may help to explain that this was, in fact, a normal 28 day cycle.

Stress

Stressful events such as the death of a close member of the woman's family may provoke a menstrual bleed. In susceptible women, this may even occur in association with aeroplane journeys or other apparently innocuous events.

Miscalculation of a normal cycle

Women may claim to have a cycle of 21 days when they actually mean 21 days free of bleeding. This is a common trap for doctors who are inexperienced in taking a gynaecological history and may result in unnecessary referral to a gynaecological clinic.

Prolongation of bleeding

The error of stating the number of 'clear days' instead of the true cycle may conceal the fact that the cycle has remained normal but the duration of the bleeding has increased – a woman who states that she is bleeding 'every 14 days' may actually be bleeding for 14 days in 28. This should be investigated as described elsewhere.

Intermenstrual bleeding

Having excluded the various misunderstandings, a number of women with 'frequent periods' will be found to be have bleeding between otherwise normal periods (see 'Intermenstrual bleeding', below).

Oligomenorrhoea

As already stated, the normal cycle may range from 21 to 35 days. Oligomenorrhoea is, therefore, a cycle of longer than 35 days but, usually, less than three months. A cycle of longer than three months is usually termed secondary amenorrhoea (see below).

The causes of oligomenorrhoea are essentially the same as for secondary amenorrhoea and are dealt with in that section.

ACYCLICAL PROBLEMS

Amenorrhoea

Amenorrhoea may be primary (menstrual bleeding has never occurred) or secondary (the cessation of menstrual bleeding).

Primary amenorrhoea

The age at which menstruation begins (the menarche) is very variable but, in the UK, it is now usually between 10 and 16 years. The fact that the average age has tended to become younger is often attributed to the improvement in nutritional standards but, worldwide, there is a considerable geographical variation and many of the poorest populations have early average menarches. Individual perception of the normal age also varies and, in a single clinic recently, the question 'When did you start having periods?' produced the replies 'Very early, I was only 12' and 'Quite late, 12 years old' from two different patients.

It is also important to differentiate between primary amenorrhoea (where the endometrial lining of the uterus has not bled) from cryptomenorrhoea, in which the uterine lining bleeds but the blood cannot escape due to a mechanical obstruction.

Cryptomenorrhoea

Cryptomenorrhoea as a cause of primary amenorrhoea could, theoretically, be due to obstruction at any level from the lower uterine cavity to the vulva but, in practice, the only condition likely to be encountered is the imperforate hymen.

The central part of the hymen normally breaks down during later intrauterine life but, in a few girls, this fails to occur. The condition often remains undetected until puberty when, rather than starting to menstruate, the girl will complain of severe but intermittent lower abdominal pain. The pain may not be obviously cyclical since the first few periods after the menarche are frequently irregular. Interference with bladder function may result from pressure from the pelvic mass formed by the distended vagina.

The diagnosis may be obvious if inspection of the vulva reveals a bluish swelling at the vaginal introitus (the colour is due to the retained blood seen through the stretched but intact membrane). Occasionally, the hymen may be so thick that the typical colour is not seen and, indeed, the hymen itself may not be visible until the labia are gently separated.

The treatment consists of making a stab or cruciform incision of the hymen to allow the retained blood to escape. Although this can be done under local anaesthetic, a light general anaesthetic is preferable, since it facilitates the digital evacuation of intra-vaginal blood clot. Usually, there is little fresh bleeding but, occasionally, a few small absorbable sutures may be needed to secure haemostasis at the incised margins.

Congenital vaginal septa are usually placed longitudinally and almost never obstruct the menstrual flow but very rare cases of vaginal agenesis do occur and will necessitate more extensive surgical correction.

True primary amenorrhoea

True primary amenorrhoea may result from uterine agenesis (sometimes with an associated failure of vaginal development) but can also be due to a failure of the hormonal mechanism involving the hypothalamus, pituitary gland and ovaries. The ovaries themselves may not have developed in embryonic life (ovarian agenesis or, when development is only partial, streak ovaries). Chromosomal abnormalities must also be considered since Turner's syndrome (gonadal dysgenesis), in which one of the two sex chromosomes is absent (45X–), is not rare (approximately one in 3,000 live female births). In testicular feminising syndrome, body conformation is feminine but the chromosome pattern will be that of a normal *male* (46XY), the condition apparently resulting from a failure of the embryonic and foetal tissues to respond normally to circulating testosterone.

Secondary amenorrhoea

Secondary amenorrhoea is usually defined as the cessation of menstrual bleeding for more than three months (some authorities prefer six months). It is much more common than the primary absence of menstruation; indeed, if the physiological amenorrhoea of the menopause is included, it is the inevitable accompaniment of advancing years. Secondary amenorrhoea is, of course, also associated with pregnancy, a cause which should always be considered since it is not uncommon for women to seek advice about the cessation of periods without realising that they have conceived. The menstrual cycle may also take some time to be re-established after delivery, especially if the woman breast feeds.

Amenorrhoea of pregnancy

In most cases, the menstrual cycle will be abolished by the conception of a pregnancy but it is not uncommon for the pregnant woman to experience slight vaginal bleeds at the time of her first (and, sometimes, second) missed periods. These bleeds are, by definition, threatened abortions and, though they may stop spontaneously, may cause considerable anxiety. They should therefore not be dismissed lightly. Most of these are probably bleeds from that part of the uterine cavity as yet unoccupied by the gestation sac which remains unaffected but some miscarriages may be caused by bleeding at the implantation site.

Of much more significance is the fact that these early bleeds are much more common in cases of ectopic implantation of the pregnancy. It is not unusual for a woman to state that she had an apparently normal period only two or three weeks before presenting with an ectopic pregnancy which is clearly more advanced than that date would suggest.

A few women will resume a regular menstrual cycle about four weeks after the delivery of a baby but it is much more common for the first post-natal period to be delayed. If she is breast feeding her baby she may not bleed for six months or more. She should realise that ovulation may precede the first period and, unless contraception is used, she may conceive another pregnancy without menstruating in the interval.

Mechanical obstruction

In rare instances, operative damage to the cervix (for example, a cone biopsy) may cause severe stenosis of the cervical canal so that the menstrual blood is unable to escape from the uterine cavity in the usual way. The woman will experience severe, spasmodic lower abdominal pain from uterine contractions as well as from irritation of the pelvic peritoneum by blood forced along the fallopian tubes.

A rather different (and, sadly, less uncommon) mechanical interference with menstruation is the condition known as 'Asherman's syndrome', where the uterine cavity is obliterated by the opposing walls fusing together. This condition follows over enthusiastic curettage of the cavity, usually at an evacuation of retained products of conception, possibly followed by a low-grade infection. It is not often seen after curettage performed in the UK but is by no means rare in some other countries. The amenorrhoea is usually painless since there is nothing to bleed but, occasionally, islands of undamaged endometrium remain.

Hyperprolactinaemia

Breast feeding is associated with an increased production of the hormone prolactin from the anterior lobe of the pituitary gland (the name itself is derived from *pro-* (for) *lactation*) and it is probably the high level of circulating prolactin which is responsible for the associated amenorrhoea (see above). If the serum prolactin level is raised for other reasons, the menstrual cycle may be abolished. Although modest rises are seen in association with various factors, including psychological stress, the highest levels are found in the presence of an adenoma (benign tumour) of the pituitary gland. These tumours occur as micro-adenomas, small but hyperactive islands of pituitary cells, or as actual localised swellings of the gland. They can be demonstrated by various imaging techniques of which the best currently available is probably magnetic resonance imaging (MRI).

Disturbance of the pituitary-ovarian axis

The relationship between the anterior lobe of the pituitary gland and the ovaries is a complex and delicate one which is outlined in the discussion on physiology in Chapter 2. Most clinical conditions fall into one of four groups which can be defined by the levels of the pituitary hormones follicle stimulating hormone (FSH) and luteinising hormone (LH):

Hypogonadotropic:	Low FSH and LH
Normogonadotropic:	Normal levels of FSH and LH
Abnormal LH:FSH Ratio:	A ratio of >2.5:1 is usually considered abnormal
Hypergonadotropic:	High FSH and LH

Detailed consideration of these is beyond the scope of this book but it is worth mentioning that the distorted LH:FSH ratio is typically seen in cases of polycystic ovarian disease (formerly called Stein-Leventhal syndrome), a fairly common cause of both amenorrhoea and infertility. (The other features of the syndrome are obesity and hirsutism but these are not invariably present.)

Anorexia nervosa

Marked loss of body weight from any cause can result in amenorrhoea but the most important association in the Western world is with anorexia nervosa. In this condition, the girl (many sufferers are in their teenage years) or woman has a distorted body image and 'feels' herself to be overweight even though, on objective assessment, she is underweight or even grossly emaciated. In the management of these cases, close co-operation with psychologists and psychiatrists specialising in eating disorders is essential as many of them are very resistant to treatment.

Thyroid dysfunction

Both over and under activity of the thyroid gland may be associated with amenorrhoea and investigation of thyroid function is essential in many amenorrhoeic women since the cessation of the menstrual cycle may be the first indication that the thyroid gland is beginning to malfunction.

Intermenstrual bleeding (IMB)

The term intermenstrual bleeding describes the occurrence of vaginal bleeding at times other than the normal cyclical bleeds, which continue unchanged. Post-coital bleeding (see below) is a particular form of IMB and any of its causes may also result in bleeding which is not associated with sexual activity. All IMB is abnormal and further investigation may be indicated to establish the cause.

Break-through bleeding (BTB)

Break-through bleeding is an additional, and common, cause of inter-menstrual blood loss which is seen in women taking the oral contraceptive pill. It is usually associated with use of 'low dose' or 'progesterone only' preparations and, once other possible causes have been excluded, is usually cured by a change to a higher dose pill.

Post-coital bleeding (PCB)

The torn hymen

A small amount of bleeding is a common accompaniment to the rupture of a virginal hymen. Indeed, in some societies, it is the necessary conclusion to the wedding day. Unfortunately, the bleeding can occasionally be much heavier, a frightening experience for the girl and also for her partner.

The bleeding from the torn hymen can invariably be controlled by digital pressure as a first-aid measure but permanent haemostasis may require the insertion of one or more absorbable sutures. Whilst local anaesthetic may be sufficient, it is often better done under a general anaesthetic in order to enable careful examination to exclude a vaginal laceration.

Local lesions of the vagina or cervix

Lacerations

Vaginal lacerations may result from over vigorous coitus, particularly in the elderly woman and especially in association with the offence of rape. Vaginal damage can also occur if unsuitable objects are introduced into the vagina. Perhaps the most famous instance of such an injury was the death in 1921 of the Hollywood starlet Virginia Rappe (whose bladder was also lacerated). The damage was alleged to have been due to her rape with a champagne bottle wielded by the film star Roscoe 'Fatty' Arbuckle during a drunken party. (Fatty Arbuckle was ultimately acquitted.)

Cervical 'erosion'/ectropion and polyp

The normal covering of the portio vaginalis of the cervix is stratified squamous epithelium but the columnar epithelium of an erosion or ectropion is more easily damaged during sexual intercourse so that bleeding may result. The blood is bright though rarely heavy sometimes only being noticed on a condom or diaphragm. Similar symptoms may occur if a polyp is protruding from the external cervical os.

Cervical carcinoma

The early stages of cervical carcinoma are asymptomatic (hence the need for regular routine cervical cytology) but, in the later stages, malignant disease of the cervix may be associated with post-coital bleeding. All women presenting with PCB or IMB should have their cervical cytology checked.

Post-menopausal bleeding (PMB)

Vaginal bleeding occurring after an apparently normal menopause must always be taken seriously since, in a significant minority of cases, it will be due to malignant disease of the cervix or (more frequently) of the endometrium. The traditional teaching was that all cases should be investigated by a D & C. This has been modified by the development of outpatient hysteroscopy, simpler endometrial sampling methods and ultrasonographic assessment of the endometrial cavity, but the basic principle remains unchanged (though the D & C should now be accompanied by a hysteroscopy).

Vaginal lesions

Atrophic vaginitis

This condition, formerly rather tactlessly and inappropriately called 'senile' vaginitis, is due to the gradual thinning of the vaginal skin which accompanies the fall in circulating oestrogens. The thinned skin is less able to resist normal minor trauma with the result that minor bleeding occurs from the underlying small blood vessels; this may be noticed as scanty bleeding or as a blood-stained discharge. Vaginal dryness or soreness, especially during coitus, are also common symptoms.

In most cases, simple visual inspection of the vaginal walls will reveal a characteristic redness often with petechial haemorrhages. Very mild cases may only be detected on cervical or vaginal cytology but these are usually asymptomatic. Treatment is by local or systemic oestrogens.

Unfortunately, the fact that atrophic vaginitis is common, benign and easily treated sometimes traps unwary doctors into overlooking a co-existing endometrial carcinoma.

Carcinoma of the vagina

Primary carcinoma of the vagina is uncommon but secondary deposits are more frequent. In either case, lesions severe enough to cause bleeding are likely to be at an advanced stage. Treatment is usually by radiotherapy though radical surgery is sometimes undertaken.

Other vaginal and cervical lesions

The conditions described above as causes of post-coital bleeding may also give rise to post-menopausal bleeding when they occur in older women.

Foreign bodies

Plastic devices (pessaries) inserted into the vagina to control a prolapse will occasionally be forgotten and may, if left in situ for many months or years, cause ulceration of the vaginal wall and hence bleeding. Removal of the device (which may be difficult) and the treatment of any infection is all that is required but a co-existing endometrial carcinoma must, as always, be excluded.

Carcinoma of the body of the uterus

As has been stressed above, the only safe rule in the management of post-menopausal bleeding is to assume that all cases are due to malignant disease in the uterine cavity until that possibility has been positively excluded.

Some years ago, an otherwise fit and healthy woman in her early 60s consulted her general practitioner because she had noticed a bloodstained vaginal discharge. She had stopped her menstrual periods about 10 years before and, on examining her vagina, the GP noted the presence of atrophic changes. He prescribed an oestrogen cream for local application in the vagina. As the discharge persisted, the woman returned to the surgery about six weeks later when, without further examination, she was given hormone replacement therapy to take by mouth and was advised to continue using the cream. As the discharge was still unchanged, a further attendance a few months later resulted in the vaginal cream being changed to a different brand.

Not wishing to confront her GP with the continued failure of his treatment, the woman did not return until, some twelve months later, she heard that her usual doctor was away on holiday and consulted his deputy who, finding an upper abdominal mass, referred her to the local hospital. The mass proved to be her liver, which was extensively invaded by a secondary tumour from the uterine cancer which had clearly been present for a considerable time. The woman died of her malignant disease not long afterwards.

The tragedy of such a failure of care is that, if diagnosed early, cancer of the body of the uterus is often treated successfully.

PRE-MENSTRUAL SYNDROME

Pre-menstrual syndrome (PMS), also called pre-menstrual tension (PMT), typically affects women in their late 30s, though it can prove to be a problem at any age from the menarche to the menopause. The symptoms may disrupt the patient's life and characteristically occur in the seven to 10 days before the onset of menstruation, improving once the menstrual bleeding begins.

The usual complaints are of emotional instability, depression, irritability, irrational behaviour, tearfulness, fatigue, headaches, swelling or bloating of the abdomen and breast tenderness.

The cause of the condition is unknown but it does appear to be dependent upon the presence of an ovarian hormone cycle. Despite this, however, there is no conclusive evidence of any difference between PMS sufferers and other groups of women in respect of the levels of circulating hormones. It may be that symptoms are associated with variations in the hormone levels rather than the absolute value or perhaps with changes in the tissue receptors via which the hormones produce their effects. In some women, the symptoms seem to be due to a relative lack of progesterone in the second half of the menstrual cycle (though many gynaecologists would dispute this). Some theories implicate changes in the neurotransmitters within the central nervous system. It is, of course, possible that the symptoms are the clinical manifestations of a number of different underlying mechanisms, a possibility made more likely by the observation that a treatment which is effective in one woman may offer no benefit at all for another.

Management

The first priority in the management of a woman complaining of PMS is to establish the relationship between the symptoms and the menstrual bleeding. Recollection is often inaccurate and it is better to ask the woman to keep a diary of her symptoms. This may reveal that the symptoms actually have no true cyclical pattern and an alternative diagnosis should then be sought.

Differential diagnosis

PMS may be confused with a number of other conditions. If the symptoms are predominantly psychosomatic the true cause may be a psychiatric problem, especially depression, or there may be psychosexual or relationship difficulties. If the main complaint is of breast tenderness, a careful examination of the breasts (and possibly mammography) should be performed to exclude benign or malignant breast conditions. Abdominal bloating may be due to irritable bowel syndrome, abdominal tumours or even simple obesity. Anaemia or hypothyroidism (an under active thyroid gland) may mimic some of these problems.

Dysmenorrhoea is not a symptom of PMS, though PMS sufferers may, of course, also suffer from dysmenorrhoea.

Treatment

For some women, the reassurance of a thorough physical examination may be sufficient treatment but, as with most poorly understood conditions, management regimes are often unsatisfactory.

It is important that the woman's complaints are taken seriously especially as she may feel (often correctly) that her partner is unsympathetic. The clinician should reassure the woman about the nature of the condition and provide her with information about access to support groups.

The assessment of the effectiveness of the treatment of PMS demonstrates a very strong placebo effect (the patient exhibits a response to therapy even when no active substance has been administered). As many as 60% of women with PMS may report an improvement even if the treatment is only a dummy tablet. This offends the modern pseudo-scientific doctor who is constantly being encouraged to practise 'evidence-based medicine' but the improvement is no less welcome to the patient for that; unfortunately, these effects may be transient.

Many women improve with alternative therapies such as homeopathy or reflexology. Although this may also be due to the placebo response, conventional medicine cannot, at present, offer a satisfactory explanation of the mechanisms involved in PMS and women should not be discouraged from seeking alternative treatments, providing that they are not harmful.

'Over the counter' remedies

High doses of the vitamin B6 may be tried. This is thought to work by promoting the production of specific chemicals (serotonin and dopamine) in the brain.

If B6 is not helpful, the next step is often a trial of evening primrose oil, which contains essential fatty acids. These are thought to affect the cell membranes where the tissue receptors are situated and it has been postulated that an imbalance in the amounts of fatty acids may influence the effect of the circulating hormones.

Since these two therapies are available 'over the counter', the woman will often have tried them before consulting a doctor.

Hormonal regimes

If the simpler remedies fail, it is then usual to try the effect of abolishing the cyclical hormone changes that occur in the menstrual cycle and a readily available method is by administration of a combined oral contraceptive. The 'pill' provides a continuous low level of oestrogen and a progestogen throughout the month, thereby smoothing out the wide fluctuations in the hormone levels which are thought to have some causative effect in PMS. When given for this purpose, the combined pill may be taken continuously instead of for 21 days in 28.

An alternative hormonal treatment is to prescribe a progestogen for the two pre-menstrual weeks on the assumption that PMS may result from a lack of ovarian progesterone. Progestogens can be taken orally as tablets, rectally as suppositories, vaginally as pessaries or, though not commonly for this indication, as an intramuscular injection.

Although both the hormonal regimes can be helpful in relieving PMS, it is always very difficult to distinguish between a true pharmacological effect and a placebo response.

Symptomatic treatments

If the predominant symptom is breast tenderness, it may be helpful to reduce the serum prolactin level by the administration of bromocriptine. The main effect of the hormone 'prolactin' is upon the breast tissue and hence reduction of the circulating level of the hormone can relieve much of the breast discomfort associated with PMS.

Abdominal bloating is a common complaint in PMS sufferers though objective measurements usually fail to confirm the subjective feeling. Diuretics may be helpful.

Second line treatments

If troublesome symptoms persist despite treatment, other endocrine manipulation may be tried.

Danazol interrupts the normal pituitary-ovarian interaction and can be used to suppress the ovarian cycle. Unfortunately, at the high doses it can produce irritating side effects including weight gain and greasiness of the skin. These generally disappear soon after treatment is stopped but the occasional huskiness of the voice may persist. Danazol, at lower doses that do not suppress the ovarian cycle, may nevertheless be effective.

Another possible line of treatment is to provide extra oestrogen either in the form of an implant or by the same skin patches that are usually used for climacteric symptoms. Like danazol, it works by influencing the negative feedback of circulating oestrogen on the pituitary gland. This is an effective treatment but it has potential problems associated with the giving of supplementary oestrogen to a woman with no prior deficiency of the hormone. There is therefore a risk of overstimulating the uterine lining (endometrial hyperplasia) and also of increasing the risk of venous thromboembolism.

The ovarian cycle can, of course, be abolished by performing a bilateral oophorectomy. This rather drastic solution may be indicated in severe cases, especially for women in their forties. Before performing such an operation, it is often advisable to give the woman a course of gonadotrophin releasing hormone (GnRH) to help her to assess her probable response. The GnRH causes a reversible menopause and, if the woman does not have complete resolution of her PMS during treatment, the advisability of the oophorectomy should be reconsidered.

Conclusion

None of the currently available treatment options for PMS can be guaranteed to work and not all women are suitable for oestrogen implants, GnRH analogues or an oophorectomy.

Management is generally based on the simpler methods supplemented by counselling and psychological support.

CHAPTER 6

INFECTIONS

INTRODUCTION

Gynaecologists are often consulted by women who fear that they may have contracted a sexually transmitted condition for, even in these more liberated times, many people feel that there is still a stigma attached to attending a VD clinic. Perhaps as a result of this attitude, these clinics have acquired a myriad of other titles being also known as sexually transmitted disease (STD) clinics, genito-urinary medicine (GUM) clinics, special clinics or, the latest trend, sexual health clinics. These different titles probably reflect an attempt to minimise the embarrassment felt by many of the patients and even some doctors.

Among the most common problems that present to both gynaecologists and to STD clinics are vaginal discharge and vaginal irritation. The commonest causes of these two complaints are not, in fact, sexually transmitted infections and, indeed, the symptoms may not be due to a vaginal infection at all.

PHYSIOLOGICAL VAGINAL DISCHARGE

The normal healthy vagina produces a clear, mucoid discharge though some women may consider this to be abnormal, especially if they fear that they may have been exposed to the risk of infection or when they notice an increase in the discharge, as often occurs during pregnancy.

Glandular cells located near the vaginal entrance and at the uterine cervix are responsible for the production of a fluid secretion which will be manifest as a discharge. These cells respond to changes in the levels of the female hormones and an increased oestrogen level will result in the production of more secretions.

During a woman's life, her body will be exposed to varying amounts of oestrogen and other hormones. Chronologically, there are several distinct episodes of female hormonal activity (see Chapter 2). A newborn baby has recently emerged from the intrauterine environment in which it was exposed to maternal hormones. This commonly results in a newborn baby girl having a small amount of vaginal discharge. The effect rapidly disappears after birth, since the baby herself produces very little oestrogen.

This low level of oestrogen is maintained until puberty. During the changes leading up to the menarche (the onset of menstrual bleeding), the girl's ovaries begin to produce the female hormones and, not long afterwards, the ova start to develop. As the hormone level increases, the girl (or, more often, her mother) may notice some vaginal discharge.

The levels of the hormones, oestrogen and progesterone fluctuate during the monthly or menstrual cycle and the vaginal secretions consequently also vary. Some women are sufficiently aware of the cyclical properties of their vaginal discharge to be able to use these changes to predict when they are nearing ovulation and accordingly adjust their sexual activity to improve or reduce their chance of conception.

During pregnancy, the levels of both oestrogen and progesterone are increased and hence the frequently reported increase in vaginal discharge as the pregnancy proceeds.

By the age of 52 years, most women will have had their last period. The ovaries gradually stop producing both the ova and the hormones. Thus, post-menopausal women return to a low level of oestrogen in their system which will be reflected in a reduction in vaginal discharge.

Ectropion

Part of a routine gynaecological examination is the introduction of a speculum into the vagina to inspect the cervix and the vaginal walls. The visible surface of the normal cervix consists of many layers of flattened cells, whilst the canal of the cervix is lined by a single layer of cells, many of which produce mucus. In some cases, possibly under the influence of oestrogen, the mucus secreting cells spread out onto the visible surface and appear as a brighter red area contrasting with the smooth, pale pink of the normal surface. The appearance led to the term 'erosion' but the implication that the surface has been worn away is misleading and the word has largely been replaced by ectropion. The increased area of glandular cells will result in the production of a larger amount of mucus, which the woman may notice as an abnormal vaginal discharge, especially if it becomes secondarily infected.

The various infective causes for vaginal discharge must be excluded by taking the appropriate swabs (see below) and the gynaecologist can then reassure the woman that the discharge is normal. Nevertheless, some women find any sort of discharge distressing and it is possible to destroy the area of glandular cells by the application of heat (hot wire cautery or diathermy) or cold (cryocautery) or by laser evaporation. Following the treatment, the multilayered epithelium will usually grow to cover the healing area.

PATHOLOGICAL VAGINAL DISCHARGE

Non-infectious

Some non-infectious conditions can present with a vaginal discharge which may be blood stained in the presence of various cancers or of polyps. A relatively common cause of vaginal discharge is the presence of forgotten material within the vagina, most frequently a retained tampon or condom. The woman may be amazed when the offending item is retrieved!

Infections (not necessarily sexually transmitted)

Candida, also known as 'thrush' or 'monilia'

Candida albicans or 'thrush' is the most common infective cause of a vaginal discharge and vulvo-vaginal irritation. It usually causes a thick white discharge and intense itching, which may be so severe that the vulval skin becomes excoriated. The causative fungal infection is usually spread from the woman's own bowel, where it is a normal inhabitant, but it may be introduced during sexual intercourse from the penis, fingers or mouth. The spread of the organism is favoured by changes in the vaginal environment, either of an alteration in the acidity of the vagina, or a change in the normal bacterial population of the vagina. This later frequently occurs because of antibiotics taken for some other infection but sometimes after vaginal douching, especially when antiseptic solutions are used.

The vagina is normally rendered slightly acid by the cervical secretions, a condition which is ideal for the healthy *Lactobacilli*. If the acidity of the vagina is altered, then these normal bacteria may not survive and the vagina may then be colonised by opportunistic organisms. The presence of *Candida* in the bowel provides a ready source of infection.

A common cause of the loss of vaginal acidity is sexual intercourse. Semen is more alkaline than the normal vaginal pH and its effect is thus to neutralise the acidity of the vagina. In the majority of women, this will not have any noticeable effect, but a minority may suffer from bouts of 'thrush' each time they have sexual intercourse. The acidity is also altered prior to the menstrual period and some women therefore complain of a pre-menstrual irritation and vaginal discharge.

When vaginal thrush is a recurrent problem, it can give rise to psychosexual difficulties.

Bacterial vaginosis, anaerobic infections, gardnerella vaginalis

Another infection that is not sexually transmitted is bacterial vaginosis. It causes a profuse, watery discharge with a fishy odour which is frequently worse after sexual intercourse. The bacteria responsible for anaerobic infections are normally present in small numbers within the vagina and only cause symptoms if their numbers increase. Like Candida, anaerobic infections thrive in a non-acid environment, and they can also become recurrent causing psychological and psycho-sexual problems.

Anaerobic infections alone do not cause any permanent effects but they can aggravate tubal damage during an episode of pelvic inflammatory disease (see below).

Sexually transmitted infections

When a woman complains of a vaginal discharge, it is vital to elicit details of her recent sexual activity, to ascertain whether her partner has noticed any problems and to establish the interval since her last sexual intercourse with her current and previous partner. Unfortunately, many gynaecologists shy away from asking questions about sexual partners.

Herpes simplex, cold sores, genital herpes

Herpes simplex classically presents with recurrent vulval sores but the woman often complains only of vulval or vaginal irritation and may therefore be misdiagnosed as having the more common candidal infection unless a proper examination is performed. If she reports episodic problems, the gynaecologist should be alerted to the possible diagnosis and arrange to see her when she has the symptoms. This can be difficult in the gynaecology clinic with fixed weekly times and long appointment lists. It is worth considering directing the woman to an STD clinic since they frequently have a 'walk-in' facility.

Trichomonas vaginalis

Trichomonas vaginalis is sexually transmitted and causes a greenish coloured, watery vaginal discharge which is usually associated with vulval soreness. The diagnosis can often be confirmed in the clinic by microscopic examination of the discharge revealing the moving organisms. If it is detected, the sexual partner needs to be treated and the possibility that the woman may have more than one partner must be borne in mind if treatment failures are to be minimised. It is often helpful to refer the woman to a STD clinic, where they are used to dealing with all of these issues.

Gonorrhoea

Gonorrhoea is probably the most widely known cause of sexually transmitted genital infections. However, it is now uncommon in the female population outside certain high-risk groups such as prostitutes. This reduction in the number of cases is due to the fact that it is easily treated by many of the common antibiotics, but despite its reduced incidence, it remains important because it can cause severe pelvic infections which may lead to tubal damage and thus infertility. The organisms live in the cells of the cervix and urethra and therefore will only be detected if the bacteriological sample swabs are taken from these sites rather than from the vaginal walls.

Chlamydia

Chlamydia is an important cause of pelvic infection that can also give rise to infertility through causing tubal damage. Like the gonococcus, the organisms live in the cervix but, unlike gonorrhoea, it is not easily eradicated by common antibiotics and, since the symptoms may be quite mild, the woman may not seek treatment until the damage is already well advanced. Specific samples must be taken in order to detect the presence of chlamydia.

Not all women with chlamydia will develop pelvic infections and not all women with pelvic infections will develop infertility but the chance of a pelvic infection developing are increased if an operation such as a termination of pregnancy is performed when there is chlamydia present at the cervix. Women undergoing a termination of pregnancy appear to have an above average chance of harbouring chlamydial organisms and one study showed that up to one in four of women seeking a termination of pregnancy had chlamydia present.

Management of vaginal discharges

Most of the infections outlined above are relatively easy to treat with the appropriate antibiotic given for the appropriate duration to both partners. It is imperative that they abstain from sexual intercourse during the treatment time until they have both been cured otherwise the infection will be passed back and forth between them. If a specific organism is identified it is most appropriate that the woman is seen in an STD clinic as these clinics have well established contact tracing and treatment systems.

A woman at low risk of sexually transmitted diseases who is suffering from thrush should be treated with an appropriate anti-fungal therapy and also advised about measures to reduce the risk of recurrence. A disadvantage of the 'over the counter' availability of vaginal pessaries and creams is that women may misdiagnose themselves and hence fail to seek expert help for some of the more serious conditions.

Effects and sequelae of sexually transmitted infections

The most significant consequences of sexually transmitted infections are pelvic inflammatory disease (acute or chronic), pelvic adhesions and psychosexual problems.

Pelvic inflammatory disease

Strictly, this term means that some or all of the pelvic structures are affected by an inflammatory response to any sort of stimulus. In clinical practice, however, the term (often abbreviated to PID) is usually used to designate inflammation due to *infection*.

Organisms, such as the gonococcus or chlamydia, spread from the vagina through the cervical and uterine cavities to cause infection of the walls of the uterine tubes, usually on both sides. Infection of the tubes results in inflammatory swelling, pus formation and, unless effective antibiotic treatment is instituted promptly, long-term damage. Permanent damage to the tubal wall decreases fertility, increases the risk of an ectopic pregnancy and may cause complete tubal obstruction. The likelihood of permanent damage increases with the number of episodes of infection and the length of time from onset to effective treatment. The risk of permanent tubal damage after a single episode has been estimated to be about 10% but after three episodes this rises to 60%. It is important that sexual contacts of a woman with proven PID are traced and treated effectively.

It is not known why organisms such as chlamydia, which may be present in the vagina and cervix for long periods without causing any apparent problem, should, at times, spread to the relatively sensitive tubes. Certain practises such as douching have been shown to increase the chance of pelvic infection and procedures such as the insertion of an intrauterine contraceptive device or a surgical termination of pregnancy which necessitate the passage of instruments through the cervix can precipitate the condition. Prior to such procedures, the clinician should consider taking suitable swabs to search for potentially significant organisms so that appropriate treatment can be given. If the procedure is urgent, a prophylactic antibiotic may be administered.

Unfortunately, the laboratory examination of the usual 'high vaginal swab' is unreliable in demonstrating some of these organisms and specific samples taken from the cervical canal are required. The swab must also be placed in special transport medium for its journey to the laboratory. Even the best tests currently available will only detect about 70% of cases of chlamydia on one sample. New methods of detection are being evaluated.

The clinical features of pelvic infection are very variable since the signs depend on the severity of the inflammatory response which is influenced not only by the virulence of the organism but also by the individual patient's reaction. The woman may complain of lower abdominal pain and may have noticed a vaginal discharge. She may be generally unwell and may be pyrexial. Menstrual irregularity or inter-menstrual bleeding suggests that the ovaries are involved in the inflammatory process.

Vaginal examination may cause severe pain particularly if the cervix is gently rocked. This sign is called 'cervical excitation' and is a fairly reliable indication of inflammation affecting the para-cervical tissues. It is positive in most cases of PID and may be present in cases of ectopic pregnancy. Some non-gynaecological conditions such as appendicitis may cause similar inflammation.

The only real diagnostic procedure for PID is a laparoscopy. On inspection, the tubes will be red and swollen and pus may be visible draining from the fimbrial ends. This will usually be a pool of rather watery pus in the pouch of Douglas and a fibrinous exudate may be present on the peritoneal surfaces. It is reasonable to treat a patient on the clinical diagnosis initially but, if she fails to improve with antibiotic treatment or if she has recurrent symptoms, a laparoscopy should be considered in order to establish the diagnosis.

Cases of suspected PID frequently present as acute problems in the Accident and Emergency Department. In the absence of systemic symptoms and a pyrexia, many of these woman can be treated as outpatients with full courses of antibiotics, usually a tetracycline or erythromycin, for a minimum of two weeks. Arrangements should be made for the patient to be reviewed, preferably by a Sexual Health Clinic, to ensure that they respond to the treatment. More severe cases must be admitted for inpatient treatment with three or four days of intra-venous administration of antibiotics before changing to oral therapy once a definite response has been achieved.

Recurrent pelvic infection (chronic PID)

Some women in high risk situations may experience multiple episodes of re-infection but it is more common for the symptoms to recur because of inadequate treatment in the first instance. This may be because of inappropriate prescribing or because of poor patient compliance.

Some cases labelled as PID will not be due to pelvic infection at all. For example, irritable bowel syndrome (IBS) is a common cause of abdominal pain which is not only recurrent but may actually be made worse by antibiotics. A diagnostic laparoscopy is essential for these women who may otherwise suffer from persistent symptoms.

Women with low grade PID may delay seeking treatment until the disease has already become chronic. The treatment of such cases is frequently disappointing since tubal damage may already be present and symptoms often persist even if the infecting organism is successfully eradicated. The surgical division of pelvic adhesions may be necessary and removal of one or both tubes may be indicated if the damage is severe. Occasionally, the effects on the pelvic organs may be so widespread that even a hysterectomy with bilateral salpingo-oophorectomy may be required.

Pelvic adhesions

Adherence of peritoneal surfaces within the pelvis frequently causes deep dyspareunia and may give rise to pain unassociated with coitus. The mechanism for this is not properly understood, especially as it seems that some cases can remain asymptomatic for months or years before problems are experienced. Surgical division of the adhesions may be effective in relieving the symptoms but it is very difficult to prevent the re-formation of adhesions between the raw surfaces. In some instances, the dyspareunia may be due to bruising of a tethered ovary when mobilisation and lateral fixation of the ovary may be successful.

Unfortunately, many cases are labelled as 'psycho-somatic' but most have a physical basis for the pain, although psychological factors often contribute to the clinical picture.

Psycho-sexual problems

Not surprisingly, the pain experienced during coitus in the presence of pelvic inflammation may cause psychosexual difficulties, which may persist after the infection has been treated. Psychosexual problems may also be associated with other infections, of which the most notable is genital herpes.

In addition to the effect of the dyspareunia, the relationship with the sexual partner may be at risk because of suspicions of sexual infidelity.

CHAPTER 7

ENDOMETRIOSIS

Endometrial tissue forms the interior lining of the uterine cavity and endometrial cells are shed during the monthly menstrual bleed. When islands of endometrial cells are present at other sites, the condition is called 'endometriosis'.

Endometriosis usually affects women between the ages of 30 and 45 years and is an important cause of pelvic pain. It has been estimated that about one in 10 pre-menopausal women have endometriosis but the condition may be associated with difficulties in achieving a conception and the incidence may be as high as 30% in women attending infertility clinics. The incidence is high in some families but it is not known why endometriosis develops in some women but not in others.

Various theories have been proposed to explain how the endometrial cells come to be in abnormal situations. It is probable that the commonest mechanism is 'retrograde menstruation'. In the majority of menstruating women, some of the menstrual blood, instead of being evacuated through the cervical canal, passes though the tubes and into the abdominal cavity, where it is deposited on the adjacent peritoneal surfaces; this is called retrograde menstruation. The blood contains shed endometrial cells but, in most women, these cells fail to become established and are reabsorbed. In some women, however, possibly because of some fault in the immunological response, it appears that the mechanism fails and the cells become established in the new site. This mechanism certainly accords with the fact that the commonest site for endometriosis is the peritoneum of the pelvis and its contained organs and can account for endometriotic deposits at other sites within the abdominal cavity. It cannot, however, explain the rare appearance of endometriotic deposits in the lungs and in the tissues of the upper thigh. Although situated abnormally, the endometriotic cells are physiologically normal and hence respond to the endocrine changes of the menstrual cycle by bleeding and it is this trapped blood which actually causes the adverse effects.

A particular variant of endometriosis is the presence of endometrial deposits within the myometrial layer of the uterine wall. This is known as 'adenomyosis' and is especially associated with severe dysmenorrhoea and heavy menstrual blood loss.

DIAGNOSIS

The only certain way of diagnosing endometriosis is by the visual confirmation of the presence of characteristic lesions at laparoscopy or laparotomy.

Endometriosis can be recognised by the presence of the classical 'powder burn' lesions (the numerous, randomly scattered, diffuse, dark lesions being reminiscent of the effect of gunpowder at short range) or the less common florid red 'flare' lesions. Other evidence of endometriosis in the pelvis is the presence of fibrin deposition either as adhesions or a diffuse layer on the peritoneal surface, localised scar tissue associated with old, burnt out endometriotic sites or defects in the peritoneal surface. The classical lesions are easy to recognise but the other appearances may be overlooked or misdiagnosed especially by less experienced gynaecological surgeons and are particularly difficult to see if situated in the ovarian fossa the proper inspection of which may be frustrated by the ovary itself.

Endometriosis may also occur within the ovary and is one of the causes of ovarian cysts. Endometriotic cysts are called 'chocolate cysts' because they contain old, altered blood accumulated from the cyclical bleeding of the endometrial cells lining the cyst wall. This fluid has the colour and consistency of melted chocolate.

Two additional diagnostic tools may raise the suspicion of endometriosis. An ultrasonic scan may reveal the presence of an ovarian cyst with echogenic contents though it is ultrasonically not possible to differentiate positively between an endometriotic cyst and other types of echogenic ovarian cysts. Endometriosis may also be associated with a modest increase in the blood level of the tumour marker known as 'Ca 125'.

Symptoms

Women suffering from endometriosis will usually have consulted their general practitioner with the complaints of pelvic pain (especially cyclical pain including dysmenorrhoea) or infertility. Occasionally, the pelvic pain may be so severe that the woman first presents to the Accident and Emergency department of the hospital. They may however be referred to almost any hospital department because of the variety of situations in which endometriotic lesions may be found.

In some cases, however, the condition may cause very few problems and in many women endometriosis is only diagnosed when a laparoscopy is performed for some other indication.

Women may have pain during their periods (dysmenorrhoea), pain during sexual intercourse (dyspareunia) or non-specific lower abdominal pain. Dysmenorrhoea that is due to endometriosis is usually described as beginning with the onset of the menstrual bleeding and lasting throughout the period. The pain may be due to peritoneal irritation by the blood released from the endometriotic lesion but it is a frequent observation that the most severe pain often occurs with small and apparently almost insignificant lesions and this may be because a small amount of bleeding into a lesion of modest size will cause a greater pressure change than in a large lesion. The natural sequel is the deposition of fibrin and the development of scar tissue, possibly with the adherence of adjacent organs.

The disorganisation of the pelvic anatomy by endometriotic scarring may cause infertility, especially if the tubes and ovaries are involved as is often the case and actual tubal obstruction may occur. Women with endometriosis are more likely to suffer from infertility even if the tubes remain patent and there is no intra-abdominal scarring and, rather surprisingly, it has also been found that women with this condition have greater difficulty in conceiving even with in vitro fertilisation (IVF or 'test-tube baby') techniques. It must therefore be assumed that the endometriotic deposits contribute to sub-fertility in some as yet unknown way.

Extra-pelvic endometriosis can present with a variety of symptoms, for example, endometriosis in the lung can cause monthly haemoptysis (coughing up of blood) while a lesion in the umbilicus may cause a cyclical discharge from that site.

Delay in diagnosis

It is not uncommon for women to have endured pelvic pain or dysmenorrhoea for many years before the diagnosis is made. Sometimes, this is because they have been told by their female friends and relations (and sometimes, it must be said, by their medical advisors) that this is normal to experience such symptoms.

Signs

A careful vaginal examination may raise the suspicion of the diagnosis. The uterus may be fixed in retroversion (long axis directed posteriorly) and there may be tender nodules behind the uterus in the region of the uterosacral ligaments. In other cases, it may be possible to feel an ovarian cyst. Most endometriosis sufferers will evidence severe pelvic tenderness and will complain of pain if an attempt is made to move the uterus.

The presence of adenomyosis is often associated with moderate uterine enlargement and the organ is frequently exquisitely tender especially at period times.

MANAGEMENT

Once the diagnosis is made, the woman should receive a detailed explanation of the condition with particular emphasis on the extent to which she herself is affected. The information should be provided in a relaxed and unhurried fashion and the woman should be given the opportunity of asking questions. Leaflets and diagrams are often very helpful. The implication for her future fertility is an important aspect in many cases.

Although severe endometriosis can be incapacitating, there are many cases in which the condition is only of minor extent and may have little or no impact on the woman's life. If a proper explanation of the individual circumstances is not provided, many women will refer to medical texts in their local library where they may find graphic descriptions of the severest cases and may become what one of the authors has described as 'endometriosis casualties' with serious, and quite unjustified, psychological consequences.

TREATMENT

Treatment is aimed at addressing three issues: first, providing pain relief; secondly, removing or destroying the endometrial deposits; and thirdly, preserving or restoring fertility. The treatment selected will depend upon the age of the patient, their particular symptoms and the extent and severity of the condition.

Treatment may be medical or surgical, though, in many cases, both approaches may be utilised.

Medical treatment

Analgesics

The simplest drugs are analgesics that are taken during menstruation. They may be paracetemol based, with or without codeine. The non-steroidal anti-inflammatory drugs are often very helpful.

Hormones

The next group of drugs is hormonal and all act by suppressing the endocrine function of the ovaries. The most basic are the combined oral contraceptives containing both oestrogen and progesterone. The hormone levels normally fluctuate during the month allowing maturation of the egg and thickening of the uterine endometrium. Administration of a combined contraceptive maintains the hormones at a constant level, thereby preventing the ovaries from functioning and, hence, reducing the stimulation to the endometriotic deposits.

When used to treat endometriosis, the combined oral contraceptive pill is usually given continuously for three months. Longer courses of treatment can be given but break-through bleeding is common and the therapy is only effective in mild cases of the condition.

Progestogens

Continuous administration of progestogens has been used for many years. They have the advantages of few side effects and of being inexpensive (the latter making them popular in the present cost conscious environment) but, unfortunately, like the combined contraceptive pill, they are not very effective.

Danazol

Danazol is a synthetic steroid derivative. It acts by blocking the normal hormonal activity of the menstrual cycle in both the ovary and in the pituitary (see Chapter 2). Its effect is to abolish the menstrual cycle and therefore prevent the growth of the extra endometrial tissue.

Danazol is generally effective in treating endometriosis but unfortunately can have troublesome side effects in a small number of women. These include weight gain, thinning of the hair, greasy skin and, rarely, huskiness of the voice. The voice change is not always reversible on cessation of treatment. Danazol is not a contraceptive and barrier contraception should therefore be used.

Gestrione and dimetriose

These two drugs act is a similar manner to danazol, the aim being to abolish temporarily the menstrual cycle. They have similar side effects to danazol. They are administered twice weekly, which may result in doses being forgotten.

Surgical treatment

Despite the advances in the medical treatment of endometriosis in recent years, surgical methods are still important both in the management of the condition itself and also in attempts to correct the damage that endometriosis may cause.

Laparoscopy

In addition to its value as a diagnostic method, laparoscopy also has a role in allowing the surgical destruction of endometriotic lesions by the application of electrocoagulation or by laser evaporation. Unfortunately, such methods can only be applied to visible lesions and cannot treat endometriotic deposits which are buried deeply. Care must be used to avoid damage to other intra-abdominal structures especially if the endometriosis is closely adjacent

Operative laparoscopy can also be used to divide adhesions, excise endometriomata or an entire ovary and to perform tubal surgery but adhesions caused by endometriosis are often very dense and may be extremely difficult to separate, particularly if important structures are involved. Such procedures must therefore be performed (or closely supervised) only by gynaecological surgeons with appropriate training and experience.

Laparotomy

If the gynaecologist lacks endoscopic operative experience or if the clinical condition renders such methods inadvisable, it may be necessary to perform a laparotomy. Even at open operation, the division of adhesions and the excision of endometriotic deposits may be exceedingly difficult and there is certainly no justification for leaving such procedures to be performed by junior surgeons.

As well as the removal of part or all of an ovary containing endometriotic deposits, bilateral oophorectomy also has an endocrine role in management since the resulting fall in oestrogen levels withdraws the hormonal stimulation of the endometrial cells and hence regression of the endometriosis. Bilateral oophorectomy may be combined with a hysterectomy, especially in cases where the presence of adenomyosis is suspected.

LONG TERM OUTLOOK

Endometriosis can range in severity from a few tiny deposits on the peritoneum of the pouch of Douglas to extensive disruption of the greater part of the pelvic anatomy.

Minor cases will often 'burn out' spontaneously and may cause few symptoms before ceasing to be a problem when the hormonal stimulation ceases with the cessation of periods at the menopause. In contrast, women who have the misfortune to suffer from severe endometriosis may experience incapacitating dysmenorrhoea and intractable infertility as well as agonising dyspareunia and extreme gastrointestinal symptoms; furthermore, the latter two symptoms may persist even when the endometriosis has ceased to be active.

Early treatment can help to minimise the risk of progressive disease and its long term consequences. The increased range of medical methods has afforded considerable advantage not least in reducing the need for hysterectomies in young women. Recent research into a possible immunological basis for the development of endometriosis also offers the hope that, in the future, it may be feasible to identify an 'at risk' population and even to develop some form of immunisation against the condition.

CHAPTER 8

CONDITIONS OF SPECIFIC ORGANS

Most of the gynaecological organs are subject to a large number of pathological conditions (the vulva and the ovaries being prime examples) but many of these are relatively uncommon. In this book, we have made no attempt to describe all the potential changes that may affect these organs but have attempted to portray the range of conditions while emphasising those presentations which are most commonly encountered in routine gynaecological practice.

THE VULVA

The term 'vulva' refers to the external female genitalia and the surrounding skin. It includes the mons pubis, labia majora and minora, the clitoris and the vestibule of the vagina. It does not include the perineum which separates the vaginal entrance from the anus.

The skin surface of the vulva is essentially the same as that covering the rest of the body and it is therefore susceptible to the same dermatological conditions that affect other areas. In addition, some pathological changes are specific to this region. Vulval disease usually presents with the complaint of local irritation or of swelling.

Pruritis vulvae

Mild, transient vulval irritation is common but the symptom may become much more severe and persistent. The woman's sleep may be disturbed and her life disrupted.

General conditions

Vulval irritation is sometimes part of a more general condition such as severe kidney disease or diabetes. The latter may cause a typical purplish-red discoloration of the vulval skin and this appearance should always alert the gynaecologist to the need for the investigation of glucose tolerance. It was a source of some professional satisfaction to one of the authors to be able to refer a patient back to a general physician after suspecting the correct diagnosis on clinical inspection alone!

Allergic reactions

Pruritis vulvae may be due to allergic reactions to washing powder residues in underwear or to deodorants and other cosmetic preparations that may have been used on the vulva. The vulval deodorants that were widely advertised for a time some fifteen years ago were a potent cause of problems, happily, they soon disappeared from the market. Susceptible individuals should avoid the use of perfumed soaps and moisturising creams; additional rinsing of the underwear or a change of washing product may be required.

Occasionally, similar effects may result from direct chemical action on the skin rather than from a true allergic response.

Urinary incontinence may also cause vulval irritation, especially in the very elderly or infirm, as the presence of urine on the skin acts as a chemical irritant.

Infections

Vulval infections may be general skin infections or infestations (the term used to refer to parasites) or they may be specific genital tract infections. The more important specific infections are discussed in Chapter 6: Infections, and are only summarised here.

Infections may be classified according to the type of organism: viruses, bacteria, fungi or parasites.

Viral infections

Genital herpes

The herpes simplex virus (HSV) is the same virus that causes cold sores around the mouth. On the vulva, it causes localised irritation for one or two days followed by the appearance of small vesicles. The surface of the vesicles then breaks down converting them into one or more painful ulcers. The ulcers may be confluent and, if they are near the urethral meatus, may result in such severe pain on micturition that the woman is unable to empty her bladder and requires catheterisation. The primary infection, which is usually acquired by sexual contact with an infected partner, may be accompanied by a fever and a general malaise.

Even without treatment, healing occurs in about 10 days but the condition often recurs since, once present, the virus cannot be eradicated from the skin cells. Extra-genital lesions can occur, usually on adjacent skin areas but occasionally more distant.

Local treatment with acyclovir cream or ointment may prevent or shorten an attack and systemic treatment with acyclovir tablets may be warranted for women who experience frequent recurrences.

Condylomata acuminata (genital warts)

Genital warts are caused by the human papilloma virus (HPV) of which there are several types. Some are associated with an increased risk of cervical carcinoma and other malignancies. The warts are usually multiple, small, pinkish-brown lesions but may coalesce into a larger mass. The virus is usually transmitted sexually but the lesions may not appear for several months. They are influenced by the woman's immune status, sometimes disappearing spontaneously after a few weeks. Lesions may also be present on the vaginal walls, when a yellowish discharge is often noticed.

Treatment is by local destruction of the lesions using diathermy, cryocautery, laser evaporation or the application of podophyllin paint. The use of podophyllin paint is contraindicated in pregnancy because of possible teratogenic effects.

Bacterial infections

Normal skin is very resistant to bacterial infection so that the presence of such an infection is often secondary to an underlying abnormality.

Folliculitis

As on other hair bearing skin, the hair follicles may become infected causing small, sometimes tender, solitary or multiple swellings. The discovery of these lesions may cause considerable anxiety as the woman may think they are cancerous in origin. The swelling contains inspissated pus which can usually be evacuated by digital pressure.

Syphilis

The classical ulcerated lesion of primary syphilis (the 'chancre') is now rare. It appears within four weeks of infection and heals spontaneously in a further month or so. There is enlargement of the regional lymph nodes (in the groin). Unlike the herpetic ulcer, the chancre is non-tender.

Fungal infections

Monilial vulvitis

The commonest cause of vulval irritation (pruritis vulvae) in routine gynaecological practice is infection with the fungal organism *Candida*, the diagnosis and treatment of which is described in Chapter 6.

Tinea cruris ('Dhobie itch')

Tinea cruris is a superficial skin infection caused by several fungal organisms. These fungi thrive best in warm moist environments and the condition is therefore seen most often in the summer months. Obese woman or those who work in hot, damp conditions are also more likely to be affected.

The skin becomes inflamed and scratching due to the intense irritation may lead to extensive excoriation. The broken skin may then become secondarily infected by bacteria thereby complicating the picture.

The condition is treated by anti-fungal creams and by keeping the affected area as dry and free from sweat as possible. The abandonment of nylon underclothes and tights in favour of cotton pants and stockings may be helpful.

Parasitic infestations

These conditions are not necessarily sexually transmitted although they may be passed during intimate bodily contact. They were formerly extremely common but improvements in social conditions and general hygiene have decreased their incidence

Scabies

Infestation of the vulval skin with *Sarcoptes scabiei* is not common but, when it occurs, causes intense irritation. The diagnosis is made by finding the characteristic burrows in the skin.

The infestation responds to the local application of lindane or malathion.

Pediculosis pubis

The pubic or 'crab' louse is less common than in the past but can still be a cause of vulval irritation. The parasites are larger than *P capitis* (head lice) and *P corporis* (body lice) but may be less numerous.

The treatment is the same as that for scabies.

Strongyloides stercoralis

Threadworms remain common amongst schoolchildren and may be transmitted to the rest of the family. They cause irritation of the perianal region but this may mistakenly present as pruritis vulvae.

Oral treatment with mebendazole is the drug of choice but piperazine or pyrantel may also be effective. The drug treatment must be supplemented by proper hygienic measures.

Vulval dystrophies

The vulval dystrophies are disorders of the superficial skin layers. In the past, they were classified into hypertrophic or atrophic dystrophies and the distinction between individual conditions was often confused and unclear. The terminology has recently been rationalised into the three categories, lichen sclerosis et atrophicus, squamous hyperplasia and vulval intra-epithelial neoplasia, depending upon the affected skin layer and the severity of the cellular abnormality.

Both lichen sclerosis and vulval intra-epithelial neoplasia may progress to vulval carcinoma and women suffering from either of these conditions should be kept under review.

Lichen sclerosus

Lichen sclerosus can occur at any age but is most commonly seen after the menopause though it may occur at any age, even in childhood. In the early stages, it is frequently misdiagnosed as a thrush infection and is therefore often treated incorrectly. To confirm the diagnosis, the affected area of skin should be biopsied (an outpatient procedure under local anaesthetic). Although the changes cannot be totally eradicated, lichen sclerosis usually responds quite well to the local application of a strong steroid cream for three months. This may have to be repeated occasionally to keep the condition under control. Testosterone cream and surgical excision have been employed in the past.

Vulval intra-epithelial neoplasia

Vulval intra-epithelial neoplasia (VIN) must be removed by laser evaporation or by surgery. If the lesion is small, this may be performed in the outpatient department but the changes may affect multiple or large areas. Extensive disease may necessitate vulvectomy.

Vulval carcinoma

This relatively rare cancer usually affects older women. As with all cancers, treatment depends primarily upon the stage of the disease when the diagnosis is made. The disease usually responds poorly to radiotherapy and treatment is usually by radical vulvectomy. The operation is a major procedure for an elderly woman and the probability of successful outcome must be carefully balanced against the surgical morbidity.

Miscellaneous vulval swellings

Various vulval structures may be give rise to localised swelling. Examples include vulval varicose veins, endometriotic cysts and large inguinal herniae. Other important causes of vulval swelling are trauma and enlargement of Bartholin's gland.

Trauma

Trauma may be accidental or due to malicious action.

Accidental trauma to the vulva is seen in young girls who have fallen astride a solid object. Treatment requires extreme sensitivity by the most experienced gynaecologist available, preferably with the support and advice of paediatric colleagues. Trauma may also occur during vigorous sexual intercourse.

Although accidental injury certainly occurs, in every case of vulval trauma, consideration must be given to the possibility of non-accidental injury resulting from sexual or non-sexual assault.

There may be extensive bruising and the soft tissues may undergo considerable swelling. Simple contusions will resolve without treatment though the application of ice packs may help to reduce swelling. Effective analgesia is essential.

Damage to larger blood vessels may result in the formation of a localised haematoma which should be evacuated surgically and skin damage may require suturing after exploration of the wound for foreign bodies or fragments of clothing.

Abnormalities of the Bartholin's gland

Bartholin's glands (first described in women by Casper Bartholinus, a Danish anatomist, in 1675) are paired glands that produce secretions during sexual intercourse. They are located on each side of the posterior part of the vaginal introitus and their narrow ducts open within the hymeneal ring.

The opening of the duct may become blocked, when continuing secretory activity causes distension to produce a Bartholin's cyst. The blockage is frequently due to infection which may spread to involve the trapped fluid, forming a pus filled Bartholin's abscess. A Bartholin's cyst causes little or no pain but the abscess is exquisitely tender.

Cystic swellings occasionally resolve spontaneously but, especially if causing discomfort or inconvenience during coitus, may be excised surgically as an elective procedure.

Abscesses require emergency treatment by the excision of part of the abscess wall and overlying skin (preferably from the vaginal aspect). A few absorbable sutures are then placed round the cut edge. This procedure, called 'marsupialisation', allows the pus to drain out and prevents re-closure and the collection of more pus, thereby allowing the resulting cavity to heal. Simple incision of the abscess to release the pus is rarely effective and is usually followed by early recurrence. Unfortunately, attempts are often made to treat abscesses with antibiotics in the first instance. This is never successful since the pus cannot escape. Antibiotic therapy may, however, be useful after the surgical drainage has been performed.

THE VAGINA

The most common conditions affecting the vagina are infections with various organisms. Congenital abnormalities are an infrequent problem in clinical practice and vaginal neoplasms are rare.

Normal vaginal discharge

The normal healthy vagina contains a small quantity of a non-offensive discharge produced mainly by transudation of fluid through the vaginal walls with small contributions from cervical mucus and from glandular secretions. The amount varies in response to the hormone changes of the menstrual cycle and may be sufficient to escape from the vaginal introitus when it may dry to form a pale yellowish stain on the woman's underclothes. This may cause some women to fear that they have contracted a vaginal infection and they may then resort to the use of vaginal douches which, by destroying the natural protective function of the fluid, may aggravate the problem. (See, also, Chapter 6.)

Pathological vaginal discharge

Monilial vaginitis (thrush)

The characteristic discharge caused by infection with Candida albicans or other related fungal species is white, usually thick (often likened to cottage cheese, though it can be watery) and extremely irritant. However, the absence of obvious discharge does not rule out the condition, which can be demonstrated on bacteriological culture and often also on cytological smears. The vaginal walls may be inflamed and dyspareunia is common.

Formerly, the only available treatment was by the local application of fungicidal creams or pessaries. Symptomatic relief was usually achieved but complete eradication of the infection was difficult and re-infection from the patient's own bowel or from her sexual partner was common. The development of systemic treatments taken orally has greatly improved the results but it is still important that sexual partners are treated. Systemic therapy deals not only with genital infections but also with other reservoirs of infection such as the gum margins. A small proportion of cases (about 10% in London but less elsewhere in the country) will prove to be sensitive only to itraconazole.

Bacterial vaginosis

Infections with organisms such as Gardnerella vaginalis cause a profuse, watery discharge which usually has an offensive odour. Treatment with antibiotics is effective but recurrences are common.

Trichomonas vaginalis

Trichomonal vaginitis is less common than in the past but remains prevalent in some ethnic groups. The discharge is fluid, greenish in colour and may be frothy. It causes vaginal soreness rather than irritation. The diagnosis can be confirmed by the presence of motile trichomonads on the microscopic examination of an unstained sample.

Like thrush, trichomonas may be present in the mouth as well as in the vagina. Oral therapy with metronidazole is usually effective.

Chlamydia

Although the presence of chlamydia in the vagina has long been recognised, it was thought to be an occasional commensal of no clinical significance. It has now been recognised as a potential source of serious intra-pelvic infection. Affected women may notice a minor vaginal discharge and some soreness but many are symptom free.

Treatment is by tetracycline or one of its derivatives.

Other organisms

Like chlamydia, a number of other organisms can be found in the vagina and may, occasionally, cause symptoms. These include *Escherichia coli* and some streptococcal and staphylococcal strains.

Congenital defects

The developmental abnormalities which may affect the vagina are discussed elsewhere in this volume. They are not common and the only one of real clinical importance is the imperforate hymen which is a rare but important cause of cryptomenorrhoea. Primary amenorrhoea due to the retention of the menstrual fluid would also result from vaginal agenesis, were it not for the fact that the failure of vaginal development is usually accompanied by severe uterine hypoplasia (hence, no endometrial cavity and no bleeding). Duplication of the vagina or the division of the vagina by a septum is sometimes encountered but this very rarely causes any problem to the woman as the septum is flexible and will move to one side to permit normal coitus.

Utero-vaginal prolapse

Utero-vaginal prolapse is the downward displacement of the uterus and the vaginal walls towards or through the introitus. Structures lying deep to the vaginal walls are also involved.

Prolapse of the uterus is classified into 'degree' by the position occupied by the cervix. In a first degree descent, the cervix may lie in the lower vagina but does not reach the vaginal introitus, descent to the introitus constitutes second degree prolapse whereas third degree implies that the cervix protrudes from the vagina. If the whole uterus lies outside the vagina (covered by the inverted vaginal wall), the term 'procidentia' is applied.

Vaginal wall prolapse is named according to the structure behind the vaginal wall. The urethra and bladder lie behind the anterior (front) wall and the prolapse of these structures is called urethrocoele and cystocoele respectively. The rectum and the peritoneal cavity under the posterior (back) wall form a rectocoele and an enterocoele.

Causes

Of the several causes of utero-vaginal prolapse, the most important is the erect posture adopted by humans. This requires that the entire weight of the abdominal and pelvic organs is supported by a sheet of muscle that must be both elastic and also perforated by an aperture large enough to permit the passage of a baby during childbirth. This is an inherently weak design.

In addition to the postural factor, there may be a congenital weakness of the supporting structures. The situation is aggravated by childbirth, particularly a difficult birth with a long second stage, the delivery of an unusually large baby or numerous births; this is thought to be due to partial denervation of the pelvic floor muscles.

Any factor causing an increase in the intra-abdominal pressure will increase the probability of a prolapse; this includes a chronic cough, chronic constipation with repeated straining to defecate and significant obesity.

After the menopause, the fall in the oestrogen level causes a further weakening of the pelvic supports.

Symptoms

Vaginal prolapse can be asymptomatic but commonly present with the complaint of 'something coming down'. There may also be lower abdominal discomfort, often described as a feeling of 'heaviness' or 'pressure'. The woman may have noticed a swelling at the introitus and some complain of backache, particularly in the evening.

Questioning should establish whether the woman has any bladder or bowel problems. Descent of the anterior vaginal wall is frequently associated with interference with the function of the bladder neck causing 'stress incontinence' (leakage of urine from the urethra on coughing, laughing or running). Women with posterior wall prolapse may experience difficulty on defecation with incomplete evacuation of faeces from the rectum.

If urinary symptoms are present, especially if there is complaint of urgency, urgency incontinence or frequency, assessment of bladder function by urodynamic testing is advisable. By measuring bladder capacity and the associated bladder and urethral pressures, it is possible to ascertain the nature of the bladder dysfunction which can provide some guide to the most suitable method of treatment. Many cases will prove to be a combination of bladder neck descent and bladder muscle instability. If the instability predominates, the symptoms may be made worse by surgical correction of the prolapse.

Examination

The woman is usually examined lying on her side with her knees drawn up towards her chest. A speculum is introduced into the vagina and the posterior and anterior walls are held back in turn to assess the extent and type of prolapse. She should be asked to cough or bear down to exacerbate the prolapse. For this purpose, the most suitable speculum is that devised by James Marion Sims in 1845. This differs from the more commonly used Cusco's (or 'duck-billed') speculum in having one blade rather than two.

The demonstration of stress incontinence may require examination with the woman standing.

Treatment

The choice of treatment should take into account the site and severity of the prolapse as well as the woman's wish for further children.

Attempts should be made to reduce or eliminate any aggravating factors such as obesity, chronic bronchitis or constipation.

Mild prolapse may be greatly improved by pelvic floor exercises, usually under the instruction of a physiotherapist. Voluntary exercises may be assisted by the use of weighted vaginal cones or by electrical stimulation of the muscles. In some cases, this may be sufficient to cure the symptoms.

A number of vaginal pessaries have been devised to treat more severe cases. Two types in common use are the ring pessary and Simpson's shelf pessary. Ring pessaries are made from polyethylene or polyvinyl chloride and are available in a large range of sizes. They are placed in the vagina so that it lies with its upper rim in the posterior fornix and the lower rim just above and behind the symphysis pubis. Providing the correct size is selected, the vaginal walls are supported without undue pressure. Unfortunately, even a correctly chosen ring can cause pressure ulceration of the vaginal wall though the chance of this is reduced by changing the ring every three or four months. Rings are not usually very effective in treating urinary symptoms, though occasional cases may experience dramatic improvement.

Severe degrees of uterine descent may defeat the ring pessary because the large size of the ring allows the uterus to pass through. Providing the woman does not wish to have sexual intercourse, the shelf pessary may provide a satisfactory answer by bridging the defect in the pelvic floor.

The major disadvantage of the ring and shelf pessaries is the need to change the device at frequent intervals and the majority of significant prolapses are best treated by operation. In the traditional procedure, the vaginal wall is incised and dissected free from the underlying structure (bladder, urethra or bowel). The lateral tissues are sutured together in the midline to create a firm bridge and, after trimming off redundant tissue, the vaginal wall is sutured. The operations are called 'anterior colporrhaphy' (anterior wall only), 'posterior colpoperineorrhaphy' (posterior wall only) or 'anterior and posterior colpoperineorrhaphy' if both walls are involved.

In more severe cases, a 'Manchester repair' may be performed, in which the lower part of the cervix is amputated. Not only does this shorten that structure but it also affords access to the cardinal ligaments, which are then incorporated into the supporting bridge.

A vaginal hysterectomy and repair may be the most suitable choice of operation if the woman has completed her family or is post-menopausal (see Chapter 3).

A number of other operations have been devised to correct utero-vaginal prolapse, especially those cases associated with stress incontinence

Although normal childbirth is possible after a vaginal repair, there is a risk of substantial damage to the vaginal wall. Women who have been successfully treated for stress incontinence or who have had a Manchester repair should be delivered by elective Caesarean section.

Utero-vaginal prolapse is a progressive condition though the rate of progress varies considerably from one patient to another. Childbirth and the menopause may be associated with rapid change but, even without these factors, the prolapse will tend to worsen with advancing age. This process continues even after surgical correction so that the problem will gradually recur. In many cases, the operation will have restored an approximation to normal anatomy and the subsequent deterioration will be so slow that the symptoms remain in abeyance for the remainder of the woman's life. The new fibrous tissue created by the surgery takes three to four months to mature and gain its final strength. Over stressing the tissue during this period may accelerate the return of problems and it is therefore important that prolonged standing and the lifting of heavy objects is avoided after the operation.

Recurrence can be provoked even after the first few post-operative months. One patient underwent a vaginal repair with complete relief of her symptoms until, some eight months later, she returned to her previous part time job in a public house. Her duties included lifting crates of empty bottles and, within three months, her problems had returned. A second operation was also successful but she was advised to seek alternative employment.

Vaginal adenosis and clear cell carcinoma

These two rare conditions gained prominence when, in the early 1970s, it was discovered that they showed an increased incidence in women who had been exposed to diethylstilboestrol during foetal life. Diethylstilboestrol (DES), a synthetic oestrogen, had been used from the late 1940s for the treatment of women suffering from recurrent abortions and it was the daughters resulting from treated pregnancies who were affected.

Vaginal adenosis is a non-malignant condition but can cause a copious vaginal discharge and may be associated with deep dyspareunia.

Clear cell carcinomas of the vagina tend to develop during the teenage years and early twenties, the peak incidence being at about 19 years. As in the case of other malignant conditions, early diagnosis and treatment greatly improves the prognosis. Consequently, it is important that young women who are known or suspected of having foetal exposure to DES should be screened regularly by a gynaecologist who has knowledge of and an interest in the potential problems (DES Action UK keeps a register of such individuals).

Vaginal carcinoma

Primary malignant tumours of the vagina are rare and are almost always squamous cell carcinomas. With the exception of the clear cell carcinoma (see above) they occur mainly in older women. Secondary deposits (metastases) and local invasion of the vagina by primary tumours in other sites are more common.

Vaginal discharge, often offensive due to secondary infection, or vaginal bleeding are the usual presenting symptoms. Abnormal vaginal cells may be found on routine cervical cytology.

The treatment of pre-invasive and early invasive tumours is usually by radiotherapy. Surgical excision of the vagina may be performed for more advanced lesions but the procedure may be very extensive if the bladder or rectum are involved. Careful pre-operative assessment must be made as the morbidity associated with such extensive operations may not be justified if the prospects of a cure are small.

THE UTERINE CERVIX

'Erosion'/ectropion

The surface layer (epithelium) of the portio vaginalis of the uterine cervix is continuous with the surface of the adjacent vaginal wall, with which it shares the characteristic of being composed of many layers of flattened cells. It is termed a 'stratified squamous epithelium' and is similar to the external skin. Just within the external os of the normal cervix the epithelium changes abruptly to a single layer of somewhat elongated (columnar) cells which secrete mucus.

On inspection of the cervix using a vaginal speculum (for example, before taking a smear for cervical cytology), it is quite common to find that the line along which the epithelial change occurs is visible on the ecto-cervix (there is, an area of columnar epithelium is visible around the external os). This condition was formerly thought to have resulted from damage to the normal epithelium and was therefore termed an 'erosion' to indicate that the surface had been 'worn away'.

Eversion of the cervix in the region of the external os and lower canal will also cause an area of columnar epithelium to become visible in the vagina and this condition, sometimes resulting from cervical lacerations during childbirth, was called an 'ectropion'.

The realisation that an erosion was not caused by loss of the surface layer caused the name 'erosion' to fall into disfavour and most gynaecologists now use 'ectropion' to describe both of the conditions outlined in the preceding two paragraphs.

The majority of women with these conditions are asymptomatic and many will require no treatment. In some instances, however, the increased area of mucus secreting columnar epithelium causes the production of a greater amount of mucus which the woman may notice as a vaginal discharge. She is more likely to complain if the excess mucus becomes secondarily infected.

The columnar epithelium, being a single layer of cells, is also less resistant to infection and mechanical damage than stratified squamous epithelium. It may therefore allow the entry of bacteria into the deeper tissues of the cervix with the development of a true cervicitis. This is more likely to occur if the mucus is already infected. Chronic cervicitis gives the cervix an unhealthy appearance; it is bulky and is tender to touch both during clinical examination and during sexual intercourse thus being a cause of deep dyspareunia.

The columnar epithelium may also be abraded during coitus and damage to the underlying small blood vessels may give rise to post-coital bleeding.

Treatment

Symptomatic cases may require a course of appropriate antibiotics to deal with infection before the underlying condition can be treated by destruction of the columnar epithelium. This is best done by laser evaporation but, despite the considerable fall in prices in recent years, laser equipment is still expensive and hot-wire cautery, diathermy or cryocautery are still more commonly employed. Severe cervical damage due to childbirth may require surgical correction (trachelorrhaphy).

Nabothian follicles

Mild chronic cervicitis may resolve spontaneously and, in doing so, the mouths of mucus secreting crypts may become sealed off. The columnar epithelium within the crypt continues to produce mucus which can no longer escape but forms a cystic collection within the tissue of the cervix which is visible from the vaginal aspect as a smooth bulge on the cervix usually 10 mm or less in diameter. These cysts are called Nabothian follicles and may be multiple. No treatment is necessary but, if they are punctured, the inspissated mucus within can be released. They are occasionally mistaken for malignant disease.

Cervical polyps

Cervical polyps are fleshy structures usually found protruding from the external cervical os and attached to the wall of the canal by a thin stalk (pedicle). Being vascular, they often present as causes of post-coital or intermenstrual bleeding.

Most polyps can be removed by grasping them with a suitable instrument and rotating them several times. This breaks the thin stalk after first occluding the blood vessels which run within it.

Most polyps are benign but, after removal, they should always be sent for histological examination, as a very small proportion may contain malignant cells.

Cervical fibroids

The majority of fibroids arise from the myometrium of the body of the uterus and the condition is described in more detail below. Much more rarely, fibroids may develop in the cervical region when they may interfere with sexual intercourse and, because of the distortion of the cervix, may be mistaken for malignant growth.

In pregnancy, even when a fibroid has developed in the cervix, it is usually drawn up out of the pelvis by the formation of the lower uterine segment during the later weeks of the pregnancy. It is therefore extremely rare for a cervical fibroid to obstruct the progress of labour.

Exfoliative cervical cytology

Since the first description of exfoliative cervical cytology by George Papanicolaou and Herbert Tait in 1941 (Papanicolaou had actually suggested the possibility as early as 1928), the use of the technique as a screening procedure has become widely established. In many countries (including the US, where Papanicolaou worked for most of his life), the investigation is usually called the Papanicolaou (or 'Pap') smear but, in the UK, the term 'cervical smear' is more common.

The cell sample must be properly taken and this requires good visualisation of the cervix using a vaginal speculum. The sample is obtained using either a specially shaped spatula of wood or plastic or a small conical brush; sometimes both are employed. Most designs of spatula have a narrow projection which is introduced into the cervical os, the spatula then being rotated to collect cells from all parts of the region of the external os. The brush is introduced into the lower cervical canal and then rotated several times. The sample is spread on a glass slide and an alcoholic fixative is then added before the cells can undergo drying.

Figure 8.1   Cervical cytology spatulae

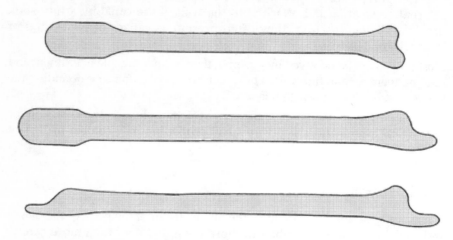

Three common patterns of wooden spatulae used for taking smears for cervical and vaginal cytology. The differently shaped ends are each suitable for use on cervices of various anatomical shapes. The rounded (top) ends of the two upper spatulae are designed for the taking of vaginal smears, for example, after hysterectomy.

For many years, the assessment of samples has depended on the expertise of specially trained laboratory workers but the number of cells that can be inspected is limited by the number of technicians employed, their concentration span and the volume of work to be performed. Recently, computerised methods of assessment have been developed which allow the scanning of very much larger numbers of cells.

The clinician responsible for taking the smear must also accept responsibility for ensuring that a reliable result has been obtained and that appropriate action is taken in the event of an abnormality being identified. Minor changes may simply necessitate early repeat of the test (usually after three or six months) but more significant findings may require referral for colposcopic assessment.

It must be remembered that cervical cytology is a *screening* test and should not form the sole basis for major treatment decisions. One of the authors remembers hearing the tragic story of a general practitioner's wife who underwent a hysterectomy because of a single abnormal cytology report. Post-operatively, she developed a deep venous thrombosis of the pelvic veins which caused a fatal pulmonary embolus but, when the cervix of the removed uterus was carefully examined, no abnormality could be found.

Cervical cytology is not infallible. It has been reported that results may be falsely reassuring in up to 30% of smears; these are false negative results. Overestimates of the severity of the condition (false positives) occur in up to 25% of assessments. A false positive result will be recognised when the smear is repeated or on colposcopy.

Following a false negative report, the true situation should be identified at the time of the next smear. Providing that routine cervical smears are taken annually or every two years, this will usually be in time to avoid any serious deterioration.

It is essential that all cytology laboratories constantly monitor performance by auditing results in an endeavour to keep the false negative rate as low as possible.

Malignant disease of the cervix

Following the stimulation of medical interest in cervical cancer by the Papanicolaou smear, a vast amount of literature has been published on pre-invasive and invasive carcinoma of the cervix. Here, it is only possible to give a brief outline of these conditions.

Most cervical malignancies are squamous cell carcinomas. The peak incidence is in the 40–55 year age range, though there is some evidence to suggest that the incidence may be rising in younger women. A number of risk factors have been identified including first sexual intercourse at a young age, multiple sexual partners, cigarette smoking and the presence of the human papilloma virus in the cervical cells.

Squamous cell carcinoma

The spectrum of this disease ranges from very mild changes in a localised area of cells within the surface epithelium to advanced, fungating tumours with metastases in bones, brain, lungs and other organs. Both for descriptive purposes and in the planning of treatment, it is necessary to classify this varied clinical picture.

Pre-invasive disease is now more correctly termed 'cervical intra-epithelial neoplasia' (CIN) and is divided into three categories. These categories are defined by histological appearances but broadly correspond to the cytological findings listed here:

CIN I   mild dysplasia

CIN II   moderate dysplasia

CIN III   severe dysplasia and carcinoma in situ

Invasive lesions are 'staged' according to the extent of the disease in accordance with a classification scheme defined by the Fédération Internationale de Gynécologie et d'Obstétrique (usually referred to as FIGO). The scheme extends from Stage Ia (microinvasive disease) to Stage IVb (metastases in distant organs). The FIGO classification actually begins with Stage 0 but this is non-invasive disease or CIN as listed above (see, also, below).

Stage 0   Cervical intra-epithelial neoplasia III.

Stage I   Disease confined to the cervix.

     Stage Ia   Microinvasive disease.

     Stage Ia1   No clinical extension but minimal microscopic disease present.

     Stage Ia2   Disease extending not more than 5 mm from the nearest basement membrane nor more than 7 mm horizontally.

     Stage Ib   All other Stage I lesions.

Stage II   Extension of disease beyond the cervix but not to the pelvic side-wall or lower third of the vagina.

     Stage IIa   No apparent involvement of the tissues around the cervix.

     Stage IIb   Involvement of the tissues around the cervix (but not extending to the pelvic side-wall).

Stage III   Extension to the pelvic side-wall or lower third of the vagina. Also includes cases with hydronephrosis or a non-functioning kidney.

     Stage IIIa   The disease reaches the lower vagina but not the pelvic side-wall.

     Stage IIIb   Other Stage III lesions.

Stage IV   Spread to other organs.

     Stage IVa   Spread to adjacent organs. Involvement of the mucosa of the bladder and/or rectum and/or extension beyond the true pelvis.

     Stage IVb   Spread to any distant organ (for example, lung or brain).

Cervical intra-epithelial neoplasia (CIN)

In this condition, previously called dysplasia or 'carcinoma in situ', the characteristic cellular changes of the neoplastic process are present in some or many of the surface cells but overall architecture of the layers remains intact and abnormal cells have not penetrated the basement membrane (see diagram).

The three grades (CIN I, II and III) denote the severity and extent of the cellular changes, CIN I being the most mild.

About 85% of cases of CIN I will probably revert to normal without treatment but the remainder may progress to more severe disease. Similar spontaneous resolution probably occurs with smaller proportions of CIN II and III but most of these will now be treated.

The disease is usually first detected on exfoliative cervical cytology. The abnormal smear must be repeated to exclude laboratory errors (both errors of assessment and also administrative mistakes such as incorrectly labelled slides) but, with the possible exception of the mildest cases, the cervical epithelium should then be inspected colposcopically and directed biopsies taken if indicated.

Colposcopy is an examination of the cervix with a specially constructed microscope and is usually carried out in the outpatient department. Prior to her appointment, the woman will usually be sent a leaflet explaining what to expect from the examination. She will be asked to lie on an examination couch and a speculum will be inserted just as if she were having a cervical smear taken. The colposcopist will then inspect the cervix to search for features indicative of abnormalities. Solutions of acetic acid or iodine (Lugol's iodine) may be used to assist in the demonstration of abnormal areas. Biopsy specimens may be taken and suitable cases may be treated at the first visit.

Many cases of CIN I may be left untreated but strict follow-up is then essential with the smear usually being repeated after an interval of three to six months. Persistent or worsening change indicates the need for re-assessment by colposcopy.

Very small lesions may be entirely removed by colposcopic biopsy but good follow-up is again necessary to ensure that the subsequent cytology remains normal. Larger areas of CIN II may be treated by various destructive techniques of which laser evaporation offers the best healing. These methods minimise the damage to cervical tissue but have the important disadvantage that no sample is available for histological examination so that the more serious cases are better managed by the taking of a cone biopsy. In this procedure, a cone shaped sample of tissue is removed from the cervix (see Figure 8.2) using a scalpel or laser. The laser offers better haemostasis (laser cone biopsies are often virtually bloodless operations) and improved post-operative healing but a thin rim of tissue is lost to histology. If the abnormality does not extend too far up the cervical canal, a 'loop excision' may be substituted for the cone biopsy. Regular smear follow-up is necessary once the healing is complete.

Figure 8.2   Cone biopsy

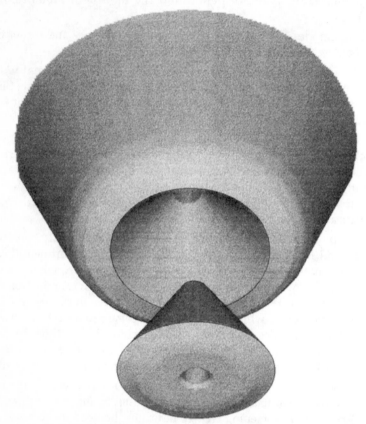

Diagrammatic illustration of the shape of the tissue sample removed from the cervix at cone biopsy. The width and length of the cone will vary with individual circumstances.

Microinvasive carcinoma (FIGO Stage Ia)

Cervical tissue obtained by local or cone biopsy is fixed, sectioned and stained before being carefully examined to determine the severity and extent of the cellular abnormality. If significant penetration of the basement membrane (5 mm or more) is found, the case is re-classified from CIN to microinvasive disease. Providing that the biopsy includes a margin of normal tissue around the lesion in all directions, the cone biopsy may still constitute sufficient treatment. If no tumour free margin is present or if involvement of lymphatic or blood vessels is seen, management will usually be as for frankly invasive disease though, in a few cases, a repeat cone biopsy may be sufficient.

Figure 8.3   CIN III

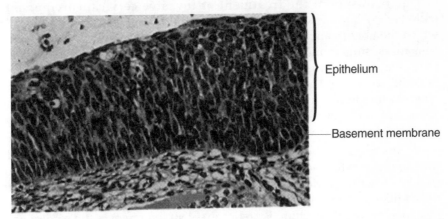

Epithelium

Basement membrane

Abnormal cells extend throughout the whole of the epithelium but have not penetrated the basement membrane

Figure 8.4   Microinvasive cancer of the cervix

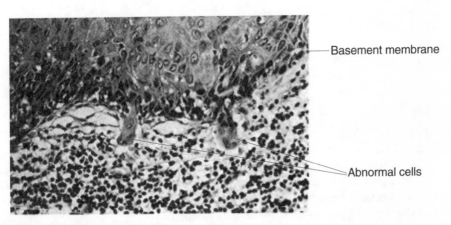

Basement membrane

Abnormal cells

'Tongues' of abnormal cells have penetrated the basement membrane and are beginning to invade the deeper tissue

Invasive cervical carcinoma

The classification of these cases is described above. Extension of the disease may be local (into the tissues around the cervix and, ultimately, out to the pelvic side-wall), lymphatic (to the lymph nodes around the iliac vessels and thence to the para-aortic nodes) or blood-borne (to distant organs, frequently to the spine, brain or lungs).

The mainstay of the treatment of invasive cervical carcinoma is radiotherapy but a few cases may be amenable to surgery, such as those in which the abnormality is very localised or if radiotherapy is not possible. Sometimes, surgery may be performed six to eight weeks after pre-operative radiotherapy but most series show this to offer little or no benefit over radiotherapy alone. The operation of extended (or Wertheim's) hysterectomy removes the uterus, upper part of the vagina and the lymph nodes on the pelvic side-wall. The ovaries are usually removed as well, though they may be conserved in younger women.

A very small number of locally advanced cases may be considered suitable for the more extensive surgical procedures if distant metastases are not present. Anterior pelvic exenteration involves an extended hysterectomy with the addition of removal of the bladder and implantation of the ureters into an ileal loop or into the rectum. Posterior exenteration removes the rectum with the creation of a colostomy. Total pelvic exenteration (pelvic clearance) is occasionally performed. These operations are associated with a high morbidity rate.

The five year survival rate is closely related to the clinical stage of the disease at the time of treatment typical figures being:

5 year survival

Stage I	85%–90 %
Stage II	70%–75 %
Stage III	30%–40 %
Stage IV	10%

Cervical adenocarcinoma

Though far less common than the squamous cell carcinoma, the incidence of cervical adenocarcinoma may be rising. The assessment and treatment is essentially similar to that for squamous carcinoma but the prognosis is a little worse, probably because changes are often not present on exfoliative cytology and the colposcopic features are usually not obvious.

Sarcoma botryoides

This extremely rare tumour occurs mainly in childhood or adolescence. The prognosis remains very poor though it has been somewhat improved by advances in chemotherapy when administered in conjunction with extended surgery.

THE UTERINE CORPUS

Functional disorders of the endometrium (dysfunctional uterine bleeding) are described elsewhere in this book (see Chapter 7).

Infections

The normal uterus is generally very resistant to infection but necrotic tissue retained within its cavity may provide an ideal breeding ground for certain types of organisms, which can then spread to involve the uterine wall itself. This is particularly likely to happen after an abortion (whether spontaneous or induced). Illegal induced abortion carries a particularly high risk as invasive procedures used to procure the termination of the pregnancy may introduce bacteria into the uterine cavity (see Chapter 13).

Because the necrotic tissue lacks a blood supply, the oxygen levels are low, favouring bacteria which multiply best in such conditions. The most dangerous of these is *Clostridium welchii* (gas gangrene), which was formerly a frequent cause of septic abortions. After an initial pyrexia, the patient's temperature may remain elevated or may fall to normal or sub-normal levels. She will experience very severe lower abdominal pain and there will be an offensive vaginal discharge. The uterus will be exquisitely tender and the presence of gas bubbles within the tissues may cause crepitus. Severe shock may develop rapidly. Although the organism is sensitive to penicillin, the infection may overwhelm the patient and prove fatal before the antibiotic can take effect.

Tuberculosis

The once common infections with the tubercle bacillus are now rare in developed countries but a mention is included here as they are occasionally seen in visitors from abroad.

Few bacteria are able to colonise the endometrium, probably because, for much of a woman's life, the greater part of the layer is shed with each menstrual bleed. Tuberculosis can be demonstrated in endometrial curettings, though the sample needs to be taken late in the menstrual cycle. There is often an associated tuberculous salpingitis and the infection can spread to the rest of the pelvis. Subsequent infertility is common.

The condition responds to treatment with isoniazid and rifampicin, which should be continued for at least nine months. Residual tubal damage may be correctable by surgery but many cases will only achieve a pregnancy with the help of in vitro fertilisation.

Endometrial hyperplasia

The internal lining of the body of the uterus, the endometrium, is sensitive to the level of circulating oestrogens which promote proliferation of the layer. Whilst this process is a normal phenomenon of the menstrual cycle, if continued beyond the normal extent it may cause hyperplasia. This is more likely to occur if the oestrogen level is abnormally high as may be the case with functioning (that is, hormone producing) tumours of the ovary though the most common association is with the use of unopposed oestrogens for hormone replacement therapy after the menopause. The addition of cyclical progestogens protects against this hazard of HRT.

The abnormally thickened endometrium is likely to give rise to irregular vaginal bleeding (or post-menopausal bleeding if normal cyclical bleeding has ended). Since the bleeding originates from within the uterine cavity, it may give rise to similar sensations to those associated with a normal period. This may mislead the woman, and sometimes her medical advisors, into assuming that the bleeding is not pathological.

Investigations may include the measurement of the endometrial thickness and the exclusion of ovarian tumours by ultrasonic scanning.

The definitive diagnosis can be made by endometrial sampling. In some cases, this may be done as an outpatient procedure either using small disposable suction sampling devices or by outpatient hysteroscopy but other cases may require hysteroscopy and D & C under a general anaesthetic.

Endometrial hyperplasia occasionally occurs in young girls soon after the menarche. This is a benign condition and regresses spontaneously without treatment.

Endometrial hyperplasia in older women is also benign but a proportion of cases may undergo malignant change and treatment is therefore advisable. The hyperplasia may regress if unopposed oestrogen HRT is stopped or if progestogens are added to the regime. Cases not associated with HRT may also respond to progestogen therapy, though many may be best treated by a hysterectomy, particularly if recurrent or associated with severe cellular atypia. Although apparently offering a good option, endometrial ablation or resection has the risk of failing to remove all the potentially pathological tissue.

Endometrial polyps

Irregular vaginal bleeding, especially post-menopausal bleeding, may be due to the presence of one or more endometrial polyps. These are usually easily removed at hysteroscopy but severe or extensive polypoid change may necessitate a hysterectomy.

Polyps are usually benign but should always be examined histologically as a few may show localised malignant change, in which case, continued follow-up is advisable.

Fibro-leiomyomata

Fibro-leiomyomata are benign tumours of the muscle wall of the uterus. Most British gynaecologists use the term 'fibroid', but in other countries 'myoma' is usually adopted. They are extremely common and it is sometimes claimed that all women over the age of 40 years will have fibroids. Fibroids are more common in women who have not borne children and show a strong racial association, being very common in most of the Negroid races but quite rare in Asians.

All fibroids begin as 'seedling fibroids' (a bad term as they are not 'seeded' from elsewhere) within the myometrium. These are firm, white nodules about 1 mm in diameter which gradually grow and may reach 30 cm or more in diameter if untreated, though most measure between 5 and 15 cm. As growth proceeds, they develop a characteristic 'whorled' appearance of the cut surface and, by differential growth, may come to lie partially within the uterine cavity (sub-mucus) or beneath the external uterine surface (sub-serous). They occasionally become pedunculated and, very rarely, pedunculated sub-serous fibroids may loose their attachment to the uterus after acquiring an alternative blood supply from adjacent tissues. Pedunculated sub-mucus fibroids are also termed 'fibroid polyps' and may be extruded through the cervix.

Most fibroids arise from the body of the uterus but they may occasionally form within the cervix.

Fibroid growth appears to be oestrogen dependent and the tumours tend to shrink after the menopause (unless HRT is used). A useful generalisation is that fibroids which have not caused symptoms before the menopause do not begin to do so afterwards. Application of this 'rule' reduces the risk of misdiagnosing ovarian tumours as fibroids and was formulated by the senior author after he had seen a post-menopausal woman (herself a doctor) with a malignant ovarian cyst treated conservatively for over twelve months on the assumption that her pelvic mass was a fibroid.

Many fibroids are asymptomatic but the resulting enlargement of the uterus may give rise to symptoms due to pressure on adjacent structures (for example, frequency of micturition due to pressure on the bladder), and sub-mucus fibroids are a common cause of menorrhagia.

Fibroids may under go a number of degenerations but most of these are of histological interest rather than clinical significance. They include hyaline, cystic, fatty and myxomatous degeneration. Calcification and, rarely, ossification can occur.

Red degeneration, which is common in pregnancy but can occur at other times, is of importance as it causes severe pain and localised tenderness (almost the only circumstance in which the fibroid itself is painful). This condition results from the growth of the fibroid exceeding the capacity of its blood supply, causing ischaemic necrosis of the central part of the tumour. Strong analgesics may be required for a few days but conservative management is appropriate as the symptoms almost always improve spontaneously. Definitive surgical treatment may be required later. In pregnancy, it may be difficult to exclude the possibility of abrutio placentae.

Sarcomatous degeneration is a rare, malignant condition. A few instances may be suspected because of unusually rapid fibroid growth but, in the majority of cases, it will be a histological finding when examining fibroids which have been removed surgically. The sarcomatous change may be restricted to part of the tumour.

Small or moderate sized fibroids causing little or no symptoms do not require treatment. Fibroids which fill or overflow the pelvis, which cause menorrhagia or pressure symptoms or which exhibit rapid growth should all be removed by myomectomy (removal of the fibroids while conserving the uterus) or by hysterectomy. In the past, myomectomy was done by open operation but improvements in endoscopy surgery have allowed many to be performed laparoscopically when the tumours may be removed piecemeal or vaporised with a laser. Intra-cavity fibroids may be removed hysteroscopically. These endoscopic techniques should only be employed by gynaecologists with the appropriate training and experience.

Some gynaecologists favour shrinking the fibroids with GnRH agonists either as the definitive management or prior to surgery. These drugs provide a useful 'first-aid' treatment if the fibroids are causing very severe menorrhagia but their use may make subsequent myomectomy more difficult.

Adenomyosis

Adenomyosis (endometriosis of the myometrium) is discussed with other types of endometriosis elsewhere in this book (see Chapter 7).

Malignant disease of the body of the uterus

Cancer of the body of the uterus is usually an adenocarcinoma (that is, derived from glandular tissue), though areas of squamous metaplasia may be present.

Compared with cancer of the uterine cervix, tumours of the body of the uterus usually arise in older women and, with improvements in life expectation, are showing an increased incidence. They commonly present with post-menopausal bleeding, though women who develop the disease before the menopause will notice inter-menstrual bleeding. Only about 50% of endometrial carcinomas will be detected on cervical cytology.

Although the majority of cases of post-menopausal bleeding will prove to have a benign cause, it is the risk that the bleeding may have originated from a malignant tumour within the uterine cavity that makes investigation essential.

Improvements in ultrasonic scanning, particularly with the introduction of vaginal probes, now permit accurate measurements of the thickness of the endometrial layer to be taken. An endometrial thickness of 4 mm or less in a post-menopausal woman is unlikely to be associated with serious pathology.

As in the case of endometrial hyperplasia, the diagnosis ultimately depends on obtaining a reliable sample from the uterine cavity (see above) and a hysteroscopy and D & C remain the procedure of choice. There was some anxiety that the use of distension fluid at hysteroscopy might encourage the spread of malignant cells along the fallopian tubes and thence into the peritoneal cavity but this does not seem to have been a problem in clinical practice.

FIGO staging

As in the case of cervical carcinoma, the Fédération Internationale de Gynécologie et d'Obstétrique has published a scheme of staging to define the extent of the disease.

Stage 0	Atypical endometrial hyperplasia.
Stage I	Disease confined to the body of the uterus.
	Stage Ia Uterine cavity 80 mm or less in length.
	Stage Ib Uterine cavity more than 80 mm in length.
Stage II	Local extension of the disease to involve the cervix.
Stage III	Extension beyond the uterus but not beyond the pelvis.
Stage IV	Spread beyond the true pelvis or involvement of the mucosal layer of the bladder and/or rectum.

Stage I is further sub-divided into Grades, according to the histological appearance of the tumour tissue:

Grade 1	Well differentiated.
Grade 2	Differentiated but with some solid areas.
Grade 3	Predominantly solid or undifferentiated tumour.

Treatment

With early diagnosis and treatment, the results are good as the disease is contained within the thick, muscular wall of the uterus but the prognosis for advanced disease is poor.

The basis of treatment is the total hysterectomy and bilateral salpingo-oophorectomy also taking a cuff of upper vagina (see Chapter 3), though there is a recent trend towards more extensive operations taking the pelvic lymph nodes as well. This is supplemented by radiotherapy before and/or after the surgery. Pre-operative radiotherapy can increase the difficulty of the operation but may reduce the risk of spreading the disease by the operative manipulations. If pre-operative treatment is given, the surgery is best planned for about six weeks after the radiotherapy when the early reactive oedema has resolved but mature fibrous tissue has not yet developed.

Many of these tumours are responsive to hormone treatment and the administration of high doses of a progestogen may be valuable in the treatment of women who are unsuitable for surgery or for palliation in advanced cases. Medroxyprogesterone acetate 400 mg daily is a common regime, though others have been described.

Most endometrial carcinomas are relatively resistant to chemotherapy.

Other malignancies of the uterine corpus

Other malignant tumours do occur but are rare.

THE FALLOPIAN TUBES

The two conditions most commonly affecting the fallopian tubes are infection (and its sequelae) and the ectopic implantation of a pregnancy. Infections are also discussed in Chapter 6 and the ectopic pregnancy is of such importance that it is accorded a chapter to itself (Chapter 14).

Infection

The fallopian tubes seem to be particularly susceptible to infection, the long-term effect of which is often obstruction of the tubal lumen and the formation of adhesions between the exterior of the tubes and other structures.

During the acute phase of tubal infection, the patient will usually be pyrexial and a blood test will show an elevated white blood cell count (leucocytosis). She will complain of lower abdominal pain and may have noticed an abnormal vaginal discharge. At laparoscopy the tubal wall is inflamed appearing red and thickened and with a rubbery texture due to oedema. There may be a thin, purulent fluid in the pouch of Douglas and inflammatory changes may be present on other peritoneal surfaces including the wall of the bowel.

After two or three days, the blocked tube becomes filled with pus, when it is called a pyosalpinx. This may measure 10 cm or more in diameter.

Prompt and energetic antibiotic therapy may prevent permanent damage (the tubal obstruction may even be corrected by resolution of the oedematous swelling) but cases which have proceeded to pyosalpinx formation will usually be left with residual damage. In time, the tube may undergo fibrous contraction or the pus may reabsorb, leaving the distended tube filled with a yellowing, watery fluid (a hydrosalpinx). Untreated or poorly treated cases may become chronic.

Fimbrial cysts

Small, smooth, thin-walled, fluid filled cysts are often present near the outer ends of the tubes and occasionally within the layers of the broad ligament. They are formed from remnants of the primitive (embryonic) tissues. They are often multiple and are invariably benign. They may be mistaken for ovarian cysts on ultrasonic scan. Fimbrial cysts rarely exceed 2 cm in diameter and are invariably benign. No treatment is needed.

Malignant disease of the tubes

Malignant tubal disease is very rare and is difficult to diagnose; most cases are not discovered until already well advanced. The tumour is usually a papillary adenocarcinoma. The age of maximal incidence is around 50 years but these tumours constitute less than 0.5% of gynaecological malignancies.

THE OVARIES

Infection

The spread of tubal infection (salpingitis) to the ovaries is common and the two structures may adhere together forming a tubovarian mass.

Ovarian inflammation (oophoritis) is occasionally associated with an appendicitis (the right ovary) or with bowel perforation due to other diseases such as diverticulitis or Crohn's disease.

Primary ovarian infection is virtually unknown.

Polycystic ovarian disease

Polycystic ovarian disease (PCOD or Stein-Leventhal syndrome) was originally described by Irving Stein and Michael Leventhal in 1934 when they presented their experience with seven cases of women with obesity, hirsutism and secondary amenorrhoea. It is now realised that the condition is more common than was formerly assumed and that the endocrine features may be present in menstruating women of normal build and hair distribution.

The PCOD ovaries are moderately enlarged and have a white, sclerotic outer surface. When cut across, there is typically a band of small cysts just below the surface layer. These cysts can also be seen on an ultrasonic scan.

The levels of circulating luteinising hormone and follicle stimulating hormone from the pituitary are moderately elevated and their relative proportions usually change so that the LH:FSH ratio equals or exceeds 3:1. In some cases, these two hormones may be normal but there is a rise in the free testosterone level.

The condition was originally thought to be caused by the formation of the sclerotic coat on the ovaries but is now known to be due to a complex disturbance in a number of inter-related hormones.

Anovulation is usual but fertility can be restored in many cases by treatment with clomiphene or tamoxifen though some may require injections of gonadotrophins. The small number of cases which fail to respond to medical treatment may resume ovulation after 'drilling' of the ovaries using a laser beam or needle diathermy.

Ovarian tumours

The ovaries are capable of developing a large number of tumours, many of which are cystic. The large range of pathological appearances provides a fruitful source of questions for examiners of medical students but has only limited effect on the clinical management.

Ovarian tumours are rare in childhood but are seen with increasing frequency as age advances. The proportion of malignancies also rises with time and ovarian cancer is typically a condition of the post-menopausal years. The family history may be important, since some families show an abnormally high incidence of malignant ovarian disease.

Complications which may affect any ovarian tumour

There are a number of potential complications that can occur to any ovarian tumours irrespective of the pathology.

Torsion

Pedunculated tumours may twist on the stalk. Rotations of a few degrees may reverse them spontaneously but, in more severe cases, the twist may obstruct the blood vessels which run within the stalk, resulting in ischaemic necrosis of the tumour. Torsion is more likely if the tumour is of small or moderate size and is benign (malignant tumours tend to be adherent to surrounding structures and therefore incapable of twisting).

Although torsion of the tumour may cause severe abdominal pain, the more serious complication is torsion of the whole ovary. On rare occasions, this may happen to a normal ovary but it is much more likely if the ovary is distorted by a small tumour. Unless an operation is carried out within one to two hours, the ovary may not be salvageable and an oophorectomy may be necessary. Unfortunately, the symptoms may resemble those of acute pelvic infection resulting in the woman being treated with antibiotics for three or four days before the correct diagnosis is appreciated. Torsion may also be misdiagnosed as the rupture of a cyst which may also result in delayed treatment.

Haemorrhage

The blood vessels in the tumour may rupture causing intra-peritoneal bleeding. In many cases, the vessel will be small and will seal spontaneously. After a few hours of lower abdominal pain, the symptoms will gradually abate. In more severe cases, operative treatment may be required in order to control the bleeding. In all but trivial cases, ultrasonic scanning will reveal the presence of fluid (blood) behind the uterus in the pouch of Douglas but this is of little practical help in reaching the diagnosis because fluid is present in this site in a number of other conditions.

Rupture

Clearly, solid tumours cannot undergo rupture but cysts and partially cystic tumours can develop a small but persistent leak or a more dramatic rupture, with discharge of the fluid contents into the peritoneal cavity.

The symptoms will depend on the degree of peritoneal irritation caused by the cyst fluid and vary from minor lower abdominal discomfort to severe pain. Dramatic rupture is associated with very sudden onset of pain.

Ultrasonic scanning may reveal fluid in the pouch of Douglas but the cyst may not be visible if its fluid contents have drained out.

Incarceration

Many enlarging pelvic tumours will extend up into the lower abdomen and, if sufficiently mobile, may come to lie entirely outside the pelvis. Others, however, may remain within the pelvic cavity which they ultimately fill. Most of these will present with symptoms of pressure on adjacent structures (usually the bladder) but a few may remain unsuspected until elongation and compression of the urethra results in the inability to void urine. Such cases require immediate catheterisation of the bladder to relieve pain and to prevent renal damage due to back pressure. This should be followed by surgical removal of the tumour.

Infection

On rare occasions, ovarian cysts may become secondarily infected. This is more common if tissue necrosis has followed torsion (see above). The infecting organisms usually originate from the bowel but may come from the genital tract; surgically introduced infection can occur if the cyst is drained but not removed.

'Physiological' cysts

During the menstrual cycle, the ovaries develop Graaffian follicles, ova are released and corpora lutea are formed. This process is sometimes faulty and either the follicle or the corpus luteum may become cystic. Because they are derived from normal cells, these cysts are often termed 'physiological'. They are smooth-walled, unilocular (but sometimes multiple) and are filled with a yellowish, watery fluid. They rarely exceed 5 cm in diameter and, because the contained fluid is non-echogenic, they are easily seen as dark, featureless areas on ultrasonic scanning.

Physiological cysts are usually asymptomatic, often being discovered on pelvic examination when the woman attends for routine cervical cytology or being seen on ultrasonic scanning for some unrelated reason. However, both follicular and luteal cysts may be functional and the hormone production may cause secondary amenorrhoea; follicular cysts may be associated with endometrial hyperplasia because of the persistent oestrogen secretion. In the absence of complications, both follicular and luteal cysts frequently resolve spontaneously.

Women suspected of having an ovarian cyst should be investigated by an ultrasonic scan. If the symptoms, if any, are not too troublesome and the cyst is 'simple' (that is, unilocular and non-echogenic) and is 5 cm or less in diameter, it is normal to warn the woman of the possible complications (see below) and arrange another scan after an interval of six to eight weeks. In many cases, the cyst will no longer be present and an unnecessary operation will have been avoided; persistent cysts should be removed. Multi-loculate cysts or those containing echogenic material or measuring over 5 cm in diameter are unlikely to resolve spontaneously.

Cysts of the corpus luteum are common in early pregnancy and their removal is normally postponed until about week 16 (by which time many will have disappeared). Luteal cysts are very common in the presence of trophoblastic disease (hydatidiform mole and choriocarcinoma – see Chapter 15).

Benign ovarian tumours

Physiological (follicular and luteal) cysts are benign tumours but they are described separately (see above) because their management differs from that of pathological neoplasms.

Endometrioma

Unlike the other tumours described in this section, the endometrioma is not a neoplasm but is a cystic tumour formed by the collection of old blood produced by an endometriotic deposit within the ovary (see, also, Chapter 7).

The altered blood forms a typical brown and slightly viscous fluid resembling melted chocolate and the alternative name for the lesion is therefore 'chocolate cyst'.

Isolated endometriomata are fairly easy to remove, though it is important to include all the active ectopic endometrium if a recurrence is to be prevented, but the condition often co-exists with more generalised pelvic endometriosis and the associated pelvic adhesions may render the operation exceedingly difficult. Removal of the whole ovary may be necessary and post-operative medical treatment is often required.

Dermoid cysts

Unlike all the other common ovarian tumours, benign cystic teratomas, commonly called 'dermoid cysts' are found most frequently in teenage girls or women in their early twenties. They are mostly small (up to 10 cm in diameter) and are unusual in that they often lie in front of the broad ligament. (The ovary is attached to the back of that structure and other ovarian cysts are usually posterior to it.) Clinically, they are usually unilateral but the other ovary should be carefully assessed as bilateral tumours are not uncommon.

The tumours are part cystic and part solid (though the proportions of each vary) and the contents are highly echogenic on ultrasonic scan.

In most of these tumours, the solid part is predominantly composed of tissue derived from skin elements (hence the name dermoid – from 'derma', Greek for 'skin'). This includes not only disorganised skin itself but also sweat and sebaceous glands, hair follicles, nail tissue and sometimes even partially formed teeth (which may be recognisable on an abdominal X-ray). Tissue may, however, be found from any other body structure the more common being brain, bone and gut. This is thought to be the origin of the rare tumour called a 'struma ovarii', in which thyroid tissue predominates; about 5% of these produce sufficient thyroid hormone to cause thyrotoxicosis.

The fluid in the cystic part of the tumour is composed of sebaceous material often mixed with copious amounts of hair.

Dermoid cysts are thought to be created by the spontaneous development of unfertilised germ cells. The fluid content is highly irritant to the peritoneum and leakage causes severe pain. It is also important to avoid spilling the fluid during surgical removal as dense pelvic adhesions may otherwise be formed. Irrigation of the pelvis at the end of the operation with Hartman's solution is a wise precaution in all cases and is essential if accidental spillage has occurred.

Fibroma

Fibromata are small medium sized, solid, white tumours which are often bilateral. They are formed from fibrous tissue and, although benign, may be associated with ascites and even pleural effusion (Meigs' syndrome) the mechanism for which is not known.

Serous cystadenoma

Serous cystadenomata are usually unilocular though they may be divided by a few septa. They contain yellowish, watery fluid and grow to moderate size (15–20 cm in diameter), though some are much larger. The wall is thin and leakage or rupture is quite common. Removal is essential since even apparently benign growths may, on histological examination, prove to contain areas of suspicious or even frankly malignant cells.

Mucinous cystadenoma

Multilocular, thin-walled and containing viscous, almost jelly-like material, mucinous cysts can attain very large size sometimes causing gross abdominal distension. The largest reported ovarian tumour was removed in 1905 and weighed over 148 kg (328 lb). The woman recovered.

The early removal of these cysts is necessary as their rupture, either spontaneous or at operation, may result in the deposition of mucin secreting cells on peritoneal surfaces. This can cause the condition of 'myxoma peritoneii', in which the abdomen repeatedly fills with unencapsulated mucin which, because of the formation of adhesions, becomes increasingly difficult to remove by paracentesis. Although remaining pathologically benign, the condition may prove fatal.

Uncommon ovarian tumours

Other benign ovarian neoplasms include the Brenner tumour, the granulosa cell tumour, the thecoma and the arrhenoblastoma. Granulosa cell tumours and thecomata are oestrogen secreting, whereas the arrhenoblastoma produces testosterone and may cause virilisation.

Malignant ovarian tumours

Many of the benign ovarian neoplasms have malignant counterparts and the histopathology of these tumours is further complicated as, not only can areas of malignant change be present within a benign growth but, in some cases, the features may lie on the borderlines of malignancy.

Endometrioid carcinoma

As already noted above, the endometrioma is a manifestation of endometriosis and not a neoplastic condition. It is therefore not surprising that malignant change in these tumours is exceedingly rare. However, neoplastic growths with histological features resembling those of uterine adenocarcinoma occasionally develop in the ovary and it is possible that these originate from endometriotic deposits.

Malignant teratoma

A very rare but highly malignant tumour which appears to have similar origins to the dermoid cyst is the malignant teratoma. Like their benign equivalent, these tumours are usually found in relatively young women and may contain tissue derived from any of the body's structures, though considerable disorganisation and lack of differentiation may render cell identification impossible. Teratomas are usually solid.

Serous and mucinous cystadenocarcinoma

Although these tumours have different origins and appearances, they are grouped together here not only because they are the commonest of the malignant ovarian tumours but because they both occur more commonly in women over the age of 50 years and also because, in their poorly differentiated forms, it may be impossible to distinguish between them.

Other ovarian malignant disease

Several other types of malignancy may arise in the ovaries but are rare.

Metastatic tumours

In common with all other tissues, the ovary can be the site of a metastatic deposit from a primary growth in some other organ system. A specialised example is the Krukenberg tumour which is a metastatic deposit in the ovary from a primary lesion in the gastro-intestinal tract (usually from the stomach).

General considerations

Most ovarian carcinomas are partly cystic and partly solid, though entirely solid tumours do occur. Spread of the disease is usually early and is by local invasion and trans-peritoneal seeding as well as by the lymphatic and blood vessels. Widespread deposits on peritoneal surfaces, including the bowel wall, are common as is involvement of the greater omentum. Ovarian malignancies, even in the early stages, are often associated with ascites which may be clinically demonstrable.

Because of late diagnosis, the prognosis for most malignant ovarian tumours is poor, but malignant change within a benign cyst may have a favourable outcome if the malignant cells have not reached the exterior surface of the tumour.

Management of suspected ovarian malignancy

Clinical examination is of limited value and special investigations are almost always required.

Special investigations

Imaging

It has been pointed out above that all ovarian tumours should be scanned ultrasonically. In many cases of malignant disease, the ultrasonic appearances will suggest the probable diagnosis. The presence of ascites may be demonstrated.

Computer automated tomography (CAT scanning) and magnetic resonance imaging (MRI) may add further useful information the MRI being particularly useful in the pre-operative assessment of possible spread. Ultrasonic scanning of the liver and contrast studies of the urinary tract (intravenous urography (IVU) – formerly called intravenous pyelography (IVP)) and of the lower bowel (by barium enema) may be indicated in some cases.

Recently, ultrasonic techniques utilising Doppler flow studies have been developed to assess the blood supply of tumours. The more vascular a tumour, the more likely it is to be malignant.

Needle biopsy

Ultrasonically or radiologically guided needle biopsy of tumour masses may be helpful in determining the histological characteristics but the findings must be interpreted with care since the sample obtained may not be representative of the whole tumour.

Paracentesis abdominis

The withdrawal of intra-peritoneal fluid by the introduction of a needle through the anterior abdominal wall under local anaesthesia allows cytological examination for malignant cells and may be helpful in relieving the discomfort of a patient with gross ascites.

Tumour markers

Abnormally increased levels of certain substances in the blood have been found to be associated with many ovarian malignancies.

Carcinoembryonic antigen (CEA) and (ovarian) cancer antigen (Ca 125) are raised in many cases. Unfortunately, these tumour markers are not entirely specific as the levels may be affected by other conditions and caution must be exercised in applying them to diagnosis. Their most useful role is in post-treatment follow-up, when they can provide a valuable early warning of recurrence.

Specific ovarian neoplasms may also be associated with changes in the blood levels of human chorionic gonadotrophin (HCG) and a-fetoprotein (AFP).

Laparoscopy

Laparoscopy can provide the opportunity for direct inspection of tumours and also for the collection of peritoneal fluid (or washings with normal saline) for cytological examination. The surface of the liver should be examined for the presence of metastases. Laparoscopy is, however, of limited application, since the same information is available at the time of definitive surgical treatment (either laparoscopic or at laparotomy).

Surgical treatment

The fact that many ovarian cancers are diagnosed late might suggest that operative treatment would have only a small part to play in their treatment. This is not the case however, because the surgical reduction of the tumour mass (de-bulking) can greatly influence the subsequent response to radiotherapy or chemotherapy. The tumours are often bilateral and may have metastasised to the uterus (possibly via the fallopian tubes but more probably by blood born spread) so that hysterectomy and bilateral salpingo-oophorectomy is usually indicated.

A few cases of early stage, low malignancy tumours in young women may be adequately treated by oophorectomy which can sometimes be performed laparoscopically. It is important that these women fully understand the possible risks of such treatment and that they continue to attend for careful follow-up.

Lymphatic spread is often to the para-aortic nodes and node biopsy in this area can offer a guide to subsequent treatment. Omentectomy is frequently indicated both to reduce the total tumour mass and also to reduce, or at least postpone, the incidence of post-operative ascites. Biopsies should be taken from any suspicious area which cannot be excised (including the liver, which should always be examined).

Radiotherapy

Radiotherapy has little part to play in the treatment of ovarian malignancy.

Treatment by external irradiation of the pelvis and abdomen may be considered if the disease has not spread too widely. The dosage is limited by the effects on bowel mucosa.

Intra-peritoneal instillation of radioactive isotopes has been used but is probably of limited value. There are practical problems with supply and with the protection of staff from exposure to the ionising radiation both during the operation and in post-operative nursing care.

Chemotherapy

The chemotherapeutic treatment of ovarian carcinoma has been considerably improved in recent years with a reduction in the incidence of unpleasant side-effects (nausea, vomiting, diarrhoea, hair loss and bone marrow depression) and better tumour response. This is primarily due to the development of regimes which combine three or more cytotoxic agents which may be administered together or sequentially.

The response to chemotherapy (and to radiotherapy) is mainly determined by the amount of malignant tumour, hence the value of surgical de-bulking.

Cytotoxic drugs can be placed in the peritoneal cavity and this may have some therapeutic value if performed at the time of operative tumour removal.

'Second look' operations

Following treatment, a further laparoscopy or laparotomy may be performed after several weeks or a few months. This allows for the re-evaluation of any residual disease and assessment of the need for further treatment. Tumour excision and the biopsy of lymph nodes and other deposits may again be indicated.

'Well woman' screening

Exfoliative cytology is well established as a screening test for carcinoma of the uterine cervix and mammography is now used to screen for breast cancer. The routine use of pelvic ultrasonic scanning in apparently healthy women offers the possibility of the early detection of ovarian disease but it is not yet sufficiently refined to offer a screening test for the general population. Ultrasonic screening should be offered to women from high risk families – 40% of women with two close relatives who have suffered from ovarian carcinoma will themselves develop the disease.

Medico-legal significance

Cancer of the ovary is an important cause of death in women and, having a peak incidence in women over the age of 50 years, may be expected to increase in frequency as life expectancy improves. A useful, though very approximate, guide is that the percentage chance of an ovarian cyst being malignant is about the same as the woman's age in years. As pointed out above, women with a strong family history of ovarian malignancy are at particular risk.

The biggest problem is the difficulty of diagnosing the growth of a tumour situated deep within the body and which frequently remains asymptomatic until an advanced stage.

Any woman suspected of having a pelvic mass must be properly investigated and this is especially true if she is post-menopausal.

The failure to offer routine ultrasonic screening may be a source of future claims.

THE PITUITARY GLAND

Although part of the endocrine system and neither a pelvic organ nor part of the reproductive tract, the pituitary gland is so intimately involved with the function of the genital organs that it merits inclusion here. The anterior part of the gland produces several hormones which affect ovarian function (see Chapter 2).

Sheehan's syndrome

In the 1930s, Harold Sheehan, a pathologist in Glasgow, noticed an unusually high incidence of ischaemic necrosis of the anterior lobe of the pituitary gland in women who had died from postpartum haemorrhage. The damage occurs because the hypotension associated with hypovolaemic shock may cause thrombosis in the blood vessels supplying the gland.

The full picture results in a failure to produce the trophic hormones with consequent impairment of the function of the ovaries and of the thyroid and adrenal glands. Lactation fails, menstruation is not re-established, secondary sexual characteristics regress and there are signs of hypothyroidism and adrenal insufficiency. Partial damage is associated with less severe changes; in these cases, reproductive function may be retained.

Improvements in care during pregnancy and labour and the better management of postpartum haemorrhage have made this a rare condition.

Pituitary adenoma

The functional (hormone producing) cells of the anterior pituitary may undergo selective overgrowth. These cases usually present to the gynaecologist with menstrual abnormalities or infertility, in which the hyperplasia affects the prolactin producing cells. The tumours are often referred to as a 'prolactinomas'. They are small, tend to be situated in the lateral part of the gland and are often multiple. Very small tumours are called 'microadenomas'.

The normal level of circulating prolactin is up to about 800 iu/l (the exact figure varies slightly between different laboratories) and can be influenced by several factors. Even the stress of attending a hospital clinic may cause a modest rise but, in the presence of a prolactinoma, the level may be 4000 iu/l or more.

In addition to measurement of the prolactin level, investigation formerly relied on X-rays of the skull to demonstrate an expansion of the bony cup containing the gland but the soft tissue itself can now be visualised by magnetic resonance imaging (MRI). This is important because upwards enlargement of the gland may result in pressure on the centre of the optic chiasma (the cross-over of the optic nerves), causing loss of peripheral vision.

Treatment was by surgical resection of part of the gland or by the insertion of radioisotope needles. Medical treatment was introduced in the mid 1970s following the discovery that a substance called bromocriptine could selectively inhibit the secretion of prolactin. Not only does bromocriptine suppress prolactin production, but, in many cases, the tumour size will decrease so that surgery and isotope therapy are less commonly required.

CHAPTER 9

SEXUAL DYSFUNCTION

In an evolutionary sense, the primary function of every plant and animal species is reproduction and to this general rule humans are no exception. We are, however, very unusual in indulging in sex for pleasure as well as for procreation. This is a behaviour trait shared by very few other species, of which the most notable is the bonobo (pigmy chimpanzee) of Central Africa. Unfortunately, for a small but significant number of individuals, sexual activity may be anything but pleasurable.

The sexual function is affected by many factors ranging from anatomical and physiological problems to social and psychological influences. Consequently, sexual difficulties must be assessed within a wider context and complaints of coital problems may sometimes be the 'public' manifestation of a dysfunctional relationship. The management of such cases may be exceedingly difficult, not least because the patient may be unwilling to recognise the true nature of the problem.

One of the authors once spent many fruitless hours attempting to treat a patient's deep dyspareunia (see definition below) only to have the symptom disappear dramatically and completely when the woman left her abusive and violent husband and entered a more satisfactory relationship.

Men may complain of the failure to achieve or to maintain penile erection or may be troubled by premature ejaculation whilst women may report the inability to allow penetration (vaginismus) or pain during intercourse (superficial or deep dyspareunia). In both sexes, the difficulty is sometimes initiated by a physical problem but perpetuated by the consequent anxiety.

Male problems will usually be referred to a urologist, preferably one with a special interest in this field, and are outside the scope of this volume.

VAGINISMUS

The semi-involuntary contraction of the pelvic floor muscles that surround the vaginal orifice is termed 'vaginismus' and the consequent narrowing of the vaginal introitus may impede or prevent penetration by the male penis. Unfortunately, the discomfort caused by attempted penetration results in increased muscular contraction, thereby aggravating the problem.

The same mechanism may render a vaginal examination difficult or even impossible though calm reassurance and a good deal of patience may help the woman to relax sufficiently for the gynaecologist to perform the examination with one finger only. Achieving this much is often a valuable first step in successful management.

Many women will present with the belief that they are anatomically abnormal. In a very few cases, there will be a physical problem such as an unusually thick or rigid hymen, which may require surgical correction. In the majority of cases, however, operative treatment should be avoided (the resulting scar tissue may even make the problem worse) and the woman must be taught to relax. This can be very time consuming and is difficult to achieve in a busy gynaecological clinic. Regular practice with a vaginal dilator in the privacy of her own home may be helpful and education of the partner in the art of foreplay may also be necessary.

Many cases of vaginismus are due to the woman's own anxieties about sexual intercourse or to her misconceptions about her anatomy but others may be due to her partner's insensitive approach. The problem can be initiated by the discomfort associated with vulvo-vaginal infections (especially thrush and herpes) but the vaginismus may then persist even after the infection has been cured. It may be secondary to the psychological trauma of attempted or actual rape.

DYSPAREUNIA

Dyspareunia means pain or discomfort during sexual intercourse. It may be due to physical abnormalities in the genital tract or, like vaginismus, it may reflect problems in the relationship with the sexual partner. Dyspareunia is described as 'superficial' if the pain is experienced at the vulva or in the vagina or 'deep' if it is within the pelvis. The two may co-exist and it may be very difficult for the woman to distinguish between them.

Superficial dyspareunia

Superficial dyspareunia may be due to vaginismus (see above) but usually implies a local problem at the vulva or in the vagina. One of the most common is the presence of sensitive scar tissue at the vaginal introitus following a tear or an episiotomy during the vaginal delivery of a baby. Some studies have reported that up to 25% of women suffer prolonged perineal pain after childbirth. This is much more likely to occur if the wound has been sutured with poor approximation of the tissues at the fourchette.

Other causes of superficial dyspareunia include vulvo-vaginal infections such as thrush or herpes or localised infections of the vulval glands. The vulval dystrophies can also cause dyspareunia. These conditions are dealt with in more detail elsewhere in this volume.

In the years following the menopause, many women experience discomfort during sexual intercourse because the reduced level of circulating oestrogen causes the vaginal walls to become thinned. The vaginal transudate is reduced so that the woman experiences 'dryness' and the nerve endings in the wall are nearer the surface causing the vagina to feel sore when stimulated by the penis.

Deep dyspareunia

In deep dyspareunia, the pain is felt in the lower abdomen; it may be unilateral or bilateral and sometimes persists for many hours after coitus has ceased. During a vaginal examination, it may be possible to reproduce the pain, though this must be attempted with care to avoid causing the patient undue distress.

Two of the possible causes of deep dyspareunia, pelvic infection and endometriosis, are important because of their potential for long term damage. Pelvic infection (also called pelvic inflammatory disease or PID) is a frequent clinical diagnosis but many women receive numerous courses of antibiotics without achieving a cure. Useful guidelines are that, in the treatment of suspected pelvic infection, courses of antibiotics should never be shorter than for 10 days (14 or even 21 days may be better) and that failure to respond to two courses is usually an indication for further investigation by laparoscopy.

Cystic swelling of an ovary may cause a localised pain during coitus, the pain often being influenced by the depth of penile penetration and hence occurring in some sexual positions and not in others. Even normal (non-cystic) ovaries may be a source of severe discomfort if bruised during sexual intercourse; this is more likely to happen if retroversion of the uterus causes them to lie in the pouch of Douglas. Ultrasonic scanning of the pelvis may be helpful in making the diagnosis.

Many gynaecologists teach that uterine retroversion itself causes no symptoms but it does seem that pain during coitus may originate from the body of the uterus if that structure lies in the long axis of the vagina.

Controversy exists among gynaecologists over whether pelvic venous congestion is a real cause of deep dyspareunia. Recent research has supported the hypothesis and one of the authors of this book has had considerable success in relieving severe symptoms by the ligation of pelvic varices.

PSYCHOSEXUAL PROBLEMS

Psychosexual counselling is a specialised area which is outside the scope of this book and, indeed, outside the professional expertise of many clinical gynaecologists. Nevertheless, it is often the gynaecologist to whom the woman first expresses her concerns and it is important to have a basic understanding of the subject.

Some reference has already been made above to the role of psychological factors in the production of physical symptoms but the range of problems is far wider. One specific problem which the gynaecologist may be called upon to address is the loss of libido or sexual drive in the peri-menopausal woman. Though one may theorise about the psychological effects of the impending change in the woman's social role, it is perhaps reassuring to find that many will respond to treatment with oestrogen replacement therapy (HRT) and that, for those who do not recover their sexual enthusiasm with oestrogen alone, the addition of a small dose of male hormone may be very effective.

TREATMENT OF SEXUAL DYSFUNCTION

In recent years, there have been considerable advances both in the management of psychosexual problems and in the training of counsellors and therapists. Specialised clinics are now available to which gynaecologists, general practitioners and others may make referrals. Unfortunately, the waiting lists for such clinics are often long, a reflection of the increased demand. It remains uncertain whether this increased demand represents a true increase in psychopathology or simply a greater awareness and acceptance of the problems.

Although explicit discussions of sexual problems are now common place on late evening cable and satellite television, there remains a considerable reticence about sexual matters in this country.

A small proportion of gynaecologists will have received psychosexual training but, for the majority, their role is primarily to exclude physical problems, to recognise the need for counselling and to encourage the patient to co-operate in therapy. Successful treatment often depends on the willing participation of both partners and the gynaecologist may also play a part in the preliminary discussions with the male partner.

Many gynaecologists, whether because of temperament or training, will be unsuited to dealing with psychosexual dysfunction. This need not necessarily prove a problem so long as they are competent to recognise when such difficulties exist and to refer patients appropriately.

CHAPTER 10

CONTRACEPTION

The ideal contraceptive would be 100% effective, free of all side effects, completely reversible, and independent of sexual intercourse. It would also be inexpensive and easily available without the need for medical or nursing involvement. No such contraceptive yet exists and all the currently available methods involve some degree of compromise. For some couples, the prevention of a pregnancy may not be the most important consideration and they may therefore be content to use a less effective contraceptive that has the advantage of fewer side effects. It should also be remembered that some forms of contraception may not be acceptable because of cultural or religious beliefs.

The effectiveness of a contraceptive method is expressed as the Pearl Index (PI), which is defined as the number of conceptions which would be expected in '100 women years' (that is, 100 women using the method for 12 months, 50 women for two years or 20 women using the method for five years). The Pearl Index allows the effectiveness of different methods to be compared, though, when considering individual requirements, the age of the woman must also be considered as her natural fertility will diminish with advancing age. The Index is also used for male contraceptive methods and would therefore be better defined in terms of 'couple years'.

The following table gives approximate failure rates for some examples of the various types of contraception available in the UK. The term progestogen is used as this refers to a variety of synthetic hormones that are based upon the hormone progesterone.

Method	Type	Pearl index
No contraception aged 25	'Baseline' fertility	80–90
No contraception aged 40	'Baseline' fertility	40–50
Others	'Natural'	15
Spermicides (only)	Chemical	12
Coitus interruptus	'Natural'	7
'Persona'	'Natural'	6
Condoms	Male barrier	4
Diaphragm	Female barrier	2
Copper IUCD	Intrauterine	1.5
Progestogen only pill	Hormonal	1.2
Progestogen injection	Hormonal	1
Combined pill	Hormonal	0.2
Female sterilisation	Permanent	0.1
Progestogen IUCD	Intrauterine + hormonal	0.02
Male sterilisation	Permanent	0.02

COUNSELLING AND CONSENT

Proper counselling should precede the provision of any contraceptive measures. The available methods should be explained and adequate time allowed for the discussion of their benefits, risks and disadvantages. Depending on the methods being considered, contraindications may have to be excluded.

Particular care must be taken in the counselling of women who request sterilisation as the request is sometimes prompted by the hope that a sterilisation will contribute to the salvation of a foundering relationship. This is almost never effective and the acquisition of a new partner after separation or divorce may cause the woman to return seeking reversal of the sterilisation, a very unsatisfactory situation.

Most contraceptive methods do not require formal written consent but it should be obtained in all cases of sterilisation and also before the fitting of an intrauterine contraceptive device in the occasional instance where this is to be done under general anaesthesia.

In the past, the sterilisation of a married woman required the prior consent of her husband (the woman's consent to her husband's sterilisation has never been required). Although this is no longer necessary, it is clearly preferable that the partner's agreement should be obtained before any permanent removal of fertility is carried out.

'NATURAL' BIRTH CONTROL

During the six months or so following the delivery of a baby, a lactating, amenorrhoic woman will have greatly reduced fertility, the most 'natural' contraception of all.

Coitus interruptus

Coitus interruptus (popularly known as 'withdrawal' or 'being careful' and sometimes abbreviated to CI) depends on the man withdrawing his penis from the vagina before ejaculation. The method has the advantage of requiring no preparation, is immediately available and is free, considerations which make it popular with some couples. It is, however, unreliable, probably because fertile semen can escape from the penis prior to ejaculation itself.

The 'rhythm' method

The 'rhythm' method of birth control, and the related 'Billings' method, are important because they may be the only methods available to some religious groups. The female egg normally remains viable for only 24–48 hours after ovulation and sperm usually survive in the vagina for only six hours due to the acidity of the vaginal secretions (though active sperm have been found as long as seven days after coitus). To use these 'natural' methods, the woman must know of the length of her menstrual cycle and preferably also be able to recognise the changes that occur in the cervical mucous prior to ovulation; she may also measure her basal body temperature. The chance of conception may then be reduced by abstaining from sexual intercourse during the potentially fertile phase of the menstrual cycle.

The 'Persona'

The 'Persona' is another natural contraceptive method which became available recently. The necessary equipment can be purchased 'over the counter' without prescription and is designed to detect the woman's cyclical changes by measuring the hormone levels in a morning urine sample thereby aiming to predict for her fertile days. The method is quoted to be 94% effective but is not inexpensive.

THE MALE CONDOM ('SHEATH')

The male condom is the oldest method of contraception having first been used in Roman times to prevent the transmission of sexual diseases. Condoms have been made from many different materials including linen (in the 14th century), animal intestine and bladder wall, and, more recently, from rubber. In the last decade, condoms have experienced a dramatic return to popularity, largely prompted by concerns about the spread of human immunodeficiency virus (HIV) and the associated acquired immune deficiency syndrome (AIDS), while marketing techniques have changed their image from the barber's sotto voce offer of 'Something for the weekend, Sir?' almost to the status of a fashion accessory.

Condom usage varies geographically. In Japan, 75% of couples use the method whilst, in Africa, the Middle East and in South America, the corresponding figure is only about 2%. In the UK, condoms are used by about 20% of couples, being particularly popular amongst those under the age of 21.

Although often considered to be one of the less effective methods (some studies have reported failure rates as high as 30%), reliable research in well motivated couples give figures of about four conceptions per 100 women years. Even better results are obtained amongst the older (and, therefore, less fertile) women over the age of 35.

Disadvantages of condoms are that they must be obtained in advance and that their use causes an unwelcome interruption in sexual foreplay. They must obviously be used for every occasion of intercourse and have to be put onto the erect penis before any semen leaks out into the vagina (as sperm are often present in the pre-ejaculate – see 'Coitus interruptus', above). The male partner may complain of reduced sensitivity.

The advantages are that they are widely available, can be bought without prescription and are relatively inexpensive. Apart from occasional allergic reactions, they have no medical side effects and are acceptably reliable in preventing conception if used consistently and correctly. They also offer considerable protection against sexually transmitted diseases.

VASECTOMY (MALE STERILISATION)

Some gynaecologists carry out vasectomies but the procedure is much more frequently performed by urological surgeons. Nevertheless, anyone offering contraceptive advice should have some knowledge of the technique.

The operation is usually performed under local anaesthetic, unlike female sterilisation which usually requires general anaesthesia, and normally takes only a few minutes. The patient can return to work afterwards and is likely to experience only minor discomfort from post-operative bruising which resolves in a few days. It is, however, important that the patient understands that the operation is not immediately effective but that it is necessary to wait two or even three months until the semen no longer contains spermatozoa. The operation occasionally fails because of the congenital re-duplication of the vas deferens on one or both sides; in such cases, re-exploration of the scrotum may be required (usually under a general anaesthetic).

In straightforward cases, after cleansing the scrotal skin and surrounding area with an antiseptic solution, towels are placed in position to provide a sterile field. The surgeon then identifies the vas deferens by palpating it through the scrotal skin and holds it in position while the area is infiltrated with local anaesthetic. After waiting for a few moments to allow the anaesthetic to take effect, the sink is then incised, the vas identified, ligated twice and divided between the ligatures. For greater security, each end is usually folded back for a few millimetres and sutured in place. The scrotal skin is sutured and the procedure then repeated on the other side.

The popularity of vasectomy varies. One author has worked in two very different areas. In one, where the population was heterogeneous with generally low average income, educational attainments and marriage rates and a high immigrant component, requests for vasectomy were infrequent and the suggestion of the operation often met with rejection. In the other, a more homogenous group of mostly married couples with higher income and education, vasectomy was very popular. This may, however, have reflected a greater acceptance of marital infidelity in the second group, since requests for the sterilisation of both partners was not uncommon.

A vasectomy, although intended to be a permanent method of sterilisation, is probably more reversible than are female sterilisations. However, the man will sometimes have developed anti-sperm antibodies so that the reappearance of motile sperm in the semen after a reversal is not always associated with a return of fertility.

FEMALE BARRIER METHODS

Like the male condom, vaginal barrier methods of contraception can also be traced back to ancient times but, again like the condom, it was the discovery, by Charles Goodyear in 1839, of the vulcanisation of rubber which ultimately led to the manufacture of the device that is known as the diaphragm. The diaphragm, is placed in the vagina to cover the cervix prior to sexual intercourse and acts as a physical barrier to the sperm. It is usually used in conjunction with a spermicidal cream or gel placed on the device as added protection against the passage of sperm.

Contraceptive chemical vaginal pessaries (no longer popular) only became widely available in the UK in the 1920s and then only to married women. The provision of contraception was greatly influenced by the social attitudes and politics of the times and there were many (mainly male) opponents who feared the consequences of allowing free rein to women's 'baser instincts'! The development of the diaphragm contributed to the emancipation of women by providing them with a means of controlling their fertility. The device reached its peak of popularity in the late 1950s but, with the advent of the oral contraceptive pill, the use of the diaphragm declined to less than 5% of the UK's contraceptive users.

Although the diaphragm is the most widely used of the vaginal methods, there are other devices that are designed to cover the cervix. These include the cervical cap, the vault cap and the vimule. US women usually use these terms correctly but, in the UK, the diaphragm is often, incorrectly, called a 'cap'.

The fact that the diaphragm provides contraception which is under the woman's control may be useful (this can be an important consideration especially if the male partner is prone to alcohol or drug abuse, rendering condom use unreliable). It has few side effects beyond the occasional allergy to the spermicidal preparation (and, rarely, to the material of the diaphragm itself). It offers protection against sexually transmitted diseases and may reduce the incidence of premalignant changes to the cervical cells. It can be inserted up to 4 hours before intercourse and, once correctly positioned, is not usually felt by either partner. It is acceptably effective if used with care but it is more reliable in the older woman whose fertility is declining. Some experience is required in its use, rather higher failure rates being quoted in women who have used the method for less than two years.

The principle disadvantage is that the appropriate size must first be assessed by a suitably trained doctor or nurse. It is unsuitable for women who are not comfortable with touching their genital area and is therefore more likely to be rejected by women who do not use tampons. Its use is somewhat inconvenient and it can occasionally cause pressure upon the bladder neck leading to urinary tract infections. Small abrasions may occur within the vagina during insertion or removal especially in pre-menopausal women in whom the falling level of circulating oestrogens has caused thinning of the vaginal skin.

Vaginal barrier methods of contraception share many of the disadvantages of the male condom whilst not having the benefit of being available without prescription. The female condom was developed in order to fill this gap in the contraceptive market, but despite being available since the early 1990s, it has not proved to be widely popular.

INTRAUTERINE CONTRACEPTIVE DEVICES (IUCDS)

The use of the abbreviation IUCD is strongly advised rather that the equally, or perhaps more widely, used IUD as the latter may be confused with 'intrauterine death' of a foetus in pregnancy. The terms 'coil' or 'loop' are often used by the lay public.

Intrauterine contraceptive devices are solid objects retained within the uterine cavity that either prevent implantation or occasionally fertilisation. Various types of device have been used since the 19th century, but they have only been widely accepted since the early 1960s when the Lippes' Loop was devised by Jack Lippes. One reason for their previous unpopularity was that they had been used to aid (illegal) abortions and were therefore associated with serious, life threatening infections and with abnormal vaginal bleeding. As with other contraceptive methods, usage of the IUCD varies greatly from country to country, in the UK about 5% of the fertile population use the method but it is much more popular in China.

Types of IUCD

Although other gynaecologists, mainly in Germany, were using intrauterine contraceptive devices from the beginning of this century, it was the painstaking research carried out by Ernst Grafenberg (1881–1957) which laid the groundwork for later developments. Grafenberg first used a device of silkworm gut but later changed to a ring of German silver (its 26% copper content accidentally anticipating subsequent discoveries).

The first generation of the modern plastic devices was piloted by the Japanese physician, Tenrei Ota but only gained wide acceptance when the US gynaecologist, Jack Lippes, introduced the Lippes' Loop in 1959. This was a double 'S' shaped device designed to conform to the shape of the uterine cavity with a thread attached for easy removal. Numerous other designs followed, though none gained greater worldwide acceptance until the development of the copper-bearing IUCDs typified by the 'Gravigard'. The addition of a fine copper wire wound round the vertical stem improved the contraceptive effect and allowed a reduction in the overall size. Although the 'Gravigard' is no longer in production, many other similar IUCDs are still fitted.

The third generation of modern IUCDs substitute controlled progestogen release for copper wire. This not only further improves the contraceptive effectiveness but also tends to reduce menstrual bleeding. These IUCDs are sometimes referred to by the alternative title of Intrauterine System (IUS) and may be described as bioactive (meaning that they have biological activity due to the presence of the progestogen).

The IUCD is very effective, independent of intercourse, reversible and relatively inexpensive. Once inserted it requires almost no further action until it is removed to allow conception or, routinely, after four to five years. The non-bioactive devices have no apparent effects on other parts of the body and even from the progestogen releasing devices only very small amounts of the hormone are absorbed, much less than with any oral progestogen contraceptive.

A disadvantage of the IUCD is that it requires insertion by trained personnel, a procedure which may cause marked discomfort and which, especially when inexpertly carried out, may be hazardous. It may not be the best choice of contraception for the woman who has never been pregnant and side effects may prompt a request for removal of the device. In the event of contraceptive failure, there is an increased risk that the pregnancy will abort (see below).

Side effects and complications

The greatest proportion of the complications occur at or soon after insertion of the device and the procedure is therefore discussed in some detail.

Insertion

Any person inserting an IUCD into the uterine cavity should have previously received proper training in the procedure and should maintain expertise by regular insertions. The device should ideally be fitted within the first half of the menstrual cycle (except when it is used for post-coital contraception) to minimise the risk of a pre-existing pregnancy. After bimanual examination to determine the position of the uterus (that is, anteverted, axial or retroverted), the cervix should be thoroughly cleaned with antiseptic solution and a metal or plastic 'sound' passed into the uterine cavity to determine the length of the uterine cavity. The device is then inserted and the threads trimmed to approximately 5 cm from the cervix. The procedure usually causes some discomfort though this can be reduced by the use of a local anaesthetic injection into the cervix (though, for some women, the injection of the anaesthetic may be more uncomfortable than the insertion of the device). Anaesthetic is more likely to be necessary if the IUCD is inserted into a uterus which has never held a pregnancy, as the cervix may be tightly closed.

Perforation

It is possible for the device to be pushed partially or completely through the uterine wall, though this may not be appreciated at the time. Complete perforation results in placement of the device in the pelvic cavity; this may also occur with partial perforations when the device is later extruded from the uterine wall by the normal contractions of that organ. The presence of an inert plastic device (for example, Lippes' Loop) in the peritoneal cavity is usually of no significance (apart, of course, from its ineffectiveness as a contraceptive) but the woman will usually request its removal. It is usual to advise removal of second generation (copper-bearing) devices as they are more likely to cause peritoneal adhesions. Removal can usually be achieved by laparoscopic techniques.

Expulsion

Expulsion of the device into the vagina can also occur being more common if the device was inserted incorrectly or during heavy menstrual bleeding. Expulsion may not be recognised and leaves the woman without contraception; consequently, she should be advised to examine her upper vagina after each menstrual period to confirm that the threads of the IUCD remain in position at the cervix. If she is unable to locate the threads she should consider herself unprotected and should use another method of contraception.

Missing threads

If a woman attends her doctor because she has been unable to locate the IUCD string, the device may be correctly placed but with the string drawn up within the uterine cavity, the device may have been expelled or it may have perforated the uterine wall to come to lie wholly or partially within the abdominal cavity. Gentle exploration of the uterine cavity in the outpatient clinic should reveal the presence of the device but, if it cannot be reliably located, an ultrasound scan can be performed to establish the whereabouts of the device. If it is not ultrasonically visualised, an X-ray of the abdomen should be arranged. Since all IUCDs are radio-opaque, the absence of the device on X-ray may be taken as evidence that it has been expelled. However, it is important to bear in mind that the whole of the peritoneal cavity may have to be checked since devices have been known to migrate as far at the lower surface of the diaphragm.

Even a properly inserted device may later be found to have its string curled up in the uterine cavity and therefore neither visible nor palpable vaginally. Provided that correct positioning of the device can be confirmed this does not affect its effectiveness but it does make regular checking impossible. It may be possible to retrieve the string by traction with a suitable (sterile) instrument but care must be taken to avoid dislodging the device in the attempt.

The string may also be drawn up into the cavity by the enlargement of the uterus in pregnancy. A woman who had been fitted with an IUCD returned a short time later to report that the string had disappeared. The doctor assumed that the device had been expelled and fitted another but the same thing happened again. By the time the woman arrived in one of the author's outpatient clinics, her uterus contained not only a pregnancy but three IUCDs!

Pelvic infection

A variety of bacteria and other organisms may be present in the vagina but only a very small proportion of these will ever make the journey up the cervical canal, through the uterine cavity and along the fallopian tubes to cause a pelvic infection. This is probably because the cervical mucus offers a barrier which organisms find difficult to cross. If the cervix and upper vagina have been inadequately cleansed or if poor technique has caused contamination of the IUCD, the introduction of the device through the cervical canal may carry infection into the uterine cavity whence onward passage along the tubes may be easier.

The insertion of the IUCD may also cause a flare-up of pre-existing pelvic inflammation and, if the condition is suspected from the clinical history or examination, a device should not be fitted before a full treatment regime has been completed. Unfortunately, low-grade, chronic pelvic sepsis may be virtually asymptomatic and may not always be identified even with the most careful preliminaries. A wise precaution prior to the insertion of a IUCD is to test for the presence of Chlamydia (one of the commonest organism implicated in chronic pelvic infection) or to prescribe an appropriate antibiotic at the time of insertion as prophylactic therapy.

The occurrence of pelvic infection after the fitting of an IUCD may therefore be indicative of poor insertion technique (failure to adequately cleanse the vagina and cervix or failure to maintain sterile precautions), it may be a relapse of the pre-existing condition and it may be due to the intra-cavity inoculation of organisms, especially Chlamydia, already present in the cervical canal. Furthermore, it is, of course, possible that the infection is newly acquired and this is more likely to occur in women who have multiple sexual partners or who have begun a new sexual relationship within the preceding three months.

Although an IUCD does not *cause* infection if properly fitted, the presence of a device within the uterine cavity tends to exacerbate the condition and may prevent adequate treatment. If, therefore, an infection is acquired with a device in situ, prompt antibiotic treatment should be initiated and continued for at least ten days. The clinical situation reviewed 24–48 hours later and unless there has been an obvious improvement the device must be removed.

The details of recent sexual intercourse must be sought whenever an IUCD is removed and the need for post-coital hormonal contraception should also be considered.

Any pelvic inflammation may result in damage to the fallopian tubes and cause subsequent problems with the conception of pregnancy. Consequently, intra-uterine devices may not be the most suitable method of contraception for young women who have not yet had children especially as sexually transmitted infections are more common in the younger age group probably because of a greater tendency to have multiple partners.

A special problem is created by the organism *actinomycoses*, a fungal infection. This organism can cause rare but serious, sometimes life-threatening, infections of the lungs and other organs as well as of the pelvis but, in women fitted with an IUCD, it may be found in the vagina where is appears to be relatively innocuous. It seems to survive in the vagina only in the presence of a local foreign body (in addition to its association with IUCDs, one author has also found it to be present in conjunction with a ring pessary) and the incidence rises with the length of time the device has been present. Vaginal actinomycosis causes no symptoms and its significance is unclear but, because of the possible risk of spread to other pelvic structures, it is usually regarded as an indication for the removal of the device, whereupon the infestation will resolve. A new IUCD may be fitted after an interval of two to three months. Recent publications have suggested that treatment with penicillin may also be effective and that removal of the device may not always be necessary.

Menstrual problems

Approximately 50% of women will find that they experience increased menstrual bleeding (in amount, duration or both) after the fitting of an IUCD but less than 10% will consider this to be severe enough to warrant abandoning the method. Pre-existing menorrhagia is, however, a relative contraindication to the choice of this form of contraception.

If heavy bleeding proves a problem, the use of a progestogen releasing IUCD may be considered. These will usually cause increased loss in the first two or three cycles but, thereafter, the bleeding will almost always diminish and may stop altogether.

Pregnancy

In the event of contraceptive failure with an IUCD in situ, the pregnancy may implant normally or it may be extra-uterine (ectopic).

If the pregnancy is intrauterine, it is advisable to remove the IUCD providing that this can be achieved without undue difficulty as the continued presence of the device is associated with an increased risk of miscarriage and possibly a greater chance of an intrauterine infection should such a miscarriage occur. Unfortunately, the IUCD removal itself is also associated with miscarriages, though, in such cases, the risk is only transient.

If the pregnancy is terminated, it is important to remove the device at the same time. It is possible to reinsert another IUCD at the time of the termination but this is inadvisable since the incidence of complications is likely to be higher. In addition, many women will not wish to continue with a method of contraception which has already let them down.

Ectopic pregnancy

The IUCD is extremely effective in reducing the numbers of intrauterine pregnancies but has much less effect in preventing implantations outside the uterine cavity. (That there is some reduction in the incidence of ectopic pregnancies is thought to be due to increased tubal activity when a foreign body is present within the uterus.) This differential effect means that, although the absolute numbers of ectopic pregnancies are less in women with IUCDs, the chance of an ectopic is higher in the pregnancies which do occur. If a woman conceives despite the continued presence of an IUCD it is therefore essential to consider the possibility that the pregnancy is ectopic and it would be difficult to defend any failure in this respect.

Contraindications

Active or recent pelvic infection should be regarded as an absolute bar to the insertion of an IUCD though it may be reasonable to fit a device in such women if they have been symptom free for six months or more following appropriate therapy. An existing pregnancy is, of course, a contraindication (but, see 'Post-coital contraception', below).

Menorrhagia is a relative contraindication as is an increased potential risk of contracting a sexually transmitted disease. An IUCD may be an unwise choice for women who have a past history of an ectopic pregnancy and also for young women who have never been pregnant since the nulliparous uterus is less likely to tolerate the presence of the device.

Prior to the fitting of an IUCD, the woman must be warned of the risks and side effects of these devices and told to report early for medical assessment if they suspect that they may be pregnant or if they experience abdominal pain and pyrexia.

HORMONAL METHODS OF CONTRACEPTION

Hormonal methods are the most effective yet also the most reversible of all the available methods of contraception. Introduced in the 1960s, the 'pill' was an important part of the sexual revolution and, for the first time, provided an effective contraception that was under the woman's control. Hormonal methods now include a wide variety of formulations encompassing not only tablets but also injectable preparations, implants and the progestogen releasing IUCD (see above).

In tablet form, the pill may be one of two basic types either containing progestogen only (often called the 'mini pill') or containing both progestogen and oestrogen (the 'combined' pill).

Oral combined contraceptive pills (OCCPs or COCPs)

Combined oral contraceptive tablets contain both oestrogen and a progestogen. These were the first oral contraceptives to be introduced and are still the most widely used, although their popularity has varied. It is still used by approximately 30% of female contraceptive users in the UK (progestogen only tablets are used by less than 5%). With a Pearl Index (see above) of 0.2, oral contraception is more reliable than any other non-permanent method except the new hormone releasing IUCDs.

The contraceptive effect is primarily due to prevention of ovulation supplemented by the secondary mechanisms of rendering the cervical mucous less permeable to sperm and also causing the uterine lining to be less favourable to the implantation of a conceptus (the fertilised ovum) should ovulation and fertilisation occur. Prevention of ovulation is by the provision of small doses of synthetic oestrogen and progestogen hormones daily, thereby blocking the normal interaction of the hypothalamus, the pituitary gland and the ovary. The tablets are usually taken for 21 days followed by 7 tablet-free days, during which time the woman will experience vaginal bleeding. It is important to appreciate that this monthly bleeding is not a normal menstrual bleed as it does not result from the normal hormonal cycle but originates from the temporary withdrawal of the synthetic hormones in the pill-free week. It is therefore better described as a 'withdrawal bleed' than a 'period'.

Women often consider the monthly bleeding to be a reassurance though it is not essential either for a contraceptive effect or for general health.

The advantages of oral contraceptives are that they are a very effective and easily reversible form of contraception as well as being independent of sexual intercourse.

Non-contraceptive uses

In addition to their contraceptive effects, these preparations have beneficial non-contraceptive functions that are sometimes overlooked. Menstrual bleeding is usually lighter, less painful and more regular, making these preparations useful in the management of some cases of menorrhagia and dysmenorrhoea. They provide some protection against pelvic inflammatory disease (probably because of the pill's effect upon the cervical mucous) and they substantially reduce the incidence of ectopic pregnancies; these two features make oral contraceptives a popular choice for the young woman with no children.

They can be used for the treatment of endometriosis and one type is also helpful in the treatment of some forms of hirsutism. They also reduce the incidence of cysts both in the breast and the ovary as well as considerably lessening the risk of the later development of ovarian and uterine (endometrial) cancers.

Unwanted side effects

A disadvantage of the oral contraceptives is that, since they are absorbed, they can have systemic effects. These may be minor side effects or more serious complications.

A common side effect, especially with very low dose formulations, is scanty, irregular, vaginal bleeding often called 'break-through bleeding'. Women also sometimes complain of a sensation of abdominal bloating.

Infrequent but more serious effects are those on the heart and circulation, the liver, the cervix and the breast tissue.

Cardiovascular effects include an increased risk of thrombosis in the deep veins of the legs (deep venous thrombosis or DVT), whence fragments of clot may break off and travel to the lungs (pulmonary embolus or PE), an event which, in severe cases, may be fatal. Oral combined contraceptives may also cause raised blood pressure, strokes (cerebrovascular accident or CVA) and heart attacks (myocardial infarction or MI). Women with a predisposition to these conditions should therefore not use these preparations without first obtaining specialist advice. Fortunately, the conditions are uncommon in women, especially in the younger age groups, but anyone taking combined oral preparations should be warned to report the occurrence of headaches or of unexplained pain in the legs or chest.

Women at greater risk are those with other factors that increase the chance of circulatory problems. These may be related to their life style (for example, smoking), their general condition (for example, age and weight) or genetic factors as evidenced by their family history. Cigarette smokers over the age of 35 years should probably be advised to stop the combined pill but non-smokers with no other risk factors can continue it until the menopause.

Oral contraceptives increase the chance of developing a benign tumour of the liver (hepatic adenoma), though the condition remains rare even in this group. There is also a small increase in the incidence of cancer of the uterine cervix or of the breast. Women who have had abnormal cervical cytology in the past may continue to take the pill but should have annual cervical smear tests.

Assessment

Before prescribing an oral contraceptive, the doctor should take a full account of the woman's medical history. This can often be done most effectively by asking her to fill in a proforma questionnaire. If any potential problems are identified, the doctor should then obtain more detailed information to elicit the exact nature of the problem and decide whether the proposed method of contraception is still suitable. A particular example is a history of migraine associated with the loss of the use of any part of the body which may indicate an increased risk of a stroke.

The woman should then be examined and her weight and blood pressure recorded. A vaginal examination should be performed and a cervical smear taken unless it is known to have been normal within the previous two years.

The woman's understanding of her contraceptive method is often greatly improved if she is given information leaflets such as those published by the Family Planning Association but these should supplement, rather than replace, proper discussion.

Progestogen only contraceptives

Progestogens, progesterone precursors, can circumvent many of the problems of the oestrogen containing oral contraceptives. Progestogens do have some circulatory effects but these are much less pronounced than with the combined preparations. For example, a woman who has developed a raised blood pressure whilst taking a combined preparation is much less likely to remain hypertensive when changed to a progestogen only product. Progestogen methods of contraception are the 'mini pill' (or POP), long acting injections (two to three months), implants that last for five years or the progestogen releasing IUCD. These methods occasionally cause irregular bleeding or may result in the cessation of all uterine bleeding (amenorrhoea).

Oral progestogen preparations are much more 'time critical' than combined pills and should be taken at about the same time every day (certainly within about 2–3 hours). The long acting methods have the advantage of not requiring a daily regime, though the woman must still remember to attend at the appropriate intervals.

POST-COITAL CONTRACEPTION

Post-coital contraception is more widely used than is often appreciated. It may taken the form of a combined oestrogen/progestogen preparation (100 mg ethinyloestradiol and 500 mg levonorgestrel) taken within 72 hours of sexual intercourse and repeated 12 hours later. Alternatively, an intrauterine contraceptive device may be fitted up to five days after intercourse.

If a conception occurs despite hormonal post-coital measures, a termination of the pregnancy may be considered as there is a theoretical risk of foetal malformation. If an IUCD has been inserted, it should be managed as in the case of any other pregnancy with a device in situ (see above). The circumstances will often prompt the woman to seek a termination anyway.

CHAPTER 11

ELECTIVE STERILISATION

Various techniques have been employed in the attempt to offer permanent contraception. Some are now of historical interest only but the fact that several remain in current usage is evidence that no single method has proved universally suitable.

Although several of the methods were devised with the intention of offering the potential of reasonably easy reversal should the patient's circumstances or wishes change, the difficulty and unreliably of all such reversals render it sound clinical practice that no sterilisation procedure should ever be undertaken unless the patient is fully aware that the intention is to permanently remove all possibility of further fertility.

In a few cases, the sterilisation may be undertaken because of some serious medical condition which is likely to be adversely affected by the conception of a pregnancy, for example a severe and untreatable cardiac problem, but the majority are performed for what may be described as 'social' reasons where family size, financial considerations and personal preferences may be among the deciding factors.

Sterilisation may, of course, be performed on either the male or the female partner but, this being a book on gynaecology, the discussion here is be concerned with sterilisation of the woman. Nevertheless, many of the considerations apply with equal force to male sterilisation (vasectomy).

The procedures themselves are generally straightforward and are often performed by gynaecologists who have not yet acquired consultant status; this is appropriate providing the individual concerned has received the necessary training and supervision but the more difficult part of the event is the prior counselling which should take place and which requires sensitivity and experience.

Before any decision is taken concerning a request for sterilisation, a medical and social history should be obtained. A few women may resent this, seeing it as an unwarranted intrusion into their private life but it must be understood that the medical staff are responsible for their actions and that it is therefore only reasonable that they should have the opportunity of assessing the request properly. It is also important to establish that the woman does not have any unwarranted expectations concerning the sterilisation, especially with regard to its reversibility.

Most forms of elective sterilisation have a small failure rate but, in the past, this was not always explained to the patient. As a result of a number of successful claims for failed sterilisation, it is now the strong recommendation of all the medical defence societies that the woman should be told of the possibility of a failure leading to a subsequent pregnancy. This does not, of course, absolve the medical staff from carrying out the procedure with due care since a conception due to incompetence cannot be defended simply because the possibility of failure has been explained.

As with all surgical procedures, the approximate position and size of any surgical incisions should be described. In the case of sterilisations which are to be carried out laparoscopically, it is also important to establish whether, should the laparoscopic route prove impractical for any reason, the woman would wish a laparotomy to be performed or that the attempt should be abandoned.

The counselling should try to establish, so far as it is practically possible, that the woman will not afterwards have serious regrets over the loss of her fertility and, although every case must be assessed on its own merits, the senior author regards marital instability as an almost absolute contraindication to permanent sterilisation. All too often, the woman will have made the request in the hope of healing the rift with her partner only to find that the relationship breaks down anyway causing her to seek reversal of the sterilisation should she later acquire a new partner.

In the past, there was an important difference between male and female sterilisation on the matter of consent in that the sterilisation of a married woman required the prior consent of her husband whereas a man did not need to have his wife's consent to undergo a vasectomy. In these enlightened times of sexual equality, there is no obligation to even inform the other partner, though it is, of course, desirable that they should be in agreement.

Occasionally, women will request sterilisation when already pregnant or even when about to undergo a Caesarean section. Whilst there are practical advantages to tubal ligation at the Caesarean operation (only one operation is required) and to surgery during the puerperium (the need for postpartum contraception and for later re-admission are avoided), these are generally bad times to make a decision on future fertility and it is often preferable to postpone the discussion until the baby has been delivered and appears to be healthy. The failure rate of sterilisations performed in association with a recent pregnancy may also be a little higher than when they are done at other times.

The medical notes must contain a record of the discussion and should include sufficient detail to establish that proper explanations have been given. The exact form which this record should take is not fixed and clinicians will vary in the amount of detail they write but it is generally considered essential that two points are specifically noted: first, that the woman knows that the procedure is intended to be irreversible; and secondly, that she also understands the possibility of failure.

METHODS

Historical methods

A few methods of elective sterilisation are no longer practised but, because they may occasionally be encountered in the past history of older women, they are mentioned briefly.

Ovarian irradiation

The discovery that irradiation of the ovaries with X-rays caused cessation of their function was, at first, thought to offer a simple, non-surgical method of sterilisation. It was soon apparent, however, that the resulting ovarian failure affected not only the production of ova but also produced a premature menopause with all its associated disadvantages. In addition, some ovaries would not fail completely or would recover function at a later date, with the possibility that the previous irradiation of the primordial follicles might give rise to the birth of genetically abnormal progeny. Eventually, recognition of the inherent risks caused ovarian irradiation to be abandoned for this indication.

Burying of the ovaries

This operation was performed by the creation of a suitable opening in the back of the broad ligament and burying the ovary between the two leaves of that structure thereby placing the ovaries outside the peritoneal cavity and preventing the tubes from picking up the released ova. This was intended to allow easy reversal by simply bringing the ovaries out from under the peritoneum again.

Unfortunately, the release of follicular fluid within the broad ligament causes a marked inflammatory reaction which may give rise to considerable pelvic pain and which also causes the adjacent tissues to undergo fibrosis rendering later extraction of the ovaries very difficult. Post-operative cyclical pain is common and, contrary to the intention, the procedure is very difficult to reverse; consequently, it is no longer performed.

Current procedures

Methods of sterilisation currently in use may be by laparoscopy, laparotomy or culdotomy. The first of these is the most popular in the UK (and elsewhere) at present whilst the third has been widely used in some other countries.

Culdotomy is carried out by positioning the woman in the lithotomy position, placing a suitable speculum in the vagina which is then cleansed and then opening the posterior vaginal fornix to gain access to the pouch of

Douglas, where the tubes can usually be found without great difficulty. After ligation and division of the tubes, the vaginal fornix is sutured with one or two absorbable sutures allowing the patient to return home with no need for follow-up. The most important disadvantage is the risk of a pelvic infection due to the impossibility of rendering the conditions fully aseptic.

The basic techniques of laparoscopy and laparotomy are described elsewhere in this volume (see Chapter 3).

Laparoscopic sterilisation

A large number of methods have been described using laparoscopy. These include tubal cauterisation, coagulation and division of the tubes as well as the application of silastic rings or metal and plastic clips across them.

Electrocautery to the tubes

Electrocautery was the popular method of laparoscopic sterilisation in the UK during the 1970s. The technique was simple to learn and quick to perform the electrocautery current being applied to the outside of the tubes via a specially designed insulated probe introduced through a second puncture situated about 3 cm above the pubic symphysis and a little away from the midline. (Occasionally, separate punctures on each side were used but, in most cases, both tubes could be reached from one site of introduction.)

Early attempts were associated with a rather high failure rate, probably because the cauterisation was discontinued when blanching of the external surface of the tubes was seen, at which point the endosalpinx had been insufficiently coagulated to produce permanent obstruction. This was largely overcome when cauterisation was performed at two or even three sites on each tube but this resulted in destruction of a large segment of tube (by thermal conduction), so that such sterilisations are almost impossible to reverse as insufficient tube remains for re-anastomosis. Since the operation was intended to be permanent this was, perhaps, not too disadvantageous but, more importantly, a substantial number of cases of damage to other structures were reported. This could occur either because of carelessness in positioning the instrument while its tip was still hot or because of the conduction of the electrical current through the tissues, causing burns at distant sites (often in places outside the field of laparoscopy view). Damage to the bowel wall was not uncommon and might result in later perforation due to ischaemic necrosis, even if no sign of the injury was apparent at the time. Severe peritonitis could follow.

Some surgeons performed cauterisation in three places and then divided the tube at the middle site with scissors but this did not significantly improve the reliability of the operation.

Thermocoagulation and unipolar diathermy

Because of the risks associated with the use of standard electrocautery equipment, manufacturers developed special machines to supply comparatively low temperature heating to the tubes and diathermy probes which carried the electrical current in both directions (thereby avoiding conduction through the other tissues). Although unipolar diathermy is still used occasionally, neither of these methods became widely adopted because, at about the same time and for the same reasons, rings and then clips were devised which were both safer and more reliable. The senior author has had only one case of failed sterilisation of which he is aware and that was performed by thermocoagulation because the ring applicator had been broken. Happily, the patient, despite having originally requested the sterilisation, was pleased to have conceived again!

Fallope rings

A special instrument is used, which consists of grasping forceps which slide inside a long, thin, double walled cylinder. The fallopian tube is grasped about its mid-point and drawn up into the cylinder. The fallope ring, which is made of silastic and resembles a tiny rubber band, has already been loaded by stretching it over the end of the inner cylinder and is then applied to the base of the loop of tube by advancing the outer cylinder. This causes ischaemic necrosis of the underlying tissues and consequent tubal obstruction.

The method can result in troublesome bleeding if the mesosalpinx is torn as the loop of tube is created and the technique is unsuitable for bulky tubes (for example, in the puerperium) which cannot be drawn into the instrument. In addition, failures were reported due to spontaneous re-anastomosis of the tube below the ring (very much as can happen with the Madlener operation (see below). For these reasons, rings have now been superseded by clips.

Hulka and Filshie clips

Laparoscopic clip sterilisation is now the most widely practised form of female sterilisation in most developed countries. It is quick, safe and, when correctly performed, has a failure rate which is probably substantially lower than the usually quoted figure of one in 1,000.

The two popular types of clips are those described by Hulka in 1972 and by Filshie in 1974. Though differing in pattern, both work on the same principle, that of causing ischaemic necrosis of the tube (and hence obstruction) by the application of a small clamp across the mid-portion of each fallopian tube. Both have jaws lined by plastic, the Hulka clip being held closed by an external spring while the Filshie clip locks at its distal end. Both are designed to maintain pressure on the tube as the tissue enclosed within them decreases in volume.

It is important that candidates for clip sterilisation understand that this, like all other current methods, is intended to be permanent. Some patients imagine the clips to be rather like a strong clothes peg applied across a garden hose and therefore think of the method as reversible simply by removal of the clip; this misapprehension is fostered by some doctors who tell patients that the technique is easily reversible. Although it is true that the damage caused by the clip is more localised and therefore more easily excised than that produced by other methods, clip sterilisation should not be undertaken unless the woman wishes its effect to be permanent.

A few surgeons routinely apply two clips to each tube (but see 'Sterilisation failures', below).

It is essential that the spring of the Hulka clip and the locking mechanism of the Filshie are checked and confirmed to be secure before the operation can be regarded as complete, since both types have been known to fail by opening (presumably soon after the laparoscope was withdrawn).

Steptoe rods

In an attempt to devise a truly reversible sterilisation, Patrick Steptoe (who, with Robert Edwards, also developed in vitro fertilisation) tried the laparoscopically controlled insertion of a semi-rigid plastic rod into the tubal lumen from the distal end. The rod had small swellings along its length and was held in place by a non-crushing clip applied to the outside of the tube. Unfortunately, the failure rate was quite high and the presence of the rod predisposed the resulting pregnancy to implant in the tube as ectopic pregnancies.

Open operation methods

Before the popularisation of laparoscopic methods in the 1970s, sterilisations were normally performed at open operation (laparotomy) though the normal mobility of the tubes generally allowed a smaller incision than usual and this is often referred to as a 'mini-laparotomy'. These procedures are now usually reserved for occasions when a sterilisation is requested but the abdomen is being opened for some other reason, for example, at Caesarean section.

A large number of methods (more than 100) have been described and only the most popular are mentioned here.

Madlener's operation

A loop of tube about 5 cm long is lifted up, its base is crushed and a ligature of non-absorbable suture material tied around the loop. This leaves the damaged ends of the tube in close proximity, with the result that a small number may re-canalise under the ligature, allowing the passage of sperm and thus enabling a conception to take place distal to the obstruction. The fertilised egg is, however, often too big to traverse the constriction and a tubal ectopic pregnancy results.

Pomeroy's operation

Two crushing clamps are applied across the tube about 3 cm apart and the intervening tube is excised. Secure ligatures are then tied around the crushed parts of the tube.

This leaves the damaged ends of the tube separated by several centimetres, thereby avoiding the problem of the Madlener technique. Failures have been described due to the spontaneous re-opening of the proximal tubal segment (that is, the part still connected to the uterus).

Virtually the same technique is used when the approach is via a posterior culdotomy (see above).

The Oxford technique

The method of open sterilisation usually adopted by the author, and one for which there is a very low failure rate, is that first practised at the Radcliffe Infirmary in Oxford. After performing a Pomeroy operation, the cut ends of the tube are separated by the round ligament, the proximal end being sutured behind that structure whilst the distal end is secured in front.

Cornuectomy

A few gynaecologists have used cornuectomy as a method of sterilisation. In this operation, the part of the tube closest to the uterus together with that part of the uterine wall containing the intra-mural part of the tube are excised. The excised portion of the uterus is wedge shaped, so that sides can be brought together with sutures.

Bilateral salpingectomy

An uncommon but effective method of elective sterilisation is the removal of the entire tube on both sides. This leaves no possibility of reversal. (The more modern endoscopic surgery techniques allow salpingectomies to be performed laparoscopically if the surgeon is suitably trained.)

Hysteroscopic sterilisations

A small number of sterilisations have been performed hysteroscopically. This has been done by the passage of a fine, insulated probe with an exposed tip into the tube, the probe then being used to carry a cauterising electrical current. Other methods involve the intra-tubal injection of sclerosant substances or even 'super glue'. None of these techniques has found wide acceptance and they must still be considered to be experimental.

OPERATIONS FOR OTHER INDICATIONS

Bilateral oophorectomy has been used to sterilise women in the past but the associated endocrine changes may be profound and the ovaries are now only removed for other reasons such as hormone dependent breast carcinomas and a few cases of very severe endometriosis.

Removal of the uterus at hysterectomy does involve the loss of fertility which may be an extra benefit or a disadvantage depending on the circumstances.

STERILISATION FAILURES

No method of sterilisation is completely free of reported failures and the reasons for some of these are mentioned above. Probably the commonest reason for failure is that the wrong structure has been operated upon, usually the round ligament or the ovarian ligament. An essential precaution is that the tube is positively identified by looking for its fimbrial end which is quite unlike any adjacent structure. This is especially true during laparoscopy, when the view is necessarily more limited.

It is generally considered that failures occurring within the first six months of sterilisation are more likely to be due to operator failure, whereas those occurring at more than two years after the operation are more probably due to natural causes.

When acting as an independent expert, the senior author encountered one case where a particularly cautious consultant gynaecologist had sterilised a woman by the application of two Filshie clips on each side. The right tube was securely obstructed but a pregnancy occurred in the uterus because the other two clips had been placed on the left ovarian ligament; no matter how many clips are used they will fail if incorrectly used. Needless to say, the claim was settled out of court.

Ideally, sterilisation should be carried out in the first half of the menstrual cycle (prior to ovulation) to avoid the small possibility that a pregnancy may already be present within the uterus at the time of the operation. This is not always practical, especially in National Health Service practice, where the appropriate selection of the operation date may prove more difficult than in private practice, and it is a wise precaution to perform a light curettage to the endometrium at the same time.

The occurrence of a pregnancy after sterilisation is clear evidence of failure but, before any medico-legal liability can be established, it will usually be necessary to determine the reason for the failure. This may require a laparoscopy, often with the introduction of coloured fluid into the uterine cavity to demonstrate any openings in the tubes. Alternatively, a hysterosalpingogram may provide the needed information.

CHAPTER 12

INFERTILITY

Reproduction of the species is perhaps the most essential of all animal functions but human reproduction, like that of other animals, formerly depended largely on chance and it is only during the present century that 'family planning' has become a reality. For many couples, conception is still a matter of chance and, despite the availability of contraception, some pregnancies will be unwanted and may be terminated. In contrast, the inability to achieve a wanted pregnancy is a source of considerable distress to many other couples.

Some infertile couples will accept their childless lot and will not seek medical assistance but, increasingly, both men and women are coming to regard the gift of a child as a right if they so desire. Modern medical techniques have gone a long way to support that view.

DEFINITION

Whilst infertility, perhaps more optimistically termed 'sub-fertility', is obviously a difficulty in achieving a conception, there is no universally accepted definition of the time for which the couple should have been trying to conceive. In the past, couples were often advised to try for two years before investigations would be commenced but the combination of more effective treatments and greater patient expectations has tended to reduce this to nine to 12 months. The increasing trend for women to work during their 20s and 30s also means that attempts to start a family may be postponed so that there may be more urgency about identifying any problems before the inevitable fall in fertility in the late 30s or early 40s.

'Primary infertility' means that the woman has never conceived a pregnancy and 'secondary infertility' implies that she has conceived before. In clinical practice, this classification, though always emphasised in the teaching of medical students, is of no great value since the investigations are essentially the same. It may also be misleading; a woman suffering from 'secondary infertility' may not have had a child but only a miscarriage whilst another may have had pregnancies by a former partner but not in her current relationship.

ASSESSMENT

Clinical history

As with any other medical complaint, the investigation of the failure to conceive begins with the taking of an appropriate history. In this case, the history must include not only current and past medical and surgical problems but also social and sexual elements. This is often best done by the GP who will probably already know something of the couple's background.

The woman should be questioned about her past menstrual history with particular reference to any episodes of amenorrhoea and, of course, details must be elicited about any previous pregnancies. The average frequency of sexual intercourse should be determined, as should the timing of coitus in relation to the menstrual cycle. This may also provide the opportunity to resolve any misunderstandings about the physiology involved.

The male partner should be asked about any pregnancies he may have fathered with other women, though this information must be interpreted with care especially if it relates to extra-marital relationships. He should also be questioned about any problems that he may have experienced with penile erection or with ejaculation.

The family history may be relevant, especially if the woman's mother or a sister has also experienced difficulties with conception.

Examination

A general clinical examination of the woman should be performed, not only to identify any obvious factors influencing her fertility but also to look for any condition (for example, previously undetected heart disease) which might cause problems if treatment results in a pregnancy.

A gynaecological examination follows with inspection of the vulva, vagina and cervix. Bimanual pelvic examination should identify any abnormal masses or any tenderness. A smear should be taken for cervical cytology unless this has been done recently.

Any vaginal discharge should certainly be investigated by one swab for general bacteriology and another specifically for chlamydia. A good case can be made for taking these swabs in *all* cases.

The male partner should also be examined, especially with reference to any anatomical abnormality of his penis which could influence intromission or ejaculation, to assess the size and consistency of the testes and to look for any scrotal abnormality.

Special Investigations

The basic assessment of fertility can be resolved into four areas under the following headings:

(a) ovulation;

(b) semen;

(c) tubes; and

(d) sperm-mucus interaction.

Ovulation

'Ovulation' here refers not only to establishing whether an ovum is released and when in the cycle this occurs but, also, to whether the levels of the relevant hormones are appropriate. The serum level of follicular stimulating hormone (FSH), luteinising hormone (LH) and prolactin should be measured in the first half of the menstrual cycle, and the levels of thyroid stimulating hormone (TSH) and thyroxin (T4) may also be checked if thyroid dysfunction is suspected.

The serum progesterone should be assayed seven days before the start of a menstrual bleed (day 21 in a 28 day cycle and, hence, sometimes called the 'day 21 progesterone'). A level of 10 nmol/l is indicative of corpus luteum function (and, hence, probable ovulation), though a peak value of 30 nmol/l or more is necessary if a fertilised egg is to implant in the uterine cavity.

Ovulation may also be investigated by 'ovarian follicle tracking', in which ultrasonic scans of the ovaries are performed, usually on alternate days, to observe and measure the developing follicle which usually ruptures when it reaches a diameter of 23–24 mm.

The old fashioned basal body temperature chart (BBT) still has a role to play. The rising level of progesterone after ovulation causes a small but detectable rise in the body temperature of most women. This can be observed by recording the oral temperature every day (immediately after waking from sleep) and can help in attempts to predict the timing of ovulation. The principle has also been used to produce a small electronic device which, by the recording of a series of daily temperatures, can 'learn' a woman's menstrual cycle and signal the fertile period. This device can be used either for contraception or to achieve conception depending on whether the fertile period is avoided or favoured for coitus.

Semen

The production of fertile semen must be confirmed by a semen analysis. The sample should be collected into a sterile container by masturbation after three to five days of abstinence. It should preferably reach the laboratory within one hour (certainly no longer than two hours), during which time it should be kept at about body temperature. One of the authors had a patient with a persistently low sperm activity which was only explained when it was established that the semen sample was placed in the refrigerator after collection! Typical normal results are:

Volume:	2–7 ml
Sperm density:	>40 million/ml
Sperm motility:	>60%
Abnormal sperm:	<40%

The presence of pus cells may point to a chronic infection of the seminal vesicles or the prostate and should be investigated further.

All the assessment up to this point can reasonably be carried out by the GP (though the special tests are more commonly arranged after referral to a hospital clinic) but the following investigations are usually hospital based.

Tubes

Patency of at least one fallopian tube is a pre-requisite for normal conception and there are two methods generally available for the assessment of the tubal state. The first, distinguished by the imposing title of hysterosalpingography (HSG), is an radiological procedure, in which X-ray contrast medium is instilled into the uterine cavity through an instrument attached to the cervix. The flow of the contrast can be observed on screen as it passes along the tubes and spills out into the pelvic cavity. A permanent record can be made by video recording or, more usually, by taking a number of radiographs. In the past, the contrast medium was usually oil based, which gave good contrast but was too viscous to outline small abnormalities. It could also remain in a blocked tube for weeks or even months, whereas the water based media in use today are cleared in a matter of hours. Oily media were also more prone to provoke an inflammatory reaction.

A recent variant of the traditional HSG uses a fluid containing very small particles which reflect ultrasound, enabling the passage of the fluid along the tubes to be observed by real-time ultrasonic scanning. This avoids the need for X-ray exposure but cannot demonstrate as much detail as the older technique.

Hysterosalpingography is normally done as an outpatient procedure at a time when the woman is not menstruating and when she could not already be pregnant (usually, therefore, before the 11th day of the cycle). Although simple in concept, the procedure does require a certain amount of technical ability and sound interpretation of the findings also demands experience. Unfortunately, the investigation is often poorly executed and inadequately reported but, when correctly carried out, can provide valuable information, not only about tubal patency but also about the cervical canal and the uterine cavity.

The alternative method of tubal assessment is by direct inspection at laparoscopy (see Chapter 3), when a weak solution of a dye (usually methylene blue) can be introduced into the uterine cavity and observed to pass through the tubes. This gives information about the condition of the tubal wall and any surrounding adhesion which is not provided by an HSG but, on the other hand, says nothing about the uterine cavity. The laparoscopy is therefore often combined with hysteroscopy; both techniques can be carried out under mild sedation but general anaesthesia is more common in this country.

Instruments can also be introduced into the tubes themselves to examine the lumen (salpingoscopy) but these instruments are not yet widely available.

Sperm-mucus interaction

Under the influence of the rising oestrogen level, the cervical mucus becomes favourable to the sperm about four or five days before ovulation and remains so until a rising progesterone renders it inhospitable within about 36 hours of the release of the ovum. The investigation of mucus-sperm interaction must therefore be performed during the short window of opportunity; this can be a problem, especially if ovulation is irregular.

If, some hours after sexual intercourse, a sample of the mucus is examined microscopically, numerous sperm should be present, many of which should be moving actively and progressively. This is called a post-coital test (PCT) and is best performed on about day 10 (of a 28 day cycle), between four and eight hours after coitus. The absence of sperm (or the presence of only small numbers) may be due to sub-fertile semen, failure of ejaculation, anatomical abnormalities of the penis (for example, severe hypospadias) or poor mucus penetration because of anti-sperm antibodies. Sluggish or dead sperm present in good numbers may also be associated with the presence of anti-sperm antibodies, especially if the immobilised sperm are clumped together.

Further investigation may be by a 'mucus hostility test', where semen and ovulatory mucus are placed together and the sperm observed microscopically for their ability to enter and survive in the mucus. A poor result may suggest an antibody problem.

It is possible to measure the level of anti-sperm antibodies in serum, semen and mucus (though it may be difficult to obtain a sufficient sample of mucus). Although the problem is often called 'mucus hostility', this is really a misnomer since, of those couples found to have anti-sperm antibodies, in only about 10% of cases will they be present in the woman. Much more common the antibodies are present in the sperm themselves but their effect only becomes manifest when the sperm enter (normal) mucus.

Various other sophisticated tests are available both of antibody levels and of sperm motility, including computerised analysis of sperm movement.

TREATMENT

The 'treatment' of sub-fertility may require only an explanation of the physiological processes involved, so that sexual intercourse takes place at an appropriate time in the cycle, and some couples will achieve success during the course of the assessment. Increasingly, however, more active intervention will be required.

Medical treatment

In the 1950s and 1960s, medical research made considerable advances in the treatment of female infertility factors. Unfortunately, the same cannot yet be said for male sub-fertility, though some progress has taken place.

Bromocriptine

The abnormally high production of prolactin by the pituitary gland (hyperprolactinaemia) may suppress ovulation and can cause amenorrhoea. In the past, this was treated by the surgical ablation of part of the gland or by the use of local radioisotopes to subdue glandular activity. Both methods were associated with significant hazards. In the mid 1960s, it was found that the prolactin level could be reduced by the administration (in tablet form) of a substance called *bromocriptine*. This is much safer than the older treatment and the dosage can be adjusted to match the response in suitable cases. For a while following its introduction, bromocriptine was almost regarded by some as the universal panacea for all infertility problems and this still seems to be the case in some countries where it is prescribed with little regard to the problem being treated. In suitable cases, however, it is very effective.

Anti-oestrogens

Substances with partially anti-oestrogenic effects (principally, clomiphene citrate and tamoxifen) are available. These interfere with the normal negative feedback control of the pituitary-ovarian axis, resulting in an increased drive to the ovary. They may be effective in producing regular ovulation in women who otherwise ovulate infrequently or not at all.

Some concern has been expressed recently over the long term use of clomiphene citrate (for more than about 8–10 months), as it may increase the possibility of ovarian carcinoma in later life.

Exogenous FSH and LH

Not all anovulatory women respond to the anti-oestrogens and it is possible to administer both follicular stimulating hormone and luteinising hormone by injection. Unfortunately, this by-passes the safety of the negative feedback from the ovary to the pituitary gland. Unless the dosage of FSH is carefully monitored, either by daily oestrogen output measurements or by ultrasonic ovarian follicle tracking, there is a risk of ovarian over stimulation, with the possible formation of large ovarian cysts or of high orders of multiple pregnancy; this was the reason for several sets of sextuplets and octuplets some years ago, these pregnancies almost invariably failing due to miscarriage.

Mechanical treatment

In a few cases, the chance of conception may be improved by artificial insemination using the partner's semen (still called AIH, the 'H' standing for 'husband', even though now a high proportion of the couples in many infertility clinics are unmarried). If the partner produces only severely sub-fertile semen or is actually azoospermic, the same techniques can be employed to introduce donor sperm (AID).

AIH was of limited value since it merely placed the semen in the lower cervical mucus; it is now possible to introduce washed sperm directly into the uterine cavity (intra-uterine insemination or IUI). Washing is necessary because the introduction of 'raw' semen into the uterine cavity may cause severe shock.

Surgical treatment

The surgical correction of anatomical deformities and damage may be by hysteroscopy, laparoscopy or laparotomy. The hysteroscopic approach is used for abnormalities of the uterine cavity and includes the removal of endometrial polyps, submucus fibroids, a congenital septum or synaechae (intra-uterine adhesions). Intra-abdominally it may be necessary to divide adhesions, especially if they are peri-tubal (adhesiolysis), or to open the tubes (salpingostomy) or to excise a blocked segment and re-anastomose them. Some surgeons prefer to perform these procedures with the aid of the operating microscope. All tubal surgery carries an increased risk of a subsequent tubal ectopic pregnancy and the wider availability of IVF and the associated techniques have reduced the need for the surgical procedures, though they still have a place in the treatment of some cases.

Advanced treatment

The development of in-vitro fertilisation (IVF) by Patrick Steptoe and Robert Edwards in the mid 1970s caused a revolution in the management of infertility and has spawned a series of related techniques all of which are known by strange acronyms (IGI, GIFT, ICSI, etc). These specialised techniques will not be described in detail here but it may be worth pointing out that, while IVF was originally devised for cases of tubal obstruction, the methods are now also employed in many other situations, including unexplained infertility and male sub-fertility.

The first IVF baby, Louise Brown, was delivered by Caesarean section on 25 July 1978.

CHAPTER 13

ABORTION

DEFINITION

In non-medical circles, the term 'abortion' is usually used to refer to the termination of an early pregnancy by artificial means whereas 'miscarriage' is used for those pregnancy losses occurring because of natural events. The medical term for both of these is an 'abortion', the definition of which is *the termination of a pregnancy before 28 weeks* (note that there is no mention of the cause); 'miscarriage' has no medical definition. This difference in the use of the same word may give rise to confusion. A woman who is already distressed by the loss of a wanted pregnancy may be angered to discover that the medical records describe her as having had an abortion and she may, incorrectly, assume that this implies that she chose to rid herself of the pregnancy. Her anger may cause her to seek legal advice and it is important that her advisers are able to explain the true interpretation.

An abortion may be classified by *cause* (spontaneous or induced), *infection* (septic or non-septic), *stage* (threatened, inevitable, complete or missed) or *occurrence* (isolated or recurrent). Unfortunately, matters are complicated by the fact that these groups are not mutually exclusive so that, for example, an induced abortion may or may not be infected and may have proceeded to any stage.

SPONTANEOUS ABORTION

Pregnancy losses before 28 weeks due to natural causes are termed spontaneous abortions. Although they may occur at any stage of the first seven months they tend to fall into four groups.

Abortions before eight weeks may be hardly more than a slightly delayed and rather heavy menstrual loss, though the greater the delay the more bleeding tends to occur. There is an increased incidence of genetic defects in the aborted tissue and it is likely that some abortions are due to such abnormalities.

The second group tend to occur more commonly at the time of the second or third missed period (that is, at about the eighth or 12th week) and the underlying cause is usually considered to be unknown, though some gynaecologists believe that partial failure of progesterone production by the corpus luteum may play a part in some cases.

'Mid trimester' abortions most often happen at 16–18 weeks and the greater proportion of these are due to cervical incompetence when the cervix uteri fails to remain closed and, by dilating inappropriately early, removes support from the membranes surrounding the pregnancy which then rupture. The cervical weakness may be due to past surgical damage (for example, cone biopsy), previous over dilatation or, rather rarely, an intrinsic defect. Cervical incompetence is correctly (though not infallibly) treated by the insertion of a supporting suture around the cervix in the next pregnancy (usually at about 14 weeks) before the cervix has begun to dilate. Occasionally, and providing the membranes have not ruptured, the suture may be attempted when the cervix has already opened but such 'salvage sutures' have a low rate of success. The suture is called 'cervical cerclage', of which the Shirodkar and MacDonald suture are two variants.

The final group of abortions tends to take place at 22–24 weeks and most of these are due to the premature rupture of the membranes, often in association with infection.

According to the strict definition, *premature labour* cannot occur before the 28th week but, in common with all the causes just mentioned, its effects may become manifest over quite a long period, perhaps as early as twenty weeks. The author managed the fourth pregnancy of a woman whose previous three conceptions had ended in loss of the babies at 28, 27 and 24 weeks, despite cervical cerclage in the second and third. A careful history revealed that, on each occasion, on initial admission to hospital, the cervix had been closed and this was followed by the pain of uterine contractions for several hours before the abortion finally took place. This suggested that the problem was not one of cervical incompetence but rather that the uterus was going into labour too early. No suture was inserted but treatment with a tocolytic enabled the pregnancy to go on to the 36th week and resulted in the birth of a healthy daughter. This illustrates the importance of obtaining an accurate clinical history.

Septic abortion

Infection was once almost pathognomonic of the criminal abortion, the organism often being *Clostridium welchii* (gas gangrene), which grows well in the dead and damaged tissue which was often left in the uterine cavity. Such cases were frequently fatal.

With the passage of the Abortion Act in 1967 and the resulting disappearance of the back street abortionist, the majority of septic abortions are now due to secondary infection, usually by *Escherichia coli* or other bowel commensals, of the retained products of conception in incomplete, spontaneous abortions or poorly performed terminations.

Non-septic abortion

The majority of abortions, both spontaneous and induced, now remain uninfected.

The most frequently encountered classification of abortions is based on the stage to which the abortion process has progressed. This is because the extent of the progress usually has a direct bearing on the medical management.

Threatened abortion

Painless vaginal bleeding of small amount is not uncommon in early pregnancy. In some cases, the bleeding will have originated from a minor lesion on the cervix, such as an erosion (ectropion), but sometimes the bleeding will be from within the uterine cavity and a proportion of these will go on to abort. For this reason, all cases of vaginal bleeding in early pregnancy are classified as threatened abortion until an obvious alternative cause has been established.

Inevitable abortion

The diagnosis of an inevitable rather than a threatened abortion is often one of clinical judgment. Typically, the inevitable abortion is characterised by heavier bleeding, the pain of uterine contractions and the partial dilatation of the cervix but not all of these are necessarily present in every case. The diagnosis normally implies that the loss of the pregnancy will occur but has not yet taken place though there is considerable overlap with the incomplete abortion and some inevitable abortions will go on to become complete without medical intervention.

Incomplete abortion

This is probably the commonest form of miscarriage to be encountered in routine gynaecological hospital practice (threatened and complete abortions are often managed at home by the general practitioner). The use of the term 'incomplete' refers to the loss of part but not all of the products of conception. Pain may be variable but the bleeding is usually heavy. Sometimes, the use of a vaginal speculum may reveal pregnancy tissue lying in the cervical canal and protruding through the external os.

Complete abortion

In the case of the complete abortion, all the pregnancy material has been lost from the uterine cavity and expelled from the cervix. The empty uterus then usually contracts so that the bleeding diminishes and stops after a few days. The uterine contraction may cause minor lower abdominal discomfort but the pain is less than that of the spasmodic contractions which are present while the abortion is still incomplete. The cervical os may still be open if the miscarriage has only recently become complete but will close within a day or so.

Missed abortion

When a pregnancy dies but remains within the uterine cavity, the term 'missed abortion' is applied. Many of these are now diagnosed on ultrasonic scan and are then evacuated surgically but the majority, if left alone, would abort spontaneously after a variable period of time. A few, however, may remain in utero eventually undergoing changes which convert the tissue into a carneous mole. A carneous mole may be associated with scanty or absent menstrual periods and can act as an intrauterine contraceptive.

Recurrent spontaneous abortion

Recurrent abortion is defined as three or more consecutive spontaneous abortions, usually in the first trimester of pregnancy (up to 12 weeks), and occur in about 1% of women. Appropriate investigations should be offered, even though, without any treatment, the chance of a successful next pregnancy is 60%.

A couple who experience even one or two spontaneous abortions frequently experience considerable psychological upset and may request investigations into the cause of the lost pregnancies.

Chromosomal abnormalities are common in pregnancies which miscarry (though the cells may be hard to grow in the laboratory making investigation of the chromosome pattern difficult). These abnormalities may result from random variations but both parents should be checked to ensure that they are not carriers of an abnormality.

An abnormality of the uterine cavity may interfere with proper implantation of a pregnancy and may be due to developmental anomalies or to acquired conditions such as past surgical damage (perhaps at an earlier termination of pregnancy) or the growth of fibroids.

Endocrine problems may be identified and the 'inadequate luteal phase', which for many years was written off by most gynaecologists as a myth, has again been recognised as a potential cause of some early pregnancy loss.

Immunological rejection of the pregnancy has received attention in recent years and the level of anti-cardiolipin antibody is thought to be useful indicator in some cases.

The treatment of many of these conditions is still controversial and is the subject of continuing research.

Anembryonic pregnancy

Like the missed abortion, this is usually an ultrasonic diagnosis and applies to cases where, instead of containing an embryo, the gestational sac is empty or contains only a small amount of embryonic tissue. The sac is, of course, filled with liquor amnii but this is non-reflective to ultrasound and the sac therefore appears to be empty. Some authorities regard the anembryonic pregnancy as a variant of the missed abortion, believing that the embryo has simply succumbed at a very early stage but it seems more likely that most of these cases are due to the failure of the differentiating embryonic cells to develop properly or at all. Anembryonic pregnancies probably all miscarry spontaneously by about 12–14 weeks (most do so earlier).

The anembryonic pregnancy was formerly thought to be rare. Doubtless, many cases were not diagnosed because the pregnancy aborted spontaneously and, if no foetal tissue was identified, this was assumed to be because it had been passed within blood clot and simple overlooked. With the advent of routine ultrasonic scanning in early pregnancy, it was realised that it is a fairly common condition but its existence remains almost unknown to the non-medical public.

Management

Possibly the most important part of the management of an anembryonic pregnancy is to appreciate that the patient may find it exceedingly difficult to comprehend the nature of the problem. It is particularly difficult to explain because the non-medical mind usually equates 'pregnancy' to 'baby' and the concept of a genuine pregnancy unassociated with the presence of a foetus may be very confusing. Patients often assume that a pseudocyesis (false pregnancy) is what is meant but this is not the case as, in the pseudocyesis, the pregnancy test remains negative and the uterine cavity is empty (in the anembryonic pregnancy, it is the intrauterine *gestational sac* which is empty). The communication of the diagnosis therefore requires a careful and sensitive approach.

As many cases will now be diagnosed by an ultrasonic scan before the woman has experienced any untoward symptoms, it is essential that the condition is confirmed to the satisfaction not only of the gynaecologist but, also, of the woman herself. This may require that no action is taken on the first scan, especially if the pregnancy is still early, but that a second scan be performed after an interval of 10–14 days, when the sac will again be found to be empty and its growth will usually, though not always, prove to have been less than expected.

In some cases, the women may refuse intervention when, as already noted, most cases will abort spontaneously by 14 weeks. This is, however, rather unsatisfactory as vaginal bleeding may start at any time and most women, once fully convinced of the diagnosis, will elect to have the uterine contents removed surgically.

The operative procedure is exactly the same as the termination of a normal pregnancy of similar duration but it is advisable to send the evacuated tissue for both histological and cytogenetic examination. The former will confirm and document the diagnosis and, if placental cells can be cultured, the latter may provide useful information about the chromosomal pattern.

The woman should be reassured that most anembryonic pregnancies are followed by normal pregnancies with the next conception though one author has seen a woman who had three consecutive anembryonic pregnancies before achieving a normal conception (which went on to produce a healthy baby).

INDUCED ABORTION

These may be legal or criminal.

Legal termination

Legal abortions (often referred to in medical documents as 'termination of pregnancy' or 'TOP') are those carried out in accordance with the terms of the Abortion Act 1967 (subsequently amended in 1991). This required that two registered medical practitioners give prior written acknowledgment that the termination is indicated for one or more of the following reasons:

(1) the continuance of the pregnancy would involve risk to the life of the pregnant woman greater than if the pregnancy were terminated;

(2) the continuance of the pregnancy would involve risk of injury to the physical or mental health of the pregnant woman greater than if the pregnancy were terminated;

(3) the continuance of the pregnancy would involve risk of injury to the physical or mental health of the existing child(ren) of the family of the pregnant woman greater than if the pregnancy were terminated;

(4) there is a substantial risk that if the child were born it would suffer from such physical or mental abnormalities as to be seriously handicapped.

These indications were changed in 1991 to:

(a) the continuance of the pregnancy would involve risk to the life of the pregnant woman greater than if the pregnancy were terminated;

(b) the termination is necessary to prevent grave permanent injury to the physical or mental health of the pregnant woman;

(c) the pregnancy has not exceeded its 24th week and that the continuance of the pregnancy would involve risk, greater than if the pregnancy were terminated, of injury to the physical or mental health of the pregnant woman;

(d) the pregnancy has not exceeded its 24th week and that the continuance of the pregnancy would involve risk, greater than if the pregnancy were terminated, of injury to the physical or mental health of any existing child(ren) of the family of the pregnant woman;

(e) there is a substantial risk that if the child were born it would suffer from such physical or mental abnormalities as to be seriously handicapped.

The appropriate form (HSA1) must be signed by both practitioners before the abortion is performed and the person carrying out the abortion (who need not be one of the authorising practitioners) must notify specified information to the Chief Medical Officer (the Chief Medical Officer for Wales in the case of terminations performed in the Principality) within seven days of performing the operation.

It is essential that proper counselling is provided before the termination is undertaken or even agreed. The nature and extent of the counselling needed will vary with the individual circumstances of each case. Clearly, the psychological trauma may be greater when the indication for the termination of an otherwise wanted baby is the presence of a severe foetal malformation.

The actual procedure may take a number of forms.

Mifepristone (RU486)

Since about 1991 (longer in some other countries), it has been possible to perform 'medical' terminations of early pregnancies by the use of mifepristone, usually in conjunction with a prostaglandin.

The high levels of natural progesterone suppress uterine contractions in early pregnancy and mifepristone (still sometimes referred to by its research designation RU486) acts to counteract this effect (that is, it is anti-progestogenic). It is licensed for the termination of pregnancies up to 63 days (9 weeks) from the last menstrual period (or the equivalent size by ultrasonic scanning). As in other cases of termination of pregnancy, the legal provisions of the Abortion Act should be satisfied.

The usual regime commences with the oral administration of 600 mg mifepristone, often with an anti-emetic to offset the common side effects of nausea and vomiting. The woman stays in the hospital for two hours before being allowed home and then returns to the hospital after an interval of 48 hours when about 3% will have already aborted. The remainder receive an intra-vaginal pessary containing 1 mg of gemeprost (a prostaglandin ester), following which, she is observed in hospital for a further six hours, during which time about 90% will abort. A follow-up assessment to confirm (by an ultrasonic scan) that the uterine cavity is empty is carried out 8–12 days later.

The overall success rate is about 95%, the failures being terminated by surgical evacuation. Some women will also require evacuation of retained products of conception because of incomplete uterine emptying.

Complications of the method include the difficulty of providing adequate analgesia, the potential risks of retained products in the uterus and the possibility of heavy vaginal bleeding.

Despite promotion as a preferable alternative to surgical terminations, enthusiasm for the method has been limited and, where both options are available, women have tended to continue to choose the more invasive but less psychologically disturbing surgical approach. The costs of the two procedures are similar because the savings on the operative costs are offset by the staff time required to supervise the response.

Surgical termination (vaginal)

The surgical (vaginal) termination of a pregnancy is essentially the same procedure as a dilatation and curettage (D & C) but, because the wall of the pregnant uterus is much softer and more vascular than when not pregnant, the risks of perforation and haemorrhage are both much greater. For this reason, narrow instruments should be avoided (the uterine sound is not normally used) and the operator needs to have had more experience than in the case of a straightforward D & C.

To facilitate the dilatation of a small cervix, especially in very early pregnancy, preoperative cervical preparation may be used. This can be done by the administration of a prostaglandin gel or pessary into the upper vagina some hours before the operation. This softens the cervical tissues and enables the dilatation to be less traumatic.

Surgical termination is usually limited to pregnancies which are no larger than 12 or perhaps 14 weeks from the last menstrual period (10–12 weeks from conception) and, in the event of any clinical doubt about the size of the pregnancy, for example, if the patient is particularly obese, an ultrasonic scan should be performed to assess the duration of the pregnancy before the method of termination is decided.

Before other methods were developed (see 'Prostaglandin termination', below), the only alternative for a termination of pregnancy after the 14th week was a hysterotomy, to avoid which, vaginal termination was performed up to about eighteen weeks. This involves more surgical destruction of the larger foetus and is associated with a greater risk of cervical and uterine damage and fell into disuse after the 1970s. There has recently been a return to the use of the method because it avoids some of the psychological stress associated with a prostaglandin termination and also because the hospital stay tends to be shorter but it is essential that the greater surgical risks are appreciated and it remains to be seen whether the long term complication rate is acceptable.

Hysterotomy

The operation of hysterotomy involves the surgical opening of the anterior abdominal and uterine walls and the manual extraction of the pregnancy from the uterine cavity. Whilst closely resembling a Caesarean section in concept, the hysterotomy is significantly different in its implications for future pregnancies. The part of the uterine wall which is opened at a Caesarean section in late pregnancy is the 'lower segment' most of which forms from the upper part of the cervix only in the last ten or twelve weeks of pregnancy. Consequently, a hysterotomy performed at an earlier stage will involve an incision into the body of the uterus which results in a weaker scar.

There is also a risk that any fragments of the endometrial tissue accidentally left in the abdominal wound may give raise to an endometrioma. This is a collection of ectopic endometrium which will bleed at the time of menstruation giving rise to a painful tumour, perhaps necessitating surgical removal.

The reliability of termination of pregnancy by the use of prostaglandin has rendered this operation obsolete in all but a very few cases.

Prostaglandin termination

In the 1960s, it was already known that mid trimester abortion could be provoked by the injection of certain substances into the amniotic fluid. Initially hypertonic solutions of glucose were used but the resulting sugar content of the fluid provided a good medium for the growth of infecting organisms and strong solutions of urea were found to be safer. The hypertonic solutions caused more water to be drawn into the amniotic fluid by osmotic action but the method was somewhat unreliable.

Extract of the prostate gland had been found to have various biological effects and, in the 1970s, these extracts became commercially available (the extracts of animal prostates were later replaced by synthetic analogues). One of the effects is to cause uterine contractions and this is used both in the induction of labour at term and also to stimulate the uterus to contract in earlier pregnancy.

The uterus is less responsive to prostaglandins in early pregnancy than at term and the side effects, which include nausea, vomiting, diarrhoea and hypotension, were a problem. It was found that these systemic effects could be minimised if the prostaglandin was administered directly into the uterus, thereby enabling the dose to be reduced. Initially, the prostaglandin solutions were given by direct injection into the amniotic fluid via a needle introduced through the anterior abdominal wall but later administration through the cervix via a thin catheter was found to be effective and, as newer and more powerful analogues were developed, it became possible to put the preparation into the upper vagina.

Although the administration of the prostaglandin has become easier and less distressing for the patient, the subsequent induced abortion remains stressful and the uterine contractions are usually painful, requiring the administration of strong analgesics such as pethidine by intramuscular injection or, if available, epidural analgesia. Occasionally, instances of patients being refused adequate analgesia have occurred, it sometimes appearing that this has been done to 'punish' the patient for wishing to terminate the pregnancy; there is no justification for such action.

After a variable time, usually 6–10 hours, the uterine contractions have caused sufficient dilatation of the cervix to allow the foetus to be expelled into the vagina. In the past, when urea was used, the foetus was invariable already dead but this is not necessarily the case with prostaglandin. In the case of termination at 18 or 20 weeks, the neonate will succumb within a few minutes but the occasional very late termination may result in the birth of a potentially viable infant. Such terminations are usually only performed where there is prior evidence of a very serious foetal abnormality which itself may prove rapidly fatal but, where this cannot be relied upon, the foetus may be killed *in utero* before the prostaglandin is administered, a procedure termed 'foeticide'.

After expulsion of the foetus, the placenta and membranes usually follow but, sometimes, uterine emptying may be incomplete and surgical evacuation of the retained products of conception may be necessary. This is associated with all the risks and complications of the same procedure undertaken after a spontaneous abortion. These are described elsewhere but, in addition, a small number of cases have been reported where permanent damage to the cervix appears to have occurred due to the force of the prostaglandin induced contractions themselves and this may give rise to cervical incompetence in a later pregnancy.

Criminal termination

Prior to 1967, any person procuring an abortion was liable to criminal prosecution. A few were performed by reputable practitioners under the same conditions as now applied to terminations under the Act but the majority were 'back street' abortions carried out in unsterile conditions often with homemade or improvised instruments (knitting needles were commonly used to attempt to rupture the membranes but could result in perforation of the vaginal walls). Sometimes corrosive or other dangerous fluids were introduced. Deaths were common due to infection, haemorrhage and gas or fluid embolism. These cases, once an everyday feature of many large casualty departments, are now rare.

CHAPTER 14

ECTOPIC PREGNANCY

DEFINITION

An ectopic pregnancy is a conceptus which has implanted and started to grow at some site in the body other than the usual, intrauterine, position.

MEDICO-LEGAL SIGNIFICANCE

Ectopic pregnancies still represent a significant cause of death in early pregnancy (in the UK, between 1991 and 1993, they contributed nine of the 18 deaths which occurred before the 20th week of pregnancy) and, even if patients do not succumb, they may suffer considerable morbidity both in the short and long term.

The 'classical' presentation should be readily recognised but other ectopic pregnancies can be notoriously difficult to diagnose and it is essential that the appropriate investigations are carried out.

MECHANISM

Fertilisation of the ovum (egg) by a spermatozoon normally takes place in the ampullary part of the fallopian tube (not, as is commonly assumed, in the uterine cavity). Consequently, although ectopic pregnancies have been described in many different parts of the abdominal cavity, the most frequent ectopic site is in the tube where implantation can occur in the ampulla, the isthmus or the interstitial segment. Strictly, these should be described as tubal ectopic pregnancies but, because other sites are so much less common, when the term 'ectopic pregnancy' is used, it can be presumed to refer to a pregnancy in some part of the tube unless some other site is specified.

The early pregnancy erodes the mucosal lining of the tube and reaches the muscle layer. Unlike the thick uterine wall, the tube cannot contain the growing conceptus which distends the tube and ultimately may cause it to rupture. Usually, the rupture of the tube occurs on its free surface and the associated bleeding from the damaged wall of the tube is released into the peritoneal cavity. Less commonly, the breach in the tubal wall may occur into the mesosalpinx with the formation of a *broad ligament haematoma*.

Occasionally, the tubal wall does not rupture but the pregnancy sac is extruded from the fimbrial end of the tube when it is called a *tubal abortion*. Infrequently, the pregnancy may die but be retained within the tube as a *tubal mole*.

The endocrine changes associated with an ectopic pregnancy are usually less than those resulting from a normally sited conceptus and may be insufficient to maintain the uterine endometrium which then begins to break down causing vaginal bleeding. This is usually intermittent as well as being darker in colour and smaller in amount than the bleeding of a menstrual period. It should be noted that the vaginal bleeding does not originate from the site of the ectopic pregnancy and the quantity of vaginal bleeding bears no relation to the amount of any intraperitoneal haemorrhage.

PRESENTATION

The clinical presentation of an ectopic pregnancy may be acute, sub-acute or chronic.

In most cases, the menstrual period is delayed by from one to six weeks (the majority present after six to eight weeks of amenorrhoea)

Many women will experience some irregular vaginal bleeding (and may mistake this for menstrual bleeding) and some will complain of spasmodic lower abdominal pain. The pain may be felt on one side only but can be central or bilateral. This pain is probably due to spasmodic contractions of the tube.

In the *acute* presentation, the tube then ruptures with torrential bleeding into the peritoneal cavity, with the result that, in addition to experiencing severe (and now continuous) lower abdominal pain, the woman becomes shocked due to the loss of blood with facial pallor, sweating and a weak, thready pulse.

As a general rule, shocked patients should be resuscitated before submitting them to surgery but the ruptured ectopic pregnancy is sometimes an exception to this rule, as the rate of intraperitoneal haemorrhage may exceed the resuscitation capabilities. An immediate laparotomy to control the bleeding may therefore be required (resuscitative measures proceeding concurrently).

Fortunately, this dramatic presentation is not common and the *subacute* picture is more usual, in which the intraperitoneal bleeding is less severe. The patient again develops continuous lower abdominal pain and on examination the abdomen will be tender, often with guarding and rebound tenderness. Bimanual pelvic examination will reveal a tender mass to one side of the uterus which itself will be somewhat enlarged. These patients will frequently be found to have some degree of anaemia due to the internal bleeding having been in progress for a few days.

Many women with sub-acute ectopic pregnancies will experience episodes of transient faintness or dizziness and they may also complain of pain over the tip of the shoulder. This latter symptom (a form of 'referred pain') is caused by blood tracking up the paracolic gutter (usually on the same side as the pregnancy) and irritating the diaphragm; this structure is supplied with nerves originating from the fourth cervical nerve roots which also enervate the skin over the shoulder.

Chronic cases are relatively rare but may present with moderate abdominal pain, anaemia and a tender pelvic mass. In these cases, the bleeding has been slow but continuous.

DIAGNOSIS AND INVESTIGATION

The diagnosis of a ruptured tubal ectopic pregnancy in the severely shocked patient is essentially clinical and depends upon the recognition of the pattern of symptoms and signs already described. The dramatic nature of this situation impresses itself upon the mind of every medical student so that it is more often the sub-acute or chronic case that is missed.

The differential diagnosis includes:

(a) an *ovarian cyst* which has undergone *torsion, haemorrhage* or *rupture* (in these cases, the signs of pregnancy are absent);

(b) the *abortion of an intrauterine pregnancy* (the vaginal bleeding is usually heavier, there is no pelvic mass and products of conception may be seen in the cervical os);

(c) *pelvic infection (salpingitis)* (there is likely to be a pyrexia and markedly raised white blood cell count. The pain and tenderness is also, usually, bilateral and there are no pregnancy signs); and

(d) in the case of right sided ectopic pregnancies, *appendicitis*.

In the past, the definitive diagnosis ultimately relied on an exploratory laparotomy or, if the patient's condition and the available equipment and expertise were appropriate, an investigative laparoscopy. To some extent, this is still true but technical improvements in tests for pregnancy have had an influence.

In the past, pregnancy tests were insensitive and often unreliable but for several years tests have been available which are based on the detection of raised levels of the hormone human chorionic gonadotrophin (HCG) or, more accurately the fraction or a sub-unit of that fraction. These tests can be performed on urine or blood (the latter being much more precise) and may be qualitative or quantitative. The qualitative urine test (usually a somewhat more sensitive version of the home pregnancy test) can be done in the consulting room or ward but a suitably equipped pathology laboratory can provide a quantitative assay on blood in a few hours. Not all laboratories will be so equipped, however, and some may need to refer the specimen on, so that the result may not be available for a few days (typically 3–4 days as a maximum). In the case of an ectopic pregnancy, the quantitative result of the HCG assay will be inappropriately low for the estimated duration of the pregnancy (as compared with a normally sited conceptus). However, low figures may also be found in association with other complications of early pregnancy, in particular with the various types of spontaneous abortion.

The commonest reason for missing an ectopic pregnancy is probably that the diagnosis is not considered but any patient with a history that is at all suggestive of this diagnosis *must*, at the very least, have an assay of the serum (HCG).

Ultrasonic scanning is also now widely available and many suspected ectopic pregnancies will be scanned. It has long been recognised that, although an experienced ultrasonographer may identify features indicating the presence of an ectopic pregnancy, negative findings *do not exclude the diagnosis*. Some authorities state that the finding of an intrauterine pregnancy excludes an ectopic gestation but this is a dangerous teaching since the apparent gestation sac may be a 'pseudo-sac' (an appearance of the degenerating uterine lining in the early stages) and it is possible (though rare) that there may be co-existing intra- and extra-uterine twins.

MANAGEMENT

If the diagnosis is uncertain and the patient's condition is stable, it may be reasonable to postpone operative intervention and to measure the circulating level of HCG on two occasions separated by 48 hours. In the presence of a normal, early pregnancy the level will more than double even in that short time. Most ectopic pregnancies will fail to achieve the expected rise.

The surgical management of the ectopic pregnancy has undergone something of a revolution in recent years. As mentioned above, the severely shocked patient will require an immediate laparotomy to arrest the haemorrhage, but, formerly, all other cases were treated by open surgical operation though, in the sub-acute and chronic cases, full resuscitation and any necessary blood transfusion could be completed first. Furthermore, until the late 1960s it was the almost invariable practice to perform a salpingectomy, sometimes with an ipsilateral oophorectomy as well.

With the development of in-vitro fertilisation, the removal of the ovary (never universally accepted) was abandoned and, at about the same time, it became more common to conserve the tube if not too severely damaged (though the control of haemorrhage remains the first priority and may, even today, necessitate a salpingectomy).

Since the mid 1980s, advances in operative laparoscopic techniques have enabled many ectopic pregnancies to be removed endoscopically; it is essential, however, that such procedures are only performed by surgeons who have received the appropriate special training and not all hospitals will have such individuals available.

Much more recently, a small number of cases have been managed conservatively by the administration of the cytotoxic drug methotrexate.

THE 'MISSED ECTOPIC' AND CLAIMS FOR NEGLIGENCE

Depending on the symptoms and signs in individual cases, the diagnosis of an ectopic pregnancy may be blindingly obvious or exceedingly difficult and it has often been said, with justification, that no gynaecologist of any experience can honestly claim never to have missed the diagnosis. Consequently, the assessment of whether or not failure to make the diagnosis was negligent requires detailed investigation of all the information available to the medical staff involved at the time.

The possible consequences of failing to make the diagnosis range from a few days of additional pain and suffering to the death of the patient. Also, since the more conservative managements (medical treatment or surgery with conservation of the tube) depend on early diagnosis, subsequent reduction in fertility may also be a basis for claim.

CHAPTER 15

TROPHOBLASTIC DISEASE

The term 'trophoblastic disease' encompasses a spectrum of neoplastic tumours originating from pregnancy tissue and ranging from the entirely benign to the highly malignant, which share the unique characteristic of being derived from a genetically different origin to that of the host patient. The benign form is called a 'hydatidiform mole', whereas the malignant tumour is designated a 'choriocarcinoma' (or, sometimes, 'chorioepithelioma' or 'chorioblastoma'). Between these two extremes, lies a locally invasive form known as 'chorioadenoma destruens' or 'invasive mole'.

INCIDENCE

The incidence of hydatidiform mole in the UK and the US is about one in 2,000 conceptions, being rather more frequent in teenagers and in women over the age of 40 years. In Asia and the Far East, the frequency is much higher and may be up to one in 200 in some areas such as Singapore and Japan.

TYPES OF TUMOUR

Over 80% of hydatidiform moles remain benign but about 15% (untreated) will progress to become locally invasive and 2–3% will develop into choriocarcinomas. Choriocarcinoma may also arise without passing through the preceding stages and the total incidence (in the Western world) is about one in 40,000 (that is, about 50% arise *de novo* after a normal pregnancy).

Local invasion of the myometrium may open larger blood vessels causing haemorrhage and the tumour may even perforate the uterine wall and invade adjacent structures. Choriocarcinomas tend to metastasise early, predominantly by the blood vessels but also by the lymphatics. Distant deposits may be found especially in the lungs, central nervous system, liver, gastrointestinal tract and kidneys.

In most instances, the embryo never develops and the uterine cavity (or other pregnancy site, in the case of ectopic implantations) is filled by the abnormal tissue. Partial moles also occur, in which the abnormal tissue develops in only part of an otherwise normal placenta. Partial moles usually result in the subsequent demise of the foetus but, occasionally, the affected area may be small enough to allow the pregnancy to continue normally.

Abnormal numbers of chromosomes are commonly present in the cell nuclei of partial moles but complete moles usually have a normal complement (usually 46, XX). In these cases, there is some evidence to suggest that the genetic material may be exclusively paternal in origin.

CLINICAL FEATURES

Trophoblastic disease is frequently associated with vaginal bleeding in early pregnancy (usually 8–10 weeks after the missed period) and is diagnosed as a threatened abortion. The bleeding may be followed by the passage of molar tissue which typically consists of grape-like clusters of small cysts filled with clear fluid (hence the term 'hydatidiform', from the Greek for 'watery'); before the advent of ultrasonic scanning it was usually not until this point that the correct diagnosis was made.

The trophoblastic tissue is hyperactive and large amounts of the hormone human chorionic gonadotrophin (HCG) are produced. The urinary pregnancy test is therefore strongly positive and measurements of the hormone in the serum (usually by a radioimmunoassay for the β-subunit, in order to minimise cross-reaction with other hormones) give very high figures. The exaggerated endocrine changes may cause hyperemesis gravidarum or even pre-eclamptic toxaemia (PET); this is the only circumstance in which PET may develop in the first trimester of pregnancy.

On clinical examination, the uterus will be found to be larger than expected for the duration of the pregnancy. Ultrasonic scanning will usually show a typical 'snowstorm' appearance caused by the reflection of the ultrasonic beam by the multiple interfaces of the hydatidiform cysts and the foetal echoes will be absent (except for some partial moles). It must be noted that a multiple pregnancy (twins, triplets, etc) will also be associated with an unusually large uterus, a high β-HCG level and possibly with hyperemesis; the ultrasonic scan should, of course, reveal the true diagnosis. The ultrasonic scan of a choriocarcinoma is also abnormal but the snowstorm appearance is usually absent because the tumour is more solid.

Cystic enlargement of the corpus luteum in the ovary is fairly common during the first trimester of a normal pregnancy but is seen far more frequently in association with trophoblastic tumours. These cysts do not require specific treatment as they will usually resolve spontaneously once the molar tissue has been removed. This should be confirmed by a repeat ultrasonic scan of the pelvis some 3–4 weeks after the tumour tissue has been removed.

MANAGEMENT

In the absence of a living foetus, the uterine contents should be evacuated by dilatation of the cervix and vacuum aspiration. The technique is identical to that described for the legal termination of pregnancy, though the risks of haemorrhage and uterine perforation are greater. Evacuation by the prostaglandin induction of uterine contractions has also been employed but there is evidence that this may increase the likelihood of blood-borne metastases should the tumour prove to be malignant.

A second aspiration evacuation may be advised about two or three weeks after the first and is mandatory if the HCG levels fail to fall as anticipated.

The rare cases of trophoblastic disease arising in ectopic pregnancies may require removal by laparotomy.

Management of the partial mole with a living foetus is more difficult and necessitates careful consideration of the probable risks as assessed largely by the ultrasonic appearances. If it is decided to allow the pregnancy to continue, regular re-scanning is essential.

The importance of follow-up

Until the 1960s, the death rate from choriocarcinoma was amongst the highest for any malignant disease. This was especially tragic because it affected younger women than most other malignancies. The past 30 years have seen a dramatic improvement in the management of these cases and the majority will now be successfully treated. This has come about partly because of improvements in chemotherapeutic regimes but also because of the realisation that the HCG production by the tumour tissue afforded an excellent 'marker' allowing the detection of very small amounts of tumour tissue (and, therefore, the continuation of treatment until it was entirely eradicated) and the early detection of recurrence. It is therefore essential that all cases of trophoblastic disease be followed up by regular estimation of the HCG level in the urine or blood. Contraception should be employed in order to avoid a new conception for up to two years (depending on the histological appearances of the original tissue). There is some evidence that oral contraception may increase the risk of a recurrence, which should always be treated quickly and energetically.

In the developed world, the efficient administration of the appropriate follow-up routines has been greatly facilitated by the establishment of regional Trophoblastic Tumour Registration Centres, of which there are three in the UK.

In a few cases, perforation of the uterine wall may necessitate a hysterectomy. It may also be necessary to resort to operative removal of the uterus in the management of some recurrences and sometimes in the treatment of the severe haemorrhage which can result from the development of arterio-venous fistulae within the uterine wall. Nevertheless, most cases of hydatidiform mole require no long term treatment and even those with malignant potential often respond well to chemotherapy, usually courses of methotrexate combined with one or more other agents.

GLOSSARY OF TERMS

Many of these terms are described in more detail elsewhere in the book. Some terms have several interpretations but, in most cases, only those meanings relevant to gynaecology are given here.

Abbreviations

δ	The Greek letter, 'delta', often used to indicate 'diagnosis of', as in 'δ chronic pelvic infection'
κ	The Greek letter, 'kappa,' sometimes used to denote 'menstrual periods'
#	An initial '#' indicates 'fracture of', as in '# pelvis'
? PID	An initial '?' indicates an unconfirmed diagnosis (of pelvic inflammatory disease in this case)
° LKKS	No clinical enlargement of liver, kidneys or spleen
± 2 SD	Plus or minus two standard deviations (a commonly used statistical method of identifying part of a population, approximately 95%)
c chr 2 cg	With sutures of chromic catgut size 2
c int 2/0 PDS	With interrupted sutures of PDS size 00 (see, also, below)
$\frac{2}{52}$ or 2/52	Two weeks
AID	Artificial insemination by donor sperm
AIDS	Acquired immune deficiency syndrome
AIH	Artificial insemination by husband's sperm
a/v	Anteversion
BO	Bowels opened
BSO	Bilateral salpingo-oophorectomy
CEA	Carcinoembryonic antigen
CIN	Cervical intra-epithelial neoplasia
CVA	Cerebrovascular accident
D & C	Dilatation and curettage

DES	Diethylstilboestrol
DNA	Deoxyribonucleic acid
DUB	Dysfunctional uterine bleeding
DVT	Deep venous thrombosis
ERPC	Evacuation of retained products of conception (sometimes, 'ERPOC')
FIGO	Fédération Internationale de Gynécologie et d'Obstétrique
FSH	Follicle stimulating hormone
GIFT	Gamete intra-fallopian transfer
GnRH	Gonadotrophin releasing hormone
GTT	Glucose tolerance test
HCG	Human chorionic gonadotrophin
HIV	Human immuno-deficiency virus
HPL	Human placental lactogen
HPV	Human papilloma virus
HRT	Hormone replacement therapy
HSG	Hysterosalpingogram
HSV	Herpes simplex virus
ICSI	Intra-cytoplasmic sperm injection
IUCD	Intra-uterine contraceptive device
IUD	Intra-uterine death (of the foetus); unfortunately, and very confusingly, sometimes also used for 'intra-uterine contraceptive device'
IUI	Intr-uterine insemination
IVF	In-vitro fertilisation
IVP	Intravenous pyleogram
IVU	Intravenous urogram
LAVH	Laparoscopically assisted vaginal hysterectomy
LH	Luteinising hormone
LLETZ	Large loop excision of the transformation zone
LMP	Last menstrual period
MI	Myocardial infarction
MPA	Medroxyprogesterone acetate
MRI	Magnetic resonance imaging
NSAID	Non-steroidal anti-inflammatory drug

NET	Norethisterone
PE	Pulmonary embolus
PET	Pre-eclampsia toxaemia
PID	Pelvic inflammatory disease (but, outside gynaecology, also commonly used as an abbreviation for 'prolapsed intervertebral disc')
POC	Products of conception
r/v	Retroversion
T4	Thyroxine
TAH	Total abdominal hysterectomy
TOP	Termination of pregnancy
TSH	Thyroid stimulating hormone
UTI	Urinary tract infection
VIN	Vulval intra-epithelial neoplasia

Surgical sutures

The thickness of surgical sutures is usually described using the United States pharmacœpia (USP) gauge and ranges form '5' (thickest) to '11/0' (thinnest). Most gynaecological surgery employs sutures from '1' (approximately 0.5 mm in diameter) down to '4/0' (with a diameter of approximately 0.2 mm), though, especially in tubal surgery, material down to about '10/0' (0.02 mm in diameter) may be used.

A metric gauging has now been approved, which identifies the suture diameter in tenths of a millimetre. For example, metric '0.4' corresponds to a diameter of 0.04 mm (in fact, it correponds a diameter of between 0.04 and 0.049 mm).

Glossary

A

Abdomen	The part of the body between the thorax (chest) and the pelvis
Abdominal bloating	A subjective feeling of abdominal distension
Abduct	To move away from the midline
Abdominal wall:	
anterior abdominal wall	The layers of the body wall (including skin, fat, and muscles) lying anterior to the peritoneal cavity
posterior abdominal wall	The layers of the body wall behind the peritoneal cavity

Abortion	The loss of a pregnancy before the end of the 24th week (formerly the 28th week) by natural or artificial influence
complete abortion	Spontaneous abortion with loss of all the products of conception
habitual abortion	Recurrent abortion (qv)
induced abortion	Abortion brought about by intervention; often called a termination of pregnancy (TOP)
incomplete abortion	Spontaneous abortion where some of the products have been retained in the uterine cavity
inevitable abortion	Abortion in which the dilatation of the uterine cervix and/or the amount of bleeding indicate that the loss of the pregnancy will occur
mid trimester abortion	Abortion occurring between 13 and 24 weeks
missed abortion	Abortion in which the foetus has died but the products of conception are retained within the uterine cavity
recurrent abortion	Three or more spontaneous abortions at about the same stage of development
septic abortion	Infected abortion
spontaneous abortion	A miscarriage
threatened abortion	Vaginal bleeding in early pregnancy (usually without cervical dilatation) which may go on to abort
Abrasion	Wearing away by an abnormal mechanical process, often referring to damage to skin or other surface layer; a graze
Abruptio placentae, placental abruption	Partial or complete separation of the placenta from the uterine wall before delivery of the foetus
Abscess	A localised collection of pus (qv)
Acquired immune deficiency syndrome (AIDS)	Disease due to HIV infection characterised by evidence of impaired immunity
Actinomycoses	An infectious disease caused by micro-organisms of the genus *Actinomyces*
Acute	Of short duration and/or sudden onset

Acyclovir	Generic name for an anti-viral drug
Adduction	To move towards the midline
Adenocarcinoma	A malignant tumour of glandular tissue
Adenoma	A benign tumour of glandular tissue
Adenomyosis	The presence of endometrial deposits within the muscular layer of the uterine wall; endometriosis of the uterine wall
Adhesiolysis	The division of adhesions
Adhesion	An area or fibrous band by which organs or other structures are abnormally stuck together
Adnexae	Structures in close proximity to a part; in gynaecology, used for the region adjacent to the cervix and uterus – principally the tubes, ovaries and associated connective tissue (adjective: adnexal)
Adrenal (or suprarenal) gland	Bilaterally paired endocrine glands producing steroid and adrenaline based hormones
Agenesis	Failed development of an organ
Amenorrhoea	Absence of menstruation
primary amenorrhoea	Failure of menstruation to occur at puberty
secondary amenorrhoea	Cessation of menstruation (usually, for at least 3–6 months)
Ampulla	Flask shaped dilatation of a tubular structure such as the mid portion of the uterine tube
Anaemia	A reduction in the volume or number of red blood cells or in the amount of haemoglobin in the blood
Anaerobic bacterial infections	Bacterial infection by organisms not requiring oxygen to survive; commonly affect the gynaecological and digestive tracts
Anal canal	The terminal part of the digestive tract extending from the rectum to the anus
Analgesia	The relief of pain without removal of consciousness
Anatomical position	The position used for anatomical reference in which the body is standing erect with the palms facing forward
Anembryonic pregnancy	A pregnancy in which there is no foetal development

Anorexia nervosa	A condition characterised by severe and prolonged refusal to eat accompanied by a distorted body image
Anovulatory	Failure of ovulation
Anteflexion	The forward curvature of the uterus
Anterior	Situated in front
Anteversion (a/v)	The forward tilt of the uterus
Anti-sperm antibodies	Antibodies in blood, semen or female mucus that kill or immobilise sperm
Anti-oestrogen	Having an effect that opposes some or all of the actions of oestrogen
Aorta	The main blood vessel carrying oxygenated blood from the heart to the rest of the body
Arterio-venous fistula	An abnormal connection between an artery and a vein which bypasses the capillary bed
Artificial insemination by husband's (AIH) or donor (AID) semen	Introduction of semen into the upper vagina uterine cavity either to circumvent male coital problems (AIH), or to provide donor sperm in cases of azoospermia (AID) (see, also, Intra-uterine insemination)
Ascites	Free fluid in the peritoneal cavity
Assay	To determine the amount of a constituent in a mixture or the potency of a drug
Atrophy	Wasting away
Atypical	Abnormal
Autonomic	Part of the nervous system that is functionally independent and not subject to voluntary control
Axial	In line with
Azoospermia	The absence of spermatozoa in the semen

B

Bacteriology	The study of micro-organisms (mainly bacteria but also including viruses, protozoa and fungi, etc)
Bacterial vaginosis	A type of vaginal infection

Bartholin's gland	The bilaterally paired greater vestibular glands at the vaginal orifice
Bartholin's abscess	An abscess of Bartholin's gland
Bartholin's cyst	A cyst of Bartholin's gland
Basal body temperature (BBT)	The body temperature taken immediately upon waking used to help predict ovulation
Benign	Not malignant
Bilateral	Both sides (usually, of the midline)
Billing's method	A method of natural contraception, relying largely on the woman's assessment of the character of her cervical mucus
Bimanual examination	Using both hands; during a vaginal examination, one of the examiner's hands rests upon the lower abdomen
Bioactive	A substance that has an effect upon living tissue
Biopsy	Removal of tissue from the living body for further examination
Blastocyst	The conceptus 7–10 days after fertilisation of the ovum
Bone marrow depression	Reduced activity of the bone marrow resulting in decreased production of blood cells, which may cause anaemia, low resistance to infection and an increased tendency to bleed
Bowel	The intestine
small bowel	The duodenum, jejunum and ileum
large bowel	The appendix, caecum, colon, rectum and anal canal
Brenner tumour	A rare, usually benign, ovarian tumour
Broad ligament	A thin fold of peritoneum draped over the uterine tubes and extending from the uterus out to the pelvic side-wall (but note that there are similarly named structures associated with the lungs and the liver)
Bromocriptine	A drug which decreases the production of the hormone prolactin by the pituitary gland; used to suppress lactation and in the treatment of hyperprolactinaemia (qv)

C

Ca 125	A tumour marker found in the blood; raised levels may be associated with some ovarian malignancies
Caesarean section	Birth of an infant through an abdominal surgical operation
Candida	A group of yeast-like fungi, which cause various infections, the most common of which is a vaginitis
Cannula	A tube for insertion into a duct or cavity; during insertion, the lumen is usually occupied by a trocar
Carcinoembryonic antigen (CEA)	A tumour marker found in the blood
Carcinoma	A malignant growth arising from epithelial cells
Cardiac	Pertaining to the heart
cardiac irregularity	Irregular heart beat
Cardio-vascular disease	Pertaining to the heart and blood vessels
Catheter	A flexible tube passed through body channels for withdrawal or introduction of fluids
Caudal	The opposite end of the body to the head (opposite of cranial)
Cautery	The application of an instrument or agent to destroy tissue by heat, cold or chemical action
Central nervous system	The brain and spinal cord
Cerebrovascular accident	A stroke
Cervical	Pertaining to the neck or to the uterine cervix
cervical canal	The channel through the centre of the uterine cervix, leading from the uterine cavity to the vagina
cervical cerclage	A suture placed around the upper cervix in an attempt to prevent cervical incompetence (qv)
cervical cytology	Microscopic examination of a cervical (Papanicolaou) smear
cervical excitation	Pain on moving the cervix during vaginal examination

cervical incompetence	Abnormally early, spontaneous dilatation of the cervix uteri (usually during the second trimester of pregnancy), resulting in a miscarriage or the birth of a very premature infant
cervical intra-epithelial neoplasia (CIN)	Pre-malignant lesion of the cervix
cervical nerve roots	Nerves originating from the spinal cord in the region of the neck
cervical os	Unless qualified, usually refers to the external cervical os
external cervical os	The vaginal opening of the cervical canal
internal cervical os	The uterine opening of the cervical canal
Cervicitis	Inflammation of the uterine cervix
Cervix	Neck (especially of the uterus)
Chancre	The primary lesion of syphilis
Chemotherapy	Treatment of disease by chemicals; often used to refer to drug based treatment of cancer
Chlamydia	Group of obligatory intracellular bacteria; the word is frequently used alone in gynaecology to refer to *C trachomatis*, the causative organism of a number of diseases, including sexually transmitted infection, resulting in pelvic inflammatory disease
Chocolate cysts	Endometriotic cysts
Choriocarcinoma	A malignant form of trophoblastic disease
Chromosomes	The structures within the cell nucleus containing strands of DNA (qv) which transmit genetic information
Chromosomal abnormalities	An abnormality of the number or structure of the chromosomes
Chronic	Persisting for a long time
Circulatory effects	Effects upon the blood vessels
Clear cell carcinoma	A type of uterine carcinoma
Climacteric	The period of time at the end of the female reproductive era around the time of the menopause (qv)
Clinically undetectable	Not possible to find on physical examination
Clitoris	The female erectile tissue; homologue of the male penis

Clomiphene	An anti-oestrogenic drug that is used for fertility treatment
Clostridium welchii	Bacterium that causes gas gangrene
Coagulation	Formation of a clot or the precipitation of proteins
Coitus	Sexual intercourse
Colicky	Spasmodic (used to describe pain)
Colonise	To establish growth (usually refers to infecting organisms)
Colposcopy	Examination of the vaginal surface of the uterine cervix under magnification
Compliance	A measure of a patient's co-operation in treatment, especially in the taking of drugs as instructed
Conception	Fertilisation of the ovum by the sperm; the beginning of pregnancy
Conceptus	The total products of a fertilised ovum, from fertilisation until birth
Cone biopsy	The removal of a cone of tissue from the uterine cervix
Congenital	Existing at the time of birth
Conjunctiva	The delicate membrane lining the eyelids and covering the exposed part of the eyeball except for the cornea
Contact tracing	Following up people who have been in contact with sexually transmitted infections
Contraindication	A factor that renders a line of treatment unsuitable
relative contraindication	A factor that may make a treatment unsuitable
absolute contraindication	A reason for not giving a treatment
Contusion	A bruise
Cornu	The horn-like extensions of the uterus into the tubes (plural: cornua)
Cornuectomy	Removal of the cornu of the uterus
Coronal plane	An descriptive anatomical term meaning at right angles to the sagittal (median) plane
Corpus	Body (especially of the uterus)
Corpus luteum	Group of cells formed in the ovary from the Graafian follicle after ovulation has occurred

Cranial	Towards the head (opposite of caudal)
Crepitus	A crackling sound upon pressure, due to gas in the tissues
Crohn's disease	An inflammatory condition of the bowel, most frequently affecting the terminal part of the ileum
Cryo-	Cold
Cryocautery	Tissue destruction by freezing
Cryptomenorrhoea	Menstrual bleeding that is 'concealed' from the exterior, as in the case of an imperforate hymen
Culdocentesis	Puncture of the posterior vaginal fornix, usually to aspirate fluid from the pouch of Douglas (qv)
Culdotomy	An incision into the posterior fornix of the vagina to gain access to the pouch of Douglas (qv)
Curette	A spoon shaped instrument for scraping a surface
Cyclical progestogen	Progestogen given for (usually) two out of four weeks
Cyst	A fluid filled sac
Bartholin's cyst	A retention cyst of Bartholin's gland
chocolate cyst	Endometriotic cyst
dermoid cyst	Ovarian cyst containing a variety of tissues, often including hair and teeth
follicular cyst	A cyst formed from the Graafian follicle
Cystic	Containing or consisting of one or more cysts
Cystocoele	Prolapse of the upper part of the anterior vaginal wall and the underlying bladder wall
Cytogenetics	The study of chromosomes
Cytology	The study of cells

D

Danazol	Generic name for a substance which inhibits pituitary gonadotrophins; used in the treatment of endometriosis and some other conditions
De-bulking	Surgical reduction of a tumour mass

Deep venous thrombosis (DVT)	A clot in a vein, usually of the lower limb
Degeneration	A deterioration of tissue
calcified (or calcareous) degeneration	The deposition of calcium in tissue
cystic degeneration	The formation of cysts within the degenerate tissue
fatty degeneration	Deposition of fat within tissue
hyaline degeneration	The change into a homogeneous, glassy mass
myxomatous degeneration	Accumulation of mucus in the tissues
ossification degeneration	The deposition of bone in tissue
red degeneration	Vascular tissue outgrowing it's blood supply, so that ischaemic necrosis occurs at the centre of the mass
sarcomatous degeneration	Malignant change in non-epithelial tissue
Deoxyribonucleic acid	The genetic material in every cell, mainly in the chromosomes (qv)
Dermatology	The study of skin diseases
Diabetes	A disorder of carbohydrate metabolism, associated with dysfunction of the insulin producing cells in the pancreas
Diagnose	To make a diagnosis
Diagnosis	To determine the nature of the disease
differential diagnosis	A list of several conditions that are possible causes for the patient's symptoms
Diagnostic reliability	The chance that the correct diagnosis has been reached
Diagnostic tool	An aid to formulating a diagnosis
Diaphragm	(a) The fibromuscular sheet separating the thorax from the abdominal cavities; (b) a vaginal contraceptive device
Diathermy	A surgical technique for the cutting or coagulation of tissues by the passage of high frequency electromagnetic radiation or ultrasonic waves; also used at lower powers to cause warming of the tissue
bipolar diathermy	Diathermy system in which the return path for the electrical current is provided via an earth plate applied to the skin of the patient, usually on the upper thigh

unipolar diathermy	Diathermy using equipment which avoids the passage of the electric current through the patient's body
Diethylstilboestrol (DES)	A synthetic oestrogen
Digestive tract	The tube passing from the mouth to the anus and including the immediately associated organs
Digital	Using one or more fingers (eg, for examination or to separate tissue planes in surgery)
Dilatation and curettage (D&C)	Operative stretching of the cervix and scraping of the uterine lining
Diuretic	An agent that promotes urine excretion
Diverticulitis	An inflammatory condition of the large bowel
Dopamine	A chemical occurring naturally in the brain, also used as a drug to treat circulatory shock
Dorsal	Anatomical term for the posterior surface of the body
Douching	To shower or wash within the vagina
Dysfunction	Abnormal action or activity
Dysfunctional uterine bleeding (DUB)	Abnormal uterine bleeding for which no cause can be found
Dysgenesis	Defective development or a malformation
Dysmenorrhoea	Pain associated with menstruation
Dyspareunia	Pain during sexual intercourse
Dysplasia	Abnormality in the size, shape or organisation of cells
Dystrophy	See Vulval dystrophy

E

Echogenic	(In ultrasonography) giving rise to echoes (reflections) of ultrasound waves
Echotranslucent	(In ultrasonography) permitting the passage of ultrasound waves without giving rise to echoes
Ectoderm	Outermost of the three primary embryonic germ cells layers, the other two being the mesoderm (middle) and the endoderm (inner)

Ectopic	In an abnormal place
ectopic pregnancy	A pregnancy located away from the normal intrauterine position, most commonly in the uterine tube
Ectropion	Eversion or turning outwards
cervical ectropion	Eversion of the external cervical os, with exposure of the columnar epithelium lining the canal
Efficacy	Measure of efficiency (usually of drugs)
Electrocautery equipment	Apparatus for cauterising tissue by means of a platinum wire heated by an electrical current
Electrodiathermy equipment	Apparatus for the heating and destruction of tissue by the application of an electric current with specific waveform
Electrolyte	A substance that dissociates into ions in solution, thereby allowing the passage of electric current
Electroresection equipment	Apparatus for the cutting away of tissue using an electric current
Electrosurgury	Surgery performed with instruments using electrical methods
Embolism	Blockage of an artery or arteriole by material, such as a blood clot or tumour cells, that has travelled in the blood stream
Embryo	The intrauterine stage of the developing baby from shortly after conception until the end of the eighth week
Endocrine	Pertaining to internal hormonal secretions
Endocrine manipulation	Administration of exogenous substances to adjust the body's hormonal function
Endometrial	Pertaining to the endometrium (qv)
endometrial ablation	Removal of the endometrial layer
endometrial cavity	The potential cavity within the uterus
endometrial hyperplasia	Excessive increase in the number of normally formed endometrial cells
endometrial resection	Cutting away of the endometrium
Endometrioid carcinoma	A malignant ovarian tumour with features of endometrial tissue
Endometrioma	A tumour caused by endometriosis (when cystic, also known as a chocolate cyst)

Endometriosis	Ectopic endometrial deposits
Endometrium	The inner lining of the uterus
Endosalpinx	The inner lining of the uterine tube
Enterocoele	Intestinal hernia; in gynaecology, a prolapse of the upper part of the posterior vaginal wall and the underlying peritoneum of the pouch of Douglas
Epidural	Outside the spinal cord and its coverings
Episiotomy	A surgical incision into the vagina and perineum, usually to facilitate delivery of the baby; also occasionally used during surgical operations to improve access to the upper vagina
Epithelium	Layers of cells above the basement membrane; the surface covering of the internal and external body surfaces
Erect	Standing upright
Erosion (cervical)	Replacement of the squamous epithelium of the vaginal portion of the cervix by columnar epithelium
Erythromycin	Antibiotic preparation with an antibacterial spectrum similar to that of penicillin but also active against many penicillin resistant staphylococci; may be used in patients who suffer from hypersensitivity to penicillin
Essential fatty acid	An unsaturated fatty acid that cannot be formed in the body and is therefore required in the diet
Ethamsylate	A drug used in the treatment of menorrhagia to reduce capillary bleeding
Excoriated	Broken skin due to scratching
Exenteration	Surgical removal of the organs and adjacent structures of the pelvis; pelvic clearance
Exfoliative cytology	Study of the cells removed from the body for examination, such when taking a cervical smear
Exogenous	Originating outside the organism
Exophthalmos	Abnormal protrusion of the eyes

External | Outer surface
external cervical os | The vaginal opening of the cervical canal
Exudate | Viscous fluid that has escaped from blood vessels, usually during an inflammatory response, containing a large amount of cells and protein

F

Fallopian tube | The uterine tube or oviduct
Femur | The thighbone
Fibrin | An insoluble protein that is formed by the blood clotting system
Fibrinous exudate | Exudate containing fibrin
Fibroid polyp | A pedunculated submucus fibroid
Fibromyomata/fibro-
leiomyomata/fibroids | A benign tumour of the muscle wall of the uterus
Fibrosis | Formation of fibrous or scar tissue
Fibrous tissue | Tissue containing collagen fibres
Filshie clip | Type of clip used in laparoscopic female sterilisation
Fimbrial | The fringe like processes of the distal end of the uterine tube
Flexion | Bending, usually of a joint
Foeticide, feticide | The destruction of the foetus
Follicle | A sac or pouch-like depression or cavity
follicle stimulating hormone (FSH) | A hormone released from the pituitary gland that acts upon the ovary
Graafian follicle | The ovarian follicle prior to ovulation, consisting of the ovum, the follicular fluid and the surrounding cells
Follicular | Pertaining to the (ovarian) follicles
Folliculitis | Inflammation of a (hair) follicle
Forceps | A two-bladed instrument for compressing or grasping tissues or materials
Formulations | Preparations of drugs

Fornix	The space surrounding the portio vaginalis at the apex of the vagina, conventionally termed anterior and posterior fornices, and right and left lateral fornices
Fourchette	The posterior margin of the vaginal introitus
Fundus	The base of an organ; the part of the uterus above the entry of the uterine tubes
Fusion	Merging together

G

Galactorrhoea	Inappropriate milk production from the breasts
Gamete intra-fallopian transfer (GIFT)	A method of assisted conception, in which the ova and sperm are inserted into the fallopian tube
Gastro-intestinal	Pertaining to the digestive tract
Gene	The biological unit of heredity located at a definite position on a particular chromosome
Generic	Non-proprietary; used in the sense of a drug not protected by a patent
Genetics	The study of inheritance
Genital tract	The reproductive tract
Genitalia	The external sexual organs
Genitourinary medicine	The study and treatment of venereal disease
Gestation sac	The amniotic sac produced as a result of conception
Gestrione	Generic name for a drug used in the treatment of endometriosis
Gland	An aggregation of cells specialising in the secretion of natural substances
Glandular	Pertaining to a gland
Glucose tolerance test (GTT)	A test of the body's ability to metabolise sugar, used to ascertain whether or not the patient is suffering from diabetes mellitus
Glycine	A type of amino acid
Goitre	An enlargement of the thyroid gland
Gold standard	A test by which all others are judged
Gonad	An ovary or a testis

Gonadotrophin releasing hormone (GnRH)	A hormone released from the hypothalamus that influences the pituitary to release LH and FSH
gonadotrophin releasing hormone analogues	Drugs that mimic the action of gonadotrophin releasing hormone
Gonorrhoea	A sexually transmitted genital infection caused by the organism *Neisseria gonorrhoeae*
Granulation	The formation of exuberant tissue during wound healing
Granulosa cell tumour	A hormone secreting ovarian tumour
Gravigard	Trade name for one of the copper bearing intrauterine contraceptive devices

H

Haematoma	A localised collection of blood
Haemoglobin	The oxygen carrying pigment of the red blood cells
Haemoptysis	The coughing up of blood
Haemorrhage	Bleeding, usually excessive
Hepatic adenoma	Benign tumour of the liver
Hernia	A bulge of part of an organ or tissue through an abnormal opening
Herpes simplex virus (HSV)	A DNA virus; HSV Type II is usually sexually transmitted
Heterogeneous	Not of uniform quality or structure
Hirsutism	Excess body hair
Histology	The study of the minute structure of tissues
Histopathological	The study of diseased tissue
Hormone	A substance produced from one part of the body and having an effect on cells or organs at a distant site
Hulka clips	Type of clip used in laparoscopic female sterilisation

Human chorionic gonadotrophin (HCG)	A pregnancy hormone; detection of HCG in urine or serum is the basis of most test for pregnancy; present in large amounts in most cases of trophoblastic disease; also administered in certain infertility treatments
Human immuno-deficiency virus (HIV)	A viral infection that causes suppression of the host's normal defences against infections and cancers
Human papilloma virus (HPV)	A viral infection causing warts; some have a role in the development of malignancies
Human placental lactogen (HPL)	A placental hormone
Hydatidiform mole	A benign form of trophoblastic disease
Hydronephrosis	Distension of the renal pelvis often due to a blockage of the ureter
Hydrosalpinx	Accumulation of fluid in the uterine tube
Hymen	A membranous fold partially closing the vagina before the first occasion of coitus
Hymeneal	Pertaining to the hymen
hymeneal ring	The site of attachment of the hymen
hymeneal tags	Small skin tags left after the hymen is ruptured during coitus
Hyper-	Abnormally high, increased or excessive
hyperemesis gravidarum	Excessive vomiting in pregnancy
hypergonadotrophic	Abnormally increased activity of the gonads with excessive growth and precocious puberty
hyperplasia	Abnormal increase in the number of otherwise normal cells
hyperprolactinaemia	Abnormally high level of prolactin hormone in the blood
hypertension	High blood pressure
hypertonic	A solution with a higher osmotic pressure than that with which it is being compared

Hypo-	Abnormally low, reduced or deficient
hypogonadotrophic	Decreased function of the gonad with retardation of growth and of sexual development
hypoplasia	Incomplete or otherwise poor growth of an organ
hypospadias	A developmental anomaly in males, in which the urethra opens on the underside of the penis (occasionally occurs in females, when the urethra opens into the vagina)
hypotension	Low blood pressure
hypothalamus	Primitive part of the brain that integrates many autonomic (qv) functions of the body
hypothyroid	Deficiency of thyroid gland function
hypovolaemia	Decreased volume of circulating fluid (eg, blood) in the body
Hysterectomy	Removal of the uterus
abdominal hysterectomy	Removal of the uterus through an abdominal incision
sub-total hysterectomy	Removal of the uterus, including the upper part of its cervix but not the lower cervix, tubes or ovaries
total hysterectomy	Removal of the uterus (including both the corpus and cervix) but not the tubes or ovaries
vaginal hysterectomy	Removal of the uterus through a vaginal incision
Hysterosalpingogram (HSG)	An X-ray examination of the uterine cavity and tubes
Hysteroscopic	Pertaining to the hysteroscope
Hysteroscopy	An instrument passed along the cervical canal to allow visual inspection of the uterine cavity
Hysterotomy	An incision into the uterus

I

Iliac (vessels)	The major blood vessels supplying the pelvis and its contained structures, and also the lower limbs
common iliac artery	The terminal division of the aorta

external iliac vessels	The major vessels that leave the pelvis to supply the lower limb
internal iliac vessels	The major vessels supplying structures in the pelvis
Ilium	One of the three parts of the innominate or hip bone
Immune status	The body's ability to respond to an immunological stimulant
Immunological response	The body's response to an immunological stimulant
Immunology	The science dealing with the body's ability to recognise self and non-self; it includes immunity and allergy
Implant	Material inserted into the body
Implantation	The attachment and embedding of the blastocyst in the uterine lining
Incarceration	Unnatural confinement within a cavity such as the pelvis
Incise	To cut into
Inferior	Anatomical term for below
Infertility	Inability to conceive
Infestation	Parasitic subsistence on the skin or skin derivatives (eg, hair and nails)
Inflammatory response	A protective response by the body to injury
Infundibulum	Funnel shaped (especially of the distal end of the uterine tube)
Inguinal hernia	A protrusion of the peritoneal cavity along the inguinal canal in the groin
Innominate bone	The hip bone
Inspissated	Thickened, dried or made less fluid
Intermenstrual	The time between each menstrual bleed
Internal	Anatomical term for the inner layer of a cavity
internal cervical os	The opening from the cervical canal into the uterine cavity
Interstitial	Between the cells
Intervertebral foramen	The bilateral space between the vertebrae through which the spinal nerves emerge (plural: foramina)

Intracytoplasmic sperm injection (ICSI)	An infertility treatment, involving the direct injection of the sperm into the ovum
Intramural	Within a wall
Intramuscular	Within a muscle
Intrauterine	Within the uterus
intrauterine contraceptive device (IUCD)	A contraceptive device that is inserted into the uterine cavity, where it can remain for several years
intrauterine death (IUD)	Death of the foetus while still within the uterine cavity
intrauterine insemination (IUI)	The introduction of washed semen into the uterine cavity, with the intention of causing conception
Intravenous	Within or into a vein
intravenous pyelography (IVP)	Radiological study of the kidneys
intravenous urography (IVU)	Radiological study of the urinary tract
Introitus	External (vulval) opening of the vagina
Intromission	Penetration (usually of the vagina by the penis during coitus)
Invasive	The ability to spread into tissues
Invasive mole	A type of trophoblastic disease which spreads into the uterine muscle
In-vitro fertilisation (IVF)	An infertility treatment, in which the egg is fertilised by a sperm when out of the woman's body, the early embryo then being placed into the uterine cavity; popularly called 'test tube' pregnancies
Ipsilateral	Situated on the same side
Irradiation	Exposure to radiant energy, often X-rays, for diagnostic or treatment purposes
Ischaemic necrosis	Death of tissues caused by loss of their blood supply
Ischium	One of the three parts of the innominate or hip bone

Isoniazid	A drug for the treatment of tuberculosis
Isthmus	Narrow portion (of the fallopian tube)

K

Key-hole surgery	Popular term for endoscopic surgery
Krukenberg tumour	Ovarian tumour that is a metastatic deposit from another tumour, commonly from the stomach

L

Labia majora	The outer, hair covered skin folds surrounding the vaginal introitus
Labia minora	The delicate skin folds immediately surrounding the vaginal introitus
Laceration	A ragged cut or tear
Lactation	The secretion of milk
Laparoscopically assisted vaginal hysterectomy (LAVH)	A hysterectomy performed using a combination of laparoscopic operating and vaginal operating techniques
Laparoscope	An instrument for visual examination of the peritoneal cavity
Laparotomy	An incision through the anterior abdominal wall to gain access to the peritoneal cavity
Large loop excision of the transformation zone (LLETZ)	Removal by diathermy of the whole transformation zone of the cervix
Laser evaporation	To remove tissue by the application of laser energy
Lateral	A position further from the midline
Lesion	A pathological or traumatic discontinuity of tissue or the loss of function of a part
Leucocytosis	Elevated white blood cell count, often indicating infection
Libido	Sexual drive
Lichen sclerosis et atrophicus	A type of vulval dystrophy

Ligament	(a) A band of fibrous tissue connecting bones or cartilages; (b) a double layer of peritoneum from one organ to another; (c) cord like remnants of foetal structures that are non-functional after birth
ovarian ligament	Bilateral peritoneal fold from the posterior surface of the uterus to the ovary
round ligament	A fibromuscular band from the anterior uterine surface, along the inguinal canal, to the labia majora
uterosacral ligament	Bilateral fibrous band from the posterior surface of the uterus to the posterolateral pelvic wall
Ligate	To tie (especially with reference to blood vessels or other tubular structures)
Lindane	Generic name for a chemical used in a 1% solution as a topical treatment for lice and scabies
Lippe's Loop	A type of intrauterine contraceptive device
Lithotomy	The position of the woman's body during most gynaecological vaginal surgery (originally used when 'cutting for stone' – surgical treatment of bladder stones – hence, from the Greek: *lithos*, a stone)
Local	Having an effect restricted to the immediate area
local anaesthetic	Anaesthetic having its effect restricted to the area into which it is given
Luteinising hormone (LH)	A hormone released from the pituitary gland that acts upon the ovaries
Lymph	The clear, watery fluid contained within the lymphatic vessels
lymph glands	Obsolete term for lymph nodes
lymph nodes	Swellings in the lymphatic system which act as filters
Lymphatic system	A system of fine tubules that drains excess fluid from tissues and returns it to the blood system

M

MacDonald suture	One version of cervical cerclage (qv)
Madlener operation	A female sterilisation operation
Magnetic resonance imaging (MRI)	An imaging method, in which molecules are stimulated by a strong magnetic field; ionising radiation is not employed
Malathion	Generic name for a substance used in topical preparations at 0.5–1% for the treatment of lice and scabies
Malignant	Cancerous
Malignant tumour	A cancerous swelling
Mammography	X-ray examination of the breast
Marsupialisation	To open a cavity, thereby creating a pouch
Mebendazole	Generic name for a substance administered orally in the treatment of intestinal worms
Medial	Towards the midline
Median	The midline of the body
Medroxyprogesterone acetate (MPA)	A progestogen
Mefanamic acid	A non-steroidal anti-inflammatory drug, which is widely used in the treatment of menorrhagia and as a pain killer
Menarche	The onset of menstruation
Menopause	The last menstrual period
Menorrhagia	Heavy menstrual blood loss
Mesonephric duct	Wolffian duct; embryological tubal system that forms the greater part of the male genital tract; it largely regresses in the female
Mesosalpinx	Part of the broad ligament which supports the fallopian tube
Mesovarium	Part of the broad ligament extending to the ovary
Metastasise	To form new foci of disease in a distant part of the body (adjective: metastatic)
Methotrexate	A drug used in chemotherapy
Metronidazole	An antimicrobial drug, particularly effective against anaerobic bacteria and protozoa

Micro-adenoma	Very small (sometimes microscopic) benign tumours, such as a prolactinoma of the pituitary
Microinvasive disease	Microscopic extension of malignant cells into surrounding tissue
Micturition	Voiding of urine from the bladder
Migraine	Symptoms consisting of periodic headaches, often with nausea, caused by constriction and then dilation of the cerebral vessels
Mons pubis	The rounded fat pad overlying the pubic symphysis
Motility	Spontaneous movement, such as assessed in semen analysis
Mucin	A thick, rather gelatinous, yellow fluid
Mucinous	Containing or consisting of mucin
mucinous cystadenocarcinoma	A type of malignant ovarian tumour
mucinous cystadenoma	A type of benign ovarian tumour
Mucosa	A mucous-secreting layer which lines many organs
Mucus-hostility test	A test of sperm function in infertility investigations
Mullerian duct	See Paramesonephric duct
Multilocular	Having many cavities
Multiparous	A woman who has already been delivered of one or more infants
Myocardial infarction (MI)	Heart attack
Myoma	Fibro-leiomyomata/fibroid; benign tumour of the myometrium
Myomectomy	An operation to remove fibroids from the uterus
Myometrium	The middle, fibro-muscular layer of the uterine wall
Myxoma peritoneii	A non-malignant (but sometimes fatal) condition characterised by widespread deposition of mucinous material within the peritoneal cavity

N

Nabothian follicle	Benign retention cysts of the uterine cervix
Necrosis	Cellular death (adjective: necrotic)
Negative feedback	The reduction in the hormone output from a gland in response to an increase in the level of circulating hormone
Neoplasia	New growth of tissue, in which multiplication of cells is uncontrolled and progressive
Neurogenic shock	Acute circulatory failure in response to excessive nerve stimulation
Neurotransmitter	Chemical substance that is released by nerve cells and which provokes a response in another ('target') cell
Non-steroidal anti-inflammatory drug (NSAID)	Any drug having anti-inflammatory properties that is not a steroid derivative
Norethisterone (NET)	A synthetic progestogen
Nulliparous	A woman who has never borne an infant

O

Oestradiol	An naturally occurring oestrogen, also used in various therapeutic preparations, including some oral contraceptives and HRT
Oestrogen	One of a group of related female hormones, including oestradiol, oestrone and oestriol
Oligomenorrhoea	Abnormally infrequent menstruation
Oligospermia	An abnormally low sperm count
Omentectomy	Removal of the omentum
Omentum	A large fold of peritoneum extending from the lower border of the stomach and containing fat
Oophorectomy	Removal of an ovary
Oophoritis	Inflammation of an ovary
Opportunistic organisms	Organisms that thrive when conditions are suitable
Optic chiasma	The cross-over of the optic nerves which is located at the base of the brain and just above the pituitary gland
Orally	By mouth

Organ	A body part that performs a special function
Os or ostium (plural: ostia)	An orifice; the opening of a tube; a 'mouth'
Osmosis	The passage of solvent from a solution of lesser concentration of solute to one of greater concentration of the same solute (adjective: osmotic)
Osteoporosis	Abnormally reduced bone density; bone de-mineralisation
Ovarian	Pertaining to the ovaries
ovarian cycle	The monthly changes occurring in the ovary
ovarian cystectomy	Removal of a cyst and its wall from the ovary
ovarian failure	Loss of the ability of the ovary to release eggs and/or hormones
ovarian follicle tracking	Frequent (usually alternate day) ultrasonic scanning to observe the follicular growth
ovarian fossa	The depression on the side wall of the pelvis in which the ovaries normally lie
Ovaries	Bilaterally paired structures lying on each side of the uterus which produce hormones and in which the ova develop
streak ovaries	Hypoplastic ovaries
Over the counter medication	Medication that can be purchased from a chemist without a doctor's prescription
Ovulation	The release of the ovum from the Graafian follicle in the ovary
Ovulatory	Relating to ovulation
Ovum (plural: ova)	An egg
Oxford technique	A type of female sterilisation operation
Oxytocin	A hormone from the pituitary gland that causes uterine contractions

P

Papanicolaou ('Pap') smear	The cervical smear
Para-	Alongside
Para-aortic nodes	Lymph nodes near the aorta into which the lymph from the ovaries drains
Paracentesis	Surgical puncture of the abdominal wall for the aspiration of fluid from the peritoneal cavity
Paracolic gutter	Channels on both sides of the peritoneal cavity alongside the large bowel

Paramesonephric duct	Mullerian duct; an embryological structure that develops into much of the female genital tract but largely regresses in the male
Partial mole	A type of trophoblastic disease
Pathological	Abnormal
Pearl index	A measure of the efficacy of a method of contraception
Pedicle	A foot or stalk; also used, especially in surgery, to refer to a group of blood vessels supplying an organ and to the connective tissue surrounding them
Pediculosis pubis	Pubic lice
Pedunculated	On a stalk
Pelvic cavity	The lower part of the peritoneal cavity bounded by the pelvic bones
Pelvic floor	A muscular sheet composed mainly of the levator ani muscles
Pelvic inflammatory disease (PID)	Inflammation of the pelvic organs, usually due to infection
Pelvic kidney	An abnormal kidney located near or in the pelvis
Pelvic varices	Abnormally prominent pelvic veins
Perforation	An abnormal hole in a structure or organ
Perineal	Pertaining to the perineum
perineal body	Fibromuscular structure between the vaginal introitus and anus
Perineum	(a) (Anatomy) the area below the pelvic floor down to the skin of the inner thighs; (b) (gynaecology) the area between the vaginal fourchette and the anus
Peritoneal cavity	The cavity between the diaphragm and the pelvic floor
Peritoneal surface	Any surface covered by peritoneum
Peritoneum	A thin epithelial layer covering many of the abdominal and pelvic organs and lining the peritoneal cavity
parietal peritoneum	Peritoneum lining the abdominal and pelvic cavities
visceral peritoneum	Peritoneum covering the abdominal and pelvic organs

Peritonitis	Inflammation of the peritoneum (usually due to infection)
Pessary	An instrument or drug intended to be placed into the vagina
Petechial haemorrhage	A minute red spot due to the escape of a tiny amount of blood
Phenotype	The overall appearance
Physiological	Associated with normal function
Physiology	The study of the normal function of living organisms
Pill, the	Oral contraceptive tablets: 'combined' pills contain both oestrogen and progestogen; 'mini pills' contain progestogen only
Piperazine	A treatment for threadworms
Pituitary gland	An endocrine gland located at the base of the brain
Placebo	Inactive substance administered in place of an active drug or (occasionally) other treatment; often used to assess the efficacy of a drug by comparison
placebo response	The effect of a placebo
Placenta	The 'after-birth' characteristic of mammalian pregnancies
Pleural effusion	Fluid in the thoracic cavity between the lungs and chest wall
Podophyllin	A toxic substance usually used as a paint for the topical treatment of warts
Polycystic	Having many cysts
Polymenorrhoea	Abnormally frequent menstruation
Polyp	A growth arising from a surface to which it is usually attached by a stalk
Pomeroy's operation	A type of female sterilisation operation
Ponstan	Trade name for mefenamic acid, a substance having analgesic and anti-prostaglandin effects
Portio vaginalis	The part of the cervix protruding into the vagina
Post-coital	After sexual intercourse
Post-coital test	A fertility investigation performed on the woman's cervical mucous after sexual intercourse

Post-menopausal	After the final menstrual bleed
Post-natal	After childbirth, with reference to the child
Postpartum	After childbirth, with reference to the mother
Pouch of Douglas	A peritoneal sac forming the lowest part of the peritoneal cavity and lying between the reproductive and lower digestive tracts
Precocious	The unusually early development of mental or physical traits
Pre-conception priming	The use of drug therapy (usually oestrogen) prior to pregnancy that is intended to render the intrauterine status more hospitable to the conception
Pre-eclampsia toxaemia (PET)	A pregnancy-specific condition associated with a raised blood pressure, protein in the urine and peripheral oedema
Pre-ejaculate	Fluid escaping from the urethral meatus of the penis prior to ejaculation
Pre-malignant	A non-cancerous condition that may progress into a cancer
Premature	Occurring before the proper time
premature labour	Spontaneous labour occurring before the beginning of the 37th week of pregnancy
premature menopause	Menopause occurring before the age of 40 years
Pre-menstrual	Before menstruation
Primary carcinoma	The initial site of a cancer
Primary ovarian failure	Failure of ovarian function not due to the malfunction of another organ or system
Primordial follicles	Primitive ovarian follicles
Procidentia	Complete prolapse of the uterus through the vagina
Products of conception (POC)	The embryo or foetus, placenta and membranes
Progeny	Offspring
Progesterone	A steroid hormone that is produced by the corpus luteum of the ovary and by the placenta
Progestogen	A substance with progestational activity
Prolactin	A pituitary hormone

Prolapse	Downward displacement from the normal, anatomical position; in gynaecology, when unqualified, it usually refers to utero-vaginal prolapse (qv)
Prophylactic	Preventative
Prostaglandin	A group of naturally occurring substances that are widespread in the body
Prostate	The gland surrounding urethra and situated just below the bladder in the male
Proximal	Closer to a point of reference (usually the origin or the midline); opposite of distal
Pruritis	Irritation, itching
pruritis vulvae	Irritation of the vulva
Pseudocyesis	'False pregnancy'
Psychopathology	Mental illness
Psychosexual	Pertaining to the emotional aspects of sexual intercourse
Psychosomatic	Physical symptoms caused by emotional or mental disturbance
Puberty	The time of change from childhood to reproductive maturity
Pubic symphysis	The anterior joint between the two hip bones
Pubis	One of the three parts of the hip bone
Puerperium	The time following childbirth
Pulmonary embolism (PE)	An obstruction to blood flow in the lung caused by material, usually blood clot, that has travelled via the blood vessels
Pus	A fluid produced by an inflammatory process and consisting mainly of white blood cells and a thin, protein rich liquid; in infections, the causative organisms will also be present but may be dead (and, therefore, not detectable by the usual tests)
pus cells	The leucocytes, a type of white blood cell
Pyosalpinx	Accumulation of pus in the uterine tube
Pyrantel	A treatment for threadworms
Pyrexia	Elevated body temperature

R

Radical surgery	Extensive surgery used for cancer treatment
Radiograph	An X-ray film
Radioimmunoassay	A method for determining the amount of a substance, often an antibody or antigen, by the use of a radioisotope marker
Radiology	The use of radiant energy (eg, X-rays) in the diagnosis and treatment of disease
Radio-opaque	Obstructive to the passage of X-rays so that area concerned appears white on the exposed X-ray film
Radiotherapy	The use of ionising radiation for the treatment of diseases, most commonly cancer
Ramus	Branch
dorsal ramus	The posterior branch of a spinal nerve
ventral ramus	The anterior branch of a spinal nerve
Rectocoele	A prolapse of the lower part of the posterior vaginal wall and the underlying rectal wall
Rectum	The part of the large bowel between the sigmoid colon and the anal canal
Rectus abdominis	The muscle of the anterior abdominal wall extending from the costal margin to the symphysis pubis on each side of the midline
Referred pain	Pain felt in an area distant from the region in which the sensation originates
Resection	Cutting away
Retractor	Instrument for holding structures out of the field of view during surgical operations
self-retaining retractor	A retractor which does not have to be held by an assistant
Retroflexion	Backwards bend of the longitudinal axis of the uterus
Retrograde menstruation	Menstrual blood passing from the uterine cavity along the uterine tube
Retroversion (r/v)	Backward tilt of the whole uterus
Roller ball	An instrument used in endometrial ablation to destroy the endometrium by electrocoagulation
Rudimentary horn	A developmental anomaly of the uterus
Rugae	Ridges

S

Sacral plexus	A network of nerves that supply the pelvic organs
Sacro-iliac joint	The joint between the sacrum and the innominate (hip) bone
Sacrum	The triangular bone at the base of the spine formed from fusion of several of the lower vertebrae
Sagittal plane	An anatomical plane parallel to the median plane
Saline solution	Solution of salt in water
Salpingectomy	Removal of the uterine tube
Salpingitis	Inflammation of the uterine tube
Salpingoscopy	Endoscopic examination of the uterine tubes
Salpingostomy	The creation of an opening in the uterine tube
Salpingotomy	Surgical incision into the uterine tube
Sarcoptes scabiei	Scabies
Scalpel	A surgical knife
Sclerosant	A chemical irritant used to produce inflammation and subsequent fibrosis
Sclerotic	Hardened
Sebaceous gland	Gland associated with the skin and producing an oily secretion (sebum)
Secondary carcinoma	A metastasis
Secondary sexual characteristics	Breast development in women, facial hair and deepening of the voice in men and axillary and pubic hair in both sexes
Semen	The male ejaculate
Seminal vesicles	Glands situated at the base of the penis contributing seminal fluid to the ejaculate
Serosa	The peritoneal surface of an organ
Serotonin	A central nervous system chemical
Serous cystadenocarcinoma	A type of malignant ovarian tumour
Serous cystadenoma	A type of benign ovarian tumour
Serum	The fluid component of blood after the clotting factors have been removed
Shock	Acute peripheral circulatory failure

Sickle cell	Inherited condition associated with abnormal red blood cells
sickle cell crisis	Acute, sometimes fatal, condition occurring in susceptible individuals due to a change in the shape of the red blood cells in response to a change in their physical environment
Sigmoid colon	Part of the large bowel between the descending colon and the rectum
Silastic	An inert material often used in medical devices
Sloughing	Necrotic tissue separating from healthy tissue
Somatic	Pertaining to the body
Sound (instrument)	An instrument used to measure the depth of a cavity
uterine sound	An instrument designed for the measurement of the length of the uterine cavity
Speculum	An instrument used to inspect body cavities (especially the vagina)
Auvard's speculum	A weighted vaginal speculum often used to improve access during vaginal surgery
Cuscoe's speculum	A bivalve vaginal speculum
Sim's speculum	A spoon shaped vaginal speculum
Spermatozoa	The mature male germ cell in the semen
Squamous metaplasia	The change from another tissue type into squamous tissue
Stenosis	The abnormal narrowing of an opening or tube
Steroid	A large group of compounds all sharing a common molecular ring structure; includes many hormones and the bile acids
Streak ovaries	Dysplastic ovaries
Strongyloides stercoralis	Threadworms
Stump carcinoma	A carcinoma arising in the part of the cervix remaining after a sub-total hysterectomy
Subclavian vein	The main vein draining the arm
Subcutaneous	Beneath the skin
Subcuticular	Beneath the epidermal layer of the skin
subcuticular suture	A method of suturing the sub-epidermal layers with a continuous length of suture material
Subfertility	Reduced ability to conceive a pregnancy
Submucus fibroids	Fibroids in or on the inner surface of the uterus

Subserous fibroids	Fibroids in or on the outer (peritoneal) surface of the uterus
Superficial	Near to the surface
Superior	Anatomical term meaning 'above'
Supra-pubic	Above the pubic symphysis
Surgical ablation	Operative destruction or removal
Suture	A surgical stitch or the material used for it
absorbable suture	A suture that will dissolve in the body
non-absorbable suture	A suture that does not dissolve
Symphysis pubis	The joint between the innominate (hip) bones
Syndrome	A characteristic collection of symptoms and/or signs
Asherman's syndrome	The partial or complete obliteration of the uterine cavity by synechiae (qv)
Irritable bowel syndrome	A disorder of the bowel characterised by intermittent diarrhoea, nausea and abdominal bloating; previously called 'spastic colon'
Meig's syndrome	An association between an ovarian fibroma and a pleural effusion
Sheehan's syndrome	Post-partum pituitary failure
Stein-Leventhal syndrome	Polycystic ovarian syndrome characterised by hirsutism, obesity and infertility
testicular feminising syndrome	Male pseudohermaphroditism; the external features are female but the ovaries, tubes and uterus are absent and testes are present
Turner's syndrome	A chromosomal disorder with XO genotype; phenotypically female
Synechia (plural: synechiae)	An adhesion, especially adhesions within the uterine cavity
Syphilis	Infection caused by the organism *Treponema pallidum*; usually transmitted sexually or acquired in utero
Systemic	Pertaining to the whole body

T

Tamoxifen	An oestrogen receptor antagonist used in the treatment of breast cancer and also some types of infertility
Telarche	The onset of the growth of body hair at puberty
Teratogenic	Having the ability to cause malformations in the developing embryo
Teratoma	Tumour composed of tissue derived from more than one primitive body layer
benign ovarian teratoma	Dermoid cyst of the ovary
malignant ovarian teratoma	Malignant (cancerous) form of dermoid cyst
Testosterone	The principle 'male' or androgenic hormone; also present in small quantities in women
Tetracycline	A group of broad-spectrum antibiotics; should not be given to children or pregnant women because they are deposited in growing teeth and bones
Therapeutic	Used in the treatment of disease
Thermocoagulation	Tissue destruction by the application of heat
Thoracic	Pertaining to the thorax
thoracic cavity	The body cavity above the diaphragm containing the lungs and heart
thoracic duct	The final pathway for the lymphatic system as it drains into the blood
Thorax	The chest
Threatened abortion	See Abortion
Thrombosis	The formation of a blood clot, usually within a blood vessel
Thyroid gland	Gland located in the neck producing the hormones thyroxine and triiodothyronine which have wide metabolic effects
Thyroid stimulating hormone (TSH)	A hormone from the pituitary gland that regulates the function of the thyroid gland
Thyrotoxicosis	A disease caused by over activity of the thyroid gland

Thyroxine (T4)	One of the thyroid gland hormones
Tinea cruris	A fungal skin infection
Tissue	A group of similar, specialised cells functioning together
tissue receptors	Specialised areas of the cell surface which receive information and then alter activity of that cell
Torsion	Twisting, often of an organ upon its stalk
Torso	The body excluding the head and the limbs; the trunk
Trachelloraphy	Suturing of the uterine cervix
Tranexamic acid	A drug that promotes blood clotting; used in the treatment of menorrhagia
Transport medium	Solution that sustains organisms or tissues during transit
Transudate	A fluid derived from blood or lymph by passing through a membrane or tissue
Trichomonas vaginalis	A sexually transmitted protozoal organism
Trochar	A sharp pointed instrument, often equipped with a cannula, used to puncture the wall of a body cavity
Trophic hormones	Hormones that cause the growth of other tissues
Trophoblast	The layer of ectodermal tissue on the outside of the blastocyst
Trophoblastic disease	Disorders of trophoblastic tissue
Trunk	The body excluding the head and limbs; the torso
Tubal	Of or pertaining to any tube but, in gynaecology, used almost exclusively to refer to the fallopian tube or oviduct
tubal ligation	Female sterilisation by tying suture material around the fallopian tubes to occlude the lumen (in most cases, the tubes are also divided)
tubal ostium	An opening in a tube, often used to refer to the uterine opening of the fallopian tube as seen on hysteroscopy

tubal surgery	An operation performed upon the fallopian tube(s); although this could include sterilisation operations, the term is usually reserved for procedures intended to restore impaired fertility
Tubovarian mass	An inflammatory mass consisting of the fallopian tube and the ovary with exudate and/or pus
Tumour	Any swelling; often used without other qualification to refer to neoplasia (qv)
tumour marker	A substance, usually in the blood, which may be associated with the presence of a tumour

U

Ulcer	A local defect in the surface layer of an organ or tissue
Ultrasonic scanning	A means of imaging using the detection of reflected high frequency sound waves
Unilateral	On one side
Unilocular	Having one cavity
Unopposed oestrogen	Oestrogen therapy without the associated intermittent use of progesterone
Urea	Major end product of protein metabolism formed in the liver and excreted in the urine
Ureter	The tube draining urine from the kidney to the bladder
Ureteric duplication	Two ureters, rather than one, originating from the same kidney
Urethra	The tube draining urine from the bladder to the exterior of the body
Urethrocoele	Prolapse of the lower part of the anterior vaginal wall and underlying urethra
Urinary tract	The kidneys, ureters, bladder and urethra
Urinary tract infection (UTI)	A bacterial infection of the urinary tract
Urodynamic tests	Study of the dynamics of the flow of urine
Uro-genital tract	Pertaining to the urinary and genital tracts
Utero-vaginal prolapse	Downward displacement of the uterus and/or vaginal walls from the normal position (see, also, Cystocoele, Enterocoele, Rectocoele and Urethrocoele)

Utero-vesicular fold	Peritoneal fold between the uterus and bladder
Uterosacral ligament	Connective tissue thickening extending from the posterior uterine surface to the pelvic wall

V

Vacuum aspiration	Removal of the uterine contents by the application of suction through a hollow curette
Vas deferens	The male duct from the epididymis of the testis which joins the urethra in the prostate gland
Vaginal	Pertaining to the vagina
vaginal adenosis	A rare condition of the vagina seen in young women exposed to DES in utero
vaginal angles	The lateral fornices of the vagina at hysterectomy
vaginal introitus	The external opening of the vagina
vaginal prolapse	Downward displacement of the uterus and/or the vaginal walls
Vaginismus	Contraction of the pelvic floor muscles surrounding the vaginal orifice
Vascular	Pertaining to blood vessels or well supplied with blood
Vascular embolisation	A method of causing tissue destruction by obstruction of the blood supply
Vasectomy	Male sterilisation
Vault	The term applied to the closed upper vagina after hysterectomy
Ventral	Anatomical term for anterior; towards the front of the body (the opposite of dorsal)
Vertebra(e)	The component bone(s) of the spine
Vesicles	A small fluid filled sac
Vesicular	Pertaining to the urinary bladder
Vimule	An occlusive female contraceptive device
Virilization	Development of male features, especially in the female
Virulence	The ability of an organism to cause disease
Vulcanisation	Chemical process for altering the physical characteristics of rubber
Vulva	The external female genitalia

Vulval	Pertaining to the vulva
vulval dystrophy	A vulval disease characterised by a disordered growth of the vulval skin
vulval intra-epithelial neoplasia (VIN)	A pre-malignant condition of the vulva
Vulvectomy	Surgical removal of the vulva
Vulvo-vaginal	Pertaining to the vulva and vagina

W

Wertheim's hysterectomy	A radical hysterectomy in which the para-cervical tissues and pelvic lymph nodes are removed in addition to the uterus and tubes
Wolffian duct	See Mesonephric duct

A-fetoprotein (AFP)..131

Ablation, endometrial...............................64, 65

Abortion
D & C...31, 33
defined 173
induced 178–83
recurrent..56
spontaneous 173–78
uterine infections 117

Abortion Act...............................38, 174, 179

Actinomycoses 148

Acyclovir cream 97

Adenocarcinoma
cervical 116
fallopian tubes..123
uterine 120–21

Adenomas..71, 134

Adenomyosis (endometriosis
of myometrium) 62, 66, 87,
92, 120

Adenosis, vaginal 106–07

Adhesiolysis 171

Adhesions, pelvic...86

AFP (a-fetoprotein)...131

Agenesis
ovarian...69
uterine 69
vaginal...58, 69

AID (fertility treatment...............................171

Amenorrhoea (absent
periods).....................................61, 68–72, 103

Ampulla...15

Anaemia 62, 76

Anaerobic infections.......................................82

Anaesthesia..3, 31

Anal canal 19

Analgesics 90

Anatomy
defined...7
pelvic, see Pelvic anatomy

Androgen insensitivity
syndrome...20

Anembryonic pregnancy 177–78

Anomalies, developmental
fusion 57
ovarian...55

tubal...55–56
urinary tract...59
uterine 56–58
vaginal...58, 103
Wolffian duct remnants 58–59

Anorexia nervosa.......................................71–72

Anteflexion 15

Anterior position...8

Anti-fungal therapy..83

Anti-inflammatory drugs,
non-steroidal (NSAID) 63

Anti-oestrogens...170

Aorta 12

Arbuckle, Roscoe (Fatty) 73

Arteries 12,13

Arterioles 12

Asherman's sydrome 70

Atrophic vaginitis....................................73–74

Automatic nervous system 12

Back street abortions 182–83

Bacterial vaginosis.....................................82, 102

Bartholin's gland.....................................100–01

Basal body temperature
chart (BBT)...167

Benign ovarian tumours.........................127–28

Bilateral salpingectomy 161

Bladder (urinary) 18

Bleeding, abnormal,
see Menstrual disorders

Blood clots..25, 61, 62

Bones, pelvis..10–11

Break-through bleeding (BTB) 72

Breast cancer..28

Breast milk 26

Brenner tumour..128

British College of Obstetricians
and Gynaecologists.....................................1

Brittle bones (osteoporosis)...........................27

Bromocriptine...77, 170

Brown, Louise 172

BTB (break-through bleeding).......................72

Ca 125 tumour marker...............88, 131

Caesarean section 56, 156, 181

Cancers
    breast 28
    cervical 49, 51, 73,
        111–17
    endometrial 27, 29, 32, 62,
        73, 74
    lymphatic system 12
    ovaries.............................129–33
    sarcomatous degeneration.............120
    squamous cell 111–12
    uterus 74–75, 120–22
    vaginal............................74, 106–07
    vulva 100

Candida albicans (thrush)...............81, 82, 98, 102

Cap (diaphram)........................143

Capillaries 12

Carcinoembryonic antigen
  (CEA).................................131

Cardiovascular disease,
  menopause problems 27

Casper Bartholinus (anatomist) 100

CAT scanning...........................130

Caudal position........................8

CEA (carcinoembryonic
  antigen) 131

Cerebrovascular disease
  (strokes)............................28, 151

Cervical canal 15

Cervix
    anatomy 15, 18
    cancer 49, 51, 73, 111–17
    cone biopsies 38
    D & C................................33–38
    erosion..............................73, 107–08
    exfoliative cytology.................109–11
    fibroids 109
    lacerations..........................73
    polyps...............................109

Chaperones 4–5

Chemotherapy 132, 194

Childhoodphysiology 21

Chlamydia 83, 102, 147, 148, 166

Chocolate cysts........................88, 127

Chorioadenoma destruens................191

Chromosomal sexual
  differentiation 20

Chromosomes
    absent periods......................69
    physiology 19, 20
    uterine abnormalities................56

CI (Coitus interruptus) 140

CIN (cervical intra-epithelial
  neoplasia)............................111–12

Clear cell carcinoma 106–07

Clostridium welchii (gas
  gangrene).............................117, 174

Coccyx................................17

COCP (oral combined
  contraceptive pill) 150–51
  See, also, Contraceptives, oral

Coitus interruptus
  (withdrawal) 140

Colposcopy, training in 3

Combined pill.........................150
  See, also, Contraceptives, oral

Complementary therapies 76–77

Complete abortion.....................175–76

Completion of Specialist
  Training certificate (CST) 2

Computer automated
  tomography (CAT scanning) 130

Condoms...............................141–42

Condylomata acuminata
  (genital warts) 97

Cone biopsy 114

Contraceptives
    condoms.............................141–42
    counselling.........................140
    female barrier methods..............143–44
    intrauterine devices 64, 144–50
    'natural' birth control 140–41
    oral................................28, 77, 90–91, 150–53
    post-coital 153
    vasectomy...........................142–43

Cornual region 15

Cornuectomy..........................161

Coronal planes 7

Corpus, uterus........................15

Counselling...........................140, 156

Cranial position...8

Criminal terminations...........................182–83

Crohn's disease 123

Cryo-coagulation 64

Cryocautery 97

Cryptomenorrhoea......................................68–69

CST (Completion of Specialist
    Training) certificates 2

Culdotomy...157–58

Cusco's speculum...104

CVA (strokes)..28, 151

Cysts
    fimbrial...58, 123
    ovarian 62, 88, 126–27,
                                                        192
        para-cervical..59
        para-vaginal 59

Cytotoxic drugs...132

D & C (dilation and curettage)
    defined..31
    diagnostic indications..........................32–33
    endometrial hyperplasia 118
    hazards...37–38
    operation notes 38–39
    procedure...33–36
    surginal termination 180
    therapeutic indications 33
    uterine cancer...121

Danazol 64, 78, 91

Deep, defined 8

Deep venous thrombosis
    (DVT).................................25, 28, 64, 78, 151

Degeneration, fibroids 119–20

Deoxyribonucleic acid (DNA).........................19

Depression 76

Dermoid cysts 127–28

DES Action UK..107

DES (diethylstilboestrol) 106

Diabetes...95

Diaphragm (cap)...143

Diathermy...97

Diethylstilboestrol (DES)...............................106

Digestive tract..11

Dilation and curettage,
    see D & C

Dilators, cervical 35

Dimetriose...91

Discharges, vaginal
    pathological............................81–86, 102–03
    physiological...............................79–80, 101

Disorders, menstrual,
    see Menstrual disorders

Distal position 8

DNA (deoxyribonucleic acid)........................19

Doppler flow studies.......................................130

Dorsal position 8

DVT (deep venous
    thrombosis) 25, 28, 64, 151

Dysfunctional uterine
    bleeding (DUB),
    see Menstrual disorders

Dysmenorrhoea (painful periods)
    D & C...33
    endometriosis....................................88, 89
    PMS...76
    primary and secondary.................61, 65–66

Dyspareunia 27, 86, 88,
                                                        102, 136–37

Dysplasia (pre-invasive
    cervical disease)....................................111–12

Ectopic pregnancy 43, 70, 149,
                                                        185–89

Ectropion of cervix 80, 107–08

Edwards, Robert 160, 172

Electrocautery...158

Endometrial ablation 40, 64, 65

Endometrial carcinomas 27, 29, 32, 62,
                                                        73, 74

Endometrial cavity 17

Endometrial hyperplasia............29, 78, 118, 121

Endometrial polyps.........................118–19, 171

Endometrial resection 65

Endometrioid carcinoma.................................129

Endometrioma 127

Endometriosis 49, 62, 66, 87–93

Endoscopic surgery 3

Erosion, cervix......................................73, 107–08

ERPC (evacuation after
    miscarriage or abortion)...........................33

Escherichia coli 103, 174

Ethamsylate 64

Evening primrose oil..77

Exfoliative cytology..........................109–11, 132

Exophthalmos..62

External, defined 8

Fallope rings 159

Fallopian tubes
    anatomy 13, 15
    elective sterilisation....................................43
    infections...122–23
    infertility investigations 168–69

Fédération Internationale de
    Gynécologie et
    d'Obstétrique (FIGO)......................112, 121

Female barrier methods of
    contraception 143–44

Fibro-leimyomata, *see* fibroids

Fibroids
    cervical 109
    submucus...171
    uterine 62, 65, 119–20

Fibroma 128

FIGO (Fédération Internationale
    de Gynécologie et
    d'Obstétrique)...................................112, 121

Filshie sterilisation clips 159, 162

Fimbriae..13

Fimbrial cysts 58, 123

Foetuses, sexual physiology 20

Follicle stimulating hormone
    (FSH)..21, 22, 24, 26,
                        71, 167, 171

Folliculitis..97

Forceps..35

Fourchette, vaginal 17

FRCS (Fellows of the Royal
    College of Surgeons) 1

FSH (follicle stimulating
    hormone) 21, 22, 24, 26,
                        71, 167, 171

Fundus..15

Gardnerella vaginalis................................82, 102

Gastro-intestinal tract..19

General Medical Council,
    registration of doctors..................................1

General practitioners, *see* GPs

Genes...19

Genetics 19–20

Genital herpes 82

Genital warts 97

Genitalia, female 17

Genito-urinary medicine
    (GUM) clinics 79

Gestational sac...177

Gestrione 91

GIFT (infertility treatment) 172

GnRH (gonadotrophin
    releasing hormone)..........21, 22, 26, 78, 120

Goitre..62

Gonadal sexual differentiation........................20

Gonadotrophin releasing
    hormone (GnRH) 21, 22, 26, 78, 120

Gonads...19, 21

Gonorrhoea..83

Goodyear, Charles...143

GPs (general practitioners),
    referral to gynaecologists............................3

Graaffian follicles...126

Grafenberg, Ernst..144

Gravigard, the 145

GUM (genito-urinary
    medicine) clinics 79

Gynaecologists, defined 1

Haemorrhages
    ovarian tumours 125
    petechial 74
    rupture of septum 58

HCG (human chorionic
    gonadotrophin) 131, 192, 193

Heart attacks..152

Heart disease 27, 28

Heavy periods...32

Hegar (dilator)..35

Herpes simplex (HSV) 82, 96

Horizontal planes 8

Hormone replacement
    therapy (HRT)...............27–29, 118

Hot flushes.............................27, 28

House physicians (HP) 1

House surgeons (HS) 1

HP (house physicians) 1

HPL (human placental
    lactogen).....................................26

HRT (hormone replacement
    therapy)........................27–29, 118

HS (house surgeons) 1

HSG (hysterosalpingography) 168, 169

HSV (herpes simplex) 82, 96

Hulka sterilisation clips....................159, 160

Human chorionic
    gonadotrophin (HCG)............131, 192, 193

Human placental lactogen
    (HPL) 26

Hydatidiform moles........................191

Hymen
    imperforate...............................68–69
    incomplete 17
    torn..72

Hyperprolactinaemia 71

Hypoplastic ovaries............................55

Hypothyroidism 62, 76

Hyskon solution................................41

Hysterectomy
    abdominal operation 51–53
    damage caused by 18
    endometriosis..............................92
    extended................................50, 116
    fibroids 65
    heavy bleeding 63, 64–65
    operation notes 54
    ovarian cancer...........................131
    salpingectomy.............................49
    salpingo-oophorectomy 50
    sub-total abdominal 49
    total abdominal............................49
    uterine cancers 122
    vaginal...................50–51, 65, 106
    See, also, Oophorectomy

Hysterosalpingography (HSG) 168, 169

Hysteroscopy
    defined..39
    endometrial hyperplasia 118
    hazards................................42, 171
    indications 40, 63, 64–65, 73
    operation notes 42
    procedure................................40–41
    sterilisations 161–62
    uterine cancer...........................121

Hysterotomy...................................181

Imaging, see CAT scanning;
    MRI

IMB (intermenstrual bleeding)......32–33, 68, 72

Improper behaviour.........................4–5

In vitro fertilisation (IVF) 89, 171, 172

Incompetence, medical 38

Incomplete abortion 175

Incontinence 96, 105

Inevitable abortions.........................175

Inferior position 8

Infertility
    assessment...............................166
    chlamydia 83, 166
    defined 165
    endometriosis..............................87
    investigations, special.............167–70
    treatment................................170–72

Infundibulum 13, 15

Innominate bone 10

Intermenstrual bleeding (IMB) 32–33, 68, 72

Internal, defined................................8

Intervertebral foramina 13

Intra-epithelial neoplasia
    cervical (CIN).............111–12, 113–14
    vulval (VIN) 99

Intra-uterine adhesions....................171

Intrauterine devices (IUCD) 64, 144–50

Invasive cervical carcinoma............116

Investigations, infertility 167–70

Ischaemic necrosis 133

Isoniazid 117

Itraconazole 102

IUCD (intrauterine devices) 64, 144–50

IUS (Intrauterine system) 145

IVF (in vitro fertilisation) 89, 171, 172

Key-hole surgery..42
Kidney disease 95
Krukenberg tumour 129

Labia majora 17
Lactation..26
Laparoscopy
  endometriosis...92
  fallopian tube infections...........................122
  general indications 43
  hazards..............................18, 46–47, 171
  ovarian cancer..............................131, 132
  PID 85
  procedure...43–46
  sterilisation 157, 158
  use 42
Laparotomy 18, 92, 157, 171
Laser evaporation 97
Lateral position 8
LAVH (laparoscopically
  assisted vaginal hysterectomy)................65
Legal terminations.....................................178–82
Let-down reflex...26
LH (luteinising hormone) 21, 22, 24, 26,
                                               71, 167, 171
LHRH analogues 64
Lichen sclerosis 99
Lindane...98
Lippes' Loop..144, 145
Lithotomy position 34
Luteinising hormone (LH)...........21, 22, 24, 26,
                                               71, 167, 171
Lymphatic system 12

McIndoe (vaginal abnormality
  specialist) 58
Madlener's operation........................159, 160–61
Magnetic resonance imaging
  (MRI) 71, 130, 134
Malathion 98
Male sterilisation......................................142–43
Mammography 29, 76
'Manchester' repair..105
Medial position 8
Median plane...7

Medical examinations (general
  gynaecological) 3, 5
Medroxyprogesterone
  acetate (MPA)....................................64, 122
Mefenamic acid 63
Menarche, the, see Menstruation
Menopause 26–29, 55
Menorrhagia (heavy periods) 32, 61–65, 150
Menstrual cycle
  follicular phase...22
  luteal phase..25
  ovulatory phase 24, 24
  pituitary-ovarian axis 23
Menstrual disorders
  amenorrhoea 68–73
  dysmenorrhoea.....................................65–66
  IUCD problems 148–49
  menorrhagia.............................32, 61–65
  polymenorrhoea.....................................66–68
  post-menopausal bleeding 32, 73–75
  pre-menstrual syndrome 75–78
Menstruation
  non-existant 55
  physiology..21–25
  retrograde 87
Mesonephric (Wolffian) ducts........................55
Mesovarium...13
Metasteses, lymphatic system 12
Metronidazole 102
MI (myocardial infarction)............................152
Microadenomas 134
Microinvasive carcinoma 114–15
MIF (mullerian
  inhibiting factor) 20
Mifepristone (RU486)................................179–80
Mini pill 150
Minora 17
Miscarriage, see Abortion
Missed abortion 176
Moles, pregnancy tissue 191
Monilial vulvitis...........................81, 82, 98, 102
Mons pubis 17
MPA (medroxyprogesterone
  acetate)..64
MRI (magnetic resonance
  imaging)....................................71, 130, 134

Mucinous cystadenocarcinoma......................129

Mucinous cystadenoma.................................128

Mullerian ducts..55, 56

Mullerian inhibiting factor (MIF)...................20

Myocardial infarction (MI).............................152

Myomectomy 43, 65

Myometrium
    endometriosis of 62
    fibroids 119–20

Myxoma peritoneii 128

Nabothian follicles...108

National Health Service (NHS)................2, 162

Needle biopsy..130

Negative feedback 22

Negligence, missed ectopics 189

Nervous system 12–13

NET (norethisterone) 64

NHS (National Health Service)................2, 162

Non-septic abortions.......................................175

Norethisterone (NET) 64

NSAID (non-steroidal
    anti-inflammatories) 63

Obstetricians, defined 1

Obstruction, mechanical.............................70–71

OCCP (oral combined
    contraceptive pill)..150

Oestradiol production 22, 55

Oestrogen
    fibroids 119
    HRT..27
    menstrual cycle...22
    PMS treatment 78
    replacement therapy 55
    vaginal discharge 79–80

Oligomenorrhoea (light
    periods) 68

Omentectomy...131

Oophorectomy (removal of ovaries)
    endometriosis..92
    ovarian tumours...............................125, 131
    PMS..78
    salpingo..50
    sterilisation 162
    uterine cancer..122

Oophoritis 123

Operations, gynaecological
    D & C..31–39
    hysterectomy..48–54
    hysteroscopy 39–42
    laparoscopy 42–47

Oral contraceptives,
    see Contraceptives, oral

Organs, pelvic
    fallopian tubes 13–15
    ovaries 13
    overview 14
    uterus...15–16
    vagina 17

Osteoporosis
    HRT..28
    menopause problems 27

Ostium, inner tubal 15

Ota, Tenrei 144–45

Ovaries
    abnormalities...55
    agenesis...69
    anatomy 13
    burying of 157
    cancers..129–33
    cystectomy...43
    cysts 62, 88
    gonads 19, 21
    Graaffian follicles 126
    infections..123
    irradiation 157
    polycystic disease.................................71, 124
    tumours..124–32
    ureters, damage at surgery 18

Ovulation 167

Oxford technique..161

Painful periods,
    see Dysmenorrhoea

'Pap' smears..109, 111

Papanicolaou, George......................................109

Paracentesis abdominis 130

Paramesonephric
    (Mullerian) ducts...55

PCB (post-coital bleeding)..............................72

PCOD (polycystic
    ovarian disease)....................................71, 124

PCT (post-coital tests) 169

PE (pulmonary embolus) 151

Pearl Index (PI).................................139

Pediculosis pubis 98

Pelvic adhesions................................86

Pelvic anatomy
    blood supply 12
    bones......................................10–11
    external genitalia 17
    nerve supply 12–13
    organs....................................13–17
    urinary tract.........................18–19

Pelvic examinations............................3

Pelvic floor 11

Pelvic inflammatory disease...............82, 84–86,
    147–48

Perineal body....................................17

Perineum 17

Periods, *see* Menstrual cycle;
    Menstrual disorders

Peritoneum 11, 17, 92

'Persona', the 141

Pessaries 105

Pfannenstiel (German
    gynaecologist) 48

Phenotypic sexual
    differentiation 20

Physiology
    childhood....................................21
    genetics, basic........................19–20
    lactation.....................................26
    menopause..............................26–29
    menstrual cycle.....................22–25
    pregnancy..............................25–26
    puberty..................................21–22
    sexual differentiation 20
    unborn...................................20–21

PID (pelvic inflammatory
    disease)............................82, 84–86

Pill, the, *see* Contraceptives, oral

Pituitary gland
    adenoma....................................134
    disturbances 71
    Sheehan's syndrome.................133

Planes, anatomical 7–8, 9

PMB (post-menopausal
    bleeding) 32, 73, 121

PMS (pre-menstrual syndrome)....................28

Podophyllin paint.............................97

Polycystic ovarian disease
    (PCOD)...............................71, 124

Polymenorrhoea (frequent
    periods) 66–68

Polyps
    cervical 109
    endometrial 118–19, 171

Pomeroy's operation 161

Portio vaginalis 15, 73

Post-coital bleeding (PCB)...........72–73

Post-coital contraception 153

Post-coital tests (PCT) 169

Post-menopausal
    bleeding (PMB)...............32, 73, 121

Posterior position.................................8

Pouch of Douglas 19, 85, 92, 125,
    137, 157–58

Pre-menstrual syndrome
    (PMS)................................28, 75–78

Pregnancy
    amenorrhoea 70
    anembryonic 177–78
    ectopic 43, 70, 149,
    185–89
    IUCD in situ 149
    physiology...........................25–26
    See, also, Sterilisation,
    elective; Trophoblastic disease

Premature menopause......................55

Primary ovarian failure 55

Procidentia 103

Progesterone, physiology...........27, 29, 167

Progestogens 63–64, 77, 91,
    118, 152

Prolactin 26, 77, 134

Prolactinomas...................................134

Prolapse, vaginal...............................11

Prostaglandin terminations 181–82

Proximal position................................8

Pruritis vulvae.............................95, 98

Psycho-sexual problems...........86, 137–38

Puberty, physiology 21–22

Pubic symphysis 10

Pulmonary embolism (PE)..........64, 151

Radiotherapy, ovarian cancer........................132

Rami, dorsal and ventral 13

Rappe, Virginia 73

RCOG (Royal College of
    Obstetricians and
    Gynaecologists) 1, 4, 5

Read (vaginal
    abnormality specialist) 58

Rectal examinations...3

Rectum..11

Recurrent pelvic infection 85–86

Recurrent spontaneous abortion.............176–77

Registrars...2

Reproductive tract 11

Res ipse loquitur 31

Research Fellow 2

Research Registrar 2

Retroflexion 15

Rhythm method...140–41

Rifampicin...117

Ring pessaries...105

Ringer lactate solution 41

Roller ball device 64–65

Royal College of Nursing.................................53

Royal College of Obstetricians
    and Gynaecologists (RCOG) 1, 4, 5

Royal College of Surgeons 1

Royal College, the..1

'Royal College of
    Women's Health'..1

RU486 (mifepristone)................................179–80

Sacral plexus 13

Sacrum..10

Sagittal plane 7

Salpingectomy (removal of
    fallopian tubes) 49, 161

Salpingitis..123

Salpingostomy...171

Sarcoma botryoides....................................116–17

Scabies..98

Scanning, ultrasound............... 62, 63, 121, 125,
    132–33

Schauta, Friedrich 51

Scrape, the, see D & C

Screening, cervical 110

Semen analysis...167–68

Senior house officers (SHO) 1

Septate uterus...56

Septic abortions...174

Serosa 17

Serous cystadenocarcinoma...........................129

Serous cystadenoma..128

Sex chromosomes 20

Sexual dysfunction
    dyspareunia......................................136–37
    psychosexual problems...................137–38
    treatment..138
    vaginismus 135–36

Sexually transmitted diseases 82–83
    clinics (STD)..79

Sheath (male condom) 141–42

Sheehan, Harold 133

Sheehan's syndrome 133

SHO (senior house officer) 1–2

Sigmoid colon...19

Simpson's shelf pessary..................................105

Sims, James Marion 104

Somatic nervous system 12

Specialist registrars (SpRs) 2

Sperm-mucus interaction.........................169–70

SpRs (specialist registrars) 2

Squamous cell carcinoma..........................111–12

Squamous hyperplasia 99

STD (sexually transmitted
    disease) clinics..79

Stein-Leventhal syndrome......................71, 124

Steptoe, Patrick 160, 172

Steptoe rods 160

Sterilisation, elective 142–43, 155–63

Streak ovaries 55, 69

Strokes 28, 151

Strongyloides stercoralis 99

Stump carcinoma 49

Submucus fibroids..171

Superficial, defined..8

Superior position 8

Syphilis 97

TAH & BSO (removal of uterus,
  tubes and ovaries) 50

TAH (total abdominal
  hysterectomy)..............................49

Tait, Herbert.....................................109

TCRE (trans-cervical resection
  of the endometrium)......................65

Telarche (secondary sexual hair) 21

Teratoma, malignant.......................129

Terminations 178–83
  See, also, Abortion

Test tube babies................................89

Testes...19

Testicular feminising syndrome 20, 69

Testosterone.....................................20

Thermo-coagulation 64

Thermocoagulation 159

Thoracic duct....................................12

Threatened abortions 175

Thrombosis, venous..............25, 28, 64,
                                   78, 151

Thrombus..25

Thrush 81, 82, 98, 102

Thyroid gland dysfunction.................62, 72

Thyroid stimulating
  hormone (TSH) 167

Tinea cruris (Dhobie itch)....................98

TOP (termination of pregnancy)..................178

Tranexamic acid 64

Trichomonas vaginalis...............82, 102

Trophin (gonadotrophins) 21

Trophoblastic disease.................191–94
  See, also, Pregnancy

Trophoblastic Tumour
  Registration Centres....................193

TSH (thyroid stimulating
  hormone).................................167

Tuberculosis 117–18

Tubal abnormalities.....................55–56

Tumour markers (ovarian
  cancer) 88, 131

Tumours, ovarian.......................124–33
  See, also, Cancers

Turner's syndrome 69

Twilight sleep.....................................33

Ultrasound scanning.............62, 63, 121,
                              125, 132–33

Underactive thyroid 62

Unipolar diathermy.........................159

Ureters 18

Urethra..18

Urinary tract 11, 59

Uterine perforation...............37, 37, 38

Uterine tubes,
  see Fallopian tubes

Utero-vaginal prolapse 103

Uterus
  abnormalities...............................56
  anatomy 15–17, 16
  cancer 74–75, 120–22
  enlargement.................................62
  infections...............................117–18

Vagina
  adenosis....................................106
  agenesis................................58, 69
  anaerobic infections 82
  anatomy 17
  atrophic vaginitis....................73–74
  bacterial vaginosis...............82, 102
  cancer 74, 106–07
  developmental
    abnormalities 58, 103
  discharges................79–86, 101–03
  dryness 74
  foreign bodies 74, 81
  gardnerella vaginalis 82, 102
  lacerations..............................73–74
  pessaries 105
  prolapse 11, 103–06
  thrush 81, 82
  trichomonas vaginalis...............82

Vaginismus................................135–36

Vasectomy................................142–43

Vasomotor instability
  (hot flushes)..........................27, 28

Veress needle....................45, 46, 47

Vessels, iliac....................................12

VIN (intra-epithelial
    neoplasia)...99
Vitamin B6 77
Volsellum forceps...35, 36
Vulva
    carcinoma...100
    dystrophies...99
    infections
        bacterial..97
        fungal 98
        parasitic..98
        viral...96–97
    physiology..95
    pruritis vulvae 95, 96
    swellings 100
    trauma 100

'Well woman' screening.................................132
Wertheim hysterectomy...........................50, 116
Wild yam..29
Wolffian ducts.......................................55, 58–59
Womb, *see* Uterus